KILO SIERRA FIVE ONE

Policing Portsmouth in the 1980s

Steve Woodward

authorHOUSE®

AuthorHouse™ UK Ltd.
500 Avebury Boulevard
Central Milton Keynes, MK9 2BE
www.authorhouse.co.uk
Phone: 08001974150

© 2010 Steve Woodward. All rights reserved.

No part of this book may be reproduced, stored in a retrieval system, or transmitted by any means without the written permission of the author.

First published by AuthorHouse 3/16/2010

ISBN: 978-1-4490-7993-2 (sc)

Front cover photo of Volvo patrol car copyright Maurice Kime.

Dedicated to;

This book is dedicated to my wife Tricia who, like the wives of many serving Police officers, has had to suffer way too much interference and intrusion into her life just because of her husband's job.

Thanks to;

Steve Moore and Stef King for allowing me to pick their memories and to everyone who ever worked at Kilo Sierra/Victor Sierra for making this book possible.

CONTENTS

Chapter 1
   Ashford, Class 1/78 — *5*
Chapter 2
   1978. Are you the new proby? — *23*
Chapter 3
   1979. Training days with the gorilla — *63*
Chapter 4
   1980. Blue and white pandas — *86*
Chapter 5
   1981. You don't belong here — *116*
Chapter 6
   1982. We are at war — *143*
Chapter 7
   1983. Kilo Sierra is dead — *180*
Chapter 8
   1984. Arthur Scargill pays my mortgage — *199*
Chapter 9
   1985. You should be dead — *245*
Chapter 10
   1986. You're grounded — *282*
Chapter 11
   1987. Vote Docker — *315*
Chapter 12
   1988. Black Rat beckons — *347*
About the Author — *361*

Some of the names in this book have had to be changed to protect the guilty! Welcome to 21st century Britain.

FOREWORD

Fred Dinenage, Presenter of Meridian Tonight on ITV Meridian.

I am happy to write the Foreword to Steve's book for a variety of reasons.

Firstly, I've spent the past forty five years living in the Portsmouth area - and I was there when he began his career in the late 'seventies. I was a TV veteran even then! For me he's truly captured the atmosphere of the city in those days.....and since.

TV presenter Fred Dinenage

Secondly, my own son is now a policeman in Portsmouth. So I'm now more aware than ever of the pressures on the boys (and girls) in blue.

And, thirdly, I've the greatest admiration for the fantastic work ninety nine per cent of our policemen and women do. Every weekday night on the TV news programme I present for ITV Meridian I'm introducing items on the bravery, dedication and sheer brilliance of our police. And now, more than ever - in a much-troubled society - we need them.

I've enjoyed reading Steve's book. It's a real copper's book - full of drama, colour and humour. I think you'll enjoy it too.

So, off you go. And, in the words of an elderly children's television presenter: "That's HOW for now!"

Remember When?

Do you remember when all Police officers had to be a required height of at least five feet, ten inches tall and would go out on patrol wearing a tunic and a helmet and that the only item of personal protection equipment they could carry would be a wooden truncheon stuffed into their trouser pocket? Do you remember when Police cars were blue and white pandas or all over white with an orange stripe? Can you recall the days before coppers wore body armour and a utility belt that Batman would have been proud of? And that the only people to ever wear fluorescent yellow jackets were Traffic cops? Can you remember an age before the world wide web, personal computers, laptops, CCTV cameras, i-pods, cs gas, extendible batons, taser guns, ASBOs, mobile phones, ANPR, political correctness, speed cameras, DNA samples, carbon foot prints, health and safety, dynamic risk assessments, mission statements, Facebook, YouTube, PCSOs, sat-nav and digital radios? This isn't the Dixon of Dock Green era we are looking back at. It is a lot closer than you might imagine. This is the 1980s.

CHAPTER 1

Ashford, Class 1/78

"I do solemnly and sincerely declare and affirm that I will well and truly serve Our Sovereign Lady the Queen in the office of constable, without fear or affection, malice or ill will; and that I will to the best of my power cause the peace to be kept and preserved and prevent all offences against the persons and properties of Her Majesty's subjects "

The solemn oath of allegiance I took on 4th January 1978

So this is it then. I'm finally here, it's actually happening. I don't know if I'm excited or just plain scared but as I look around the classroom I reckon every one else is thinking the same thing. Four rows of desks with five new recruits in each row, all sat bolt upright in shiny black uniforms that are probably just a lighter shade of brown on the inside! We aren't all new to this game of course, having spent the last three years as a cadet it did at least give me some insight into what life in the Police force was like. As I sat at the back of the class I could see Howard Marrs at the front. He and I knew each other well having joined the cadets together and passed knowing glances towards each other. Everyone else though appeared to be strangers towards each other and like naughty school children we sat there in virtual silence, just waiting.

The regional Police Training Centre at Grosvenor Hall, Ashford in Kent took raw recruits from just about every county force in the south of England. Howard and I came from Hampshire with a few others whom we had yet to meet, together with people from Essex, Thames Valley, Sussex, Surrey, Guernsey, Kent of course and the British Transport Police. This group of twenty strangers, most of whom were still in their teenage years were about to embark upon a career in law enforcement, upholding the Queens Peace and bringing rogues and vagabonds to justice.

Still we waited in silence.

I looked around the room at my new found group of classmates. At the front of the class by the door was one of the biggest human beings I'd ever seen, he was easily six feet ten inches tall, but with a gentle looking face, very blonde hair and massive feet; size fifteen feet as it turned out! He's got the perfect attributes to be a copper I thought. He'll be one of those legendary types that everyone will talk about for years after he retires with stories like "remember that eight foot tall bobby we used to have plodding the village? He used to clip me 'round the ear every time he caught me scrumping. And I daren't go 'ome an tell me dad cos he'd have taken his belt to me. They don't make coppers like that today".

In contrast to the friendly looking giant was a young girl who looked no older than your average twelve year old with the physique to match. What use is she going to be in her first pub fight I mused, they'll just tread on her like an unwanted cockroach. And this bloke sat in front of me looks like a right yob. I mean he just has that look about him with his swept back hair, big Adams apple and that rather annoying habit of pushing his head backwards and forwards like a hungry chicken whilst saying to all that made eye contact with him "Alwight mate?"

As I glanced across to my left there was another female, with long blonde hair, immaculately tied up in a bun. She had what I suppose could be classed as child bearing hips and a rather full figure and bore an uncanny resemblance to all hotel receptionists. I wonder what she did in her previous life, I thought? Waitress maybe, no air stewardess, bank clerk, no, no I've got it, hotel receptionist, definitely. The bloke sat behind her was probably the oldest one here; in his mid thirties I'd say and ex military without doubt. His shoes glistened and the creases in his trousers were sharp enough to cut your finger on. He looked rather self assured, certainly more so than the rest of us.

And still we waited.

The door at the front of the classroom flew open and hit the wall behind it with a deafening thud. We all jumped. In marched two sergeants, one tall and old looking, the other much shorter and angry looking. They stopped as one and turned left to face us. The short one bellowed;

"STAND UP ALL THE EX-CADETS"

Howie, me and four others, including two of the four girls leapt to our feet.

"YOU KNOW FUCK ALL AND IF I HEAR ANY OF YOU SAY *'WHEN I WAS A CADET'* I'LL KICK YOUR ARSES ALL OVER THE PARADE SQUARE, DO I MAKE MYSELF CLEAR?"

"Yes sergeant" we replied as one.

"Good, you may sit"

We sat almost as quickly as we had stood. The other, worldlier looking sergeant gave us a warm smile tinged with an almost sarcastic look. He leant forward onto the lectern and spoke rather quietly.

"Welcome to Ashford boys and girls, I am Sergeant Standen and this is my colleague Sergeant Johnson. We will be your course sergeants for the next twelve weeks and we will turn you from the low lifes that you are now into Policemen. This is A Class and you will be the best at everything. The other three classes are already at a disadvantage because they don't have us teaching them. And in case you misunderstood what Sergeant Johnson said just now, he really doesn't like ex-cadets and who can blame him?"

As classroom entrances go it was pretty dramatic and the dislike of ex-cadets was a real worry, but not a surprise. As cadets we got treated like shit by many officers who used us as tea boys, errand runners and general dogs-bodies. Others were somewhat kinder and at least had the decency to teach us how the job was to be done. But there were those like Sergeant Johnson who clearly had a loathing for a scheme that was introduced during the 1960s to help attract teenagers into the Police. If they were playing the good cop, bad cop routine then Sergeant Johnson clearly wasn't the good cop. I took an instant dislike to him not just because he hated ex-cadets but more because in that rather dramatic entrance he had humiliated and even alienated the six of us in front of the rest of the class. Not only did he hate us but many of the others with any sense would also dislike us, if only to stay in favour with him. It was going to be a long twelve weeks.

And so we started, with lessons first on the structure of the Police force and what its function was. This was followed by weeks of law and procedure. And to pass the course you obviously needed to pass various exams. Every Monday morning would start with a quick examination of last weeks lessons and if you failed it, or dipped it as it was known, you had to sit it again. Fail three of those exams and there was every chance you'd be on your bike and out of the force. At the end of the course there was the final exam. Dip that and you were definitely out. In order to pass these exams you needed to learn every definition of law they presented parrot fashion, verbatim, off-by-heart, word perfect. It was the only way to fully understand the law surrounding any offence. Without that knowledge you started relying on guess work and in an instant your instructors would find you out and do their utmost to humiliate you in front of your classmates. And it was hard work, make no mistake about it. At times I found some of it relatively easy, it just flowed. But there were other definitions that drove me to the stage where I'd throw my copy of Moriarty's law book across my bedroom in shear frustration. I distinctly remember struggling on the law surrounding handling stolen goods, I simply didn't understand what it meant and as for 'making a false instrument' when it came to the law on deception, well I didn't get that one at all and I dipped my week three exam. I was marched into the Inspectors office to explain why. I didn't really have an answer for him but promised I would try harder next week.

It seemed to do the trick but I was worried that I might struggle in the future. This was only week three after all.

Every morning after breakfast all four classes from our intake, plus the four classes from the course that started six weeks before us lined up in an alley way beside an area known as the solarium. Why? Because at 0800 was morning parade where we would march out onto the parade square to the tune of 'The Old Comrades March' played over the p.a system. Now I actually like military type music and was even in a marching band as a youngster so I could already march in time to music. But if I ever hear that bloody tune again I'll scream until I'm sick. I'm sure they played it as some kind of torture treatment, designed to nullify the brain cells. Even now I can hear it droning away in the background and when I go to bed tonight I bet I can still hear it. After one lap around the square we formed up in class order and were inspected by the duty officer of the day.

Our Drill Sergeant was the extremely affable Sgt Pond, complete with slashed peak, red sash and tip staff tucked beneath his left arm pit. He bellowed out the parade square orders, interspersed with comic one-liners like "Smith you march like a fucking chimpanzee" or "Jones have you shit yourself?" "No Sergeant Pond" would be the obvious reply "Well why are you marching as if you have then?" He clearly loved his job and was king of his domain.

It was quite amusing watching those who clearly had no arm to leg coordination desperately trying to master the art of marching in time with a group of others. Left arm, left leg, right arm, right leg was the usual pattern of those who failed to grasp the concept and the funniest bit was that the person concerned knew full well that they weren't doing it correctly but seemed completely incapable of preventing it from happening. Sgt Pond, patient man though he was, was tried to the limit by some of his pupils whom he had to ensure were ready in time for the passing out parade at the end of 12 weeks.

Physical education was obviously another facet of Police training that had to be endured. And we seemed to cover every type of physical there was; swimming and life saving, circuit training, weight lifting, judo, boxing, football, rugby, hockey, cross country running (how I hated cross country) and gym work. Every day meant some different kind of activity, which I suppose got us away from the academic side of things for a while. I enjoyed most of it unless I got sent out on some pointless cross country run, through mud, up hills, across fields laden with cow pats, through farm yards knee deep in the things and finally via a bed of strategically placed stinging nettles before staggering back into the training school a humiliated last, as I invariably was. I could sprint 200 yards no problem, but after that, forget it, I was crap. And to tell me I was crap there was Sgt Webb, our resident PT instructor. He looked just like Gary Glitter with his swept back hair and his chiselled jaw, he would strut about the place wearing dark blue track suit bottoms and a white tee shirt, with suitably short sleeves to show off his bulging biceps and peps. And who was he showing off to? The girlies of course. He did love the WPCs and legend has it that a large pair of rolled up socks was placed down the front of those track suit trousers to impress them even more. Every thing he did was delivered with the aim of humiliating a male officer in front of a female officer in order to make him look great. You know the type.

But he didn't always get it his own way. A couple of years after I left Ashford we had a chap come onto my Relief by the name of Mick Keating. Now Mick was a lot older than your average recruit and was a former SAS officer, although he never talked about it and certainly didn't release any testosterone laden stories for the rest of us marvel at. However he did once relay the following tale; whilst in the gym at Ashford his class were benefiting from Sgt Webb's experience in restraining techniques and self defence. They stood in a semi circle in front of the wall bars, whilst Sgt Webb asked several of them to come and see if they could force him to release his grip from the bars and thus arrest him. It goes without saying that his victims were mainly female officers who must surely have been impressed by his strength or he picked on the weaker male officers whom he could humiliate once more. And then it happened. "Come on Keating, you think you're hard, come and do your worst" he said with a swagger as he adjusted his feet into a stronger stance. Mick shrugged his shoulders and ambled up to the wall bars. In an instant Mick had grabbed Sgt Webb's track suit bottoms and whipped them straight down to the floor. Sgt Webb's reaction was to immediately let go of the bars to pull his trousers up! Mission accomplished. The class fell about laughing and Webby left the gym in a big hurry but no one was quite sure whether or not they had seen the legendary socks! Mick's actions were a classic piece of practical policing and proved that there is definitely more than one way to skin a cat.

As the academic work continued we started doing role play scenario's to assist with our learning. The training school was laid out with various props like road signs, a court room and other buildings that could be utilised as a pub or a factory. We would have to act out roles and enforce laws with our instructors playing the opposite role. If you were doing OK they would generally be quite kind to you but start flustering or bull shitting on the law because you hadn't learned your definitions by heart and you came in for some serious piss taking, which generally continued later in the bar when your acting prowess was re-enacted for the other classes to view and further piss taking was guaranteed. But it worked. You learned from it and you didn't make the same mistake again.

I remember being tasked on one of these scenarios with delivering a death message, which let's face it is everybody's worst nightmare, having the copper turn up on your doorstep to deliver the worst news ever. There was no actual training involved believe it or not. After inspecting the 'body' in one room I had to go and knock on the relatives door across the road and deliver the news. Sgt Standen was the relative and it was his brother who was the deceased. He stood in the doorway and refused to let me in. He was drunk and clearly rather anti Police as he became ever more abusive towards me. This put me off straight away and of course I started to get flustered. All I kept saying was "calm down, calm down" and in the end he had to help me out and say "What do you want anyway?" I told him his brother had died and he shouted back "Good, didn't like the fucker anyway" and he slammed the door in my face. I was quite shocked by this but was relieved to hear from both my illustrious instructors that we had to expect a different reaction from everybody we delivered a death message to, because there were no rules to abide by, everybody reacted in a different way. With that the pair of them relayed stories of incidents they had attended over the years, some funny, some tragic, all very human. And from those stories I learned that both my instructors were superbly equipped to pass on the knowledge they had. Sgt Standen had spent most of his career policing the Medway towns of Chatham, Rochester and Gravesend dealing with "pikies and dockies" whilst Sgt Johnson had spent all his time in Brighton with its night clubs and transient bed sitter areas. My initial dislike of Sgt Johnson had now evaporated as I got to learn that part of what he and Sgt Standen were trying to achieve with us was a bit of resilience in the face of the abuse that we might face out on the street.

But not all of our training was quite so impressive. I'll never forget our single one hour lesson on drugs for example. That's right, one whole hour during which some grey chap in an even greyer suit stood at the front of our class giving us all the Home Office classifications for various drugs. He was incredibly boring to listen to and none of it was sinking in to be honest. However his *pies ta de la resistance* was to pass a wooden board around the class with real drugs sealed in small plastic bags which were pinned onto the board. The name of each drug was labelled with black Dyno tape. This was the first time I had ever clapped eyes on illicit drugs and I was fascinated. I'd clearly had a rather sheltered upbringing because there were some in my class who seemed to know rather more than I did on this subject. Three of them even coughed to smoking pot, whatever that was! It was clear that drugs were still seen as a minor problem and were told that this country would never become as bad as America and that really, as uniform Police officers we wouldn't get involved in drugs unless we joined the drug squad. There was no input into how drug dealers and users operate, no advice on how different drugs affect people or for how long, what some drugs smelt like, what drug paraphernalia was, how it affected people who drove cars afterwards, what a wrap was or any of the drug slang that we might need to know. It was amateurish at best and darn right useless as a practical tool.

Another seemingly useless series of lessons centred on the Cold War. Remember this was early 1978 and relations between the West and Moscow were still sub zero. War Duty lectures was supposed to prepare us for action in the event of a nuclear war in this country. They were an off-spin from the 1950s and 60s when the Home Office formed Police Mobile Columns, a sort of latter day reaction force to assemble large numbers of officers to send to a particular part of the country to assist the military with security issues and public order. Whilst the mobile part of the equation had been disbanded there was still a need to teach us new recruits that in the event of a super power pressing the red button, we would be expected to leave our families and head off towards the nearest mushroom cloud to clear up the mess it had left behind.

Talking of public order, one of the more humorous lessons we received was in policing events where disorder had broken out. This was at a time before the first big riots in Bristol, Toxteth, Brixton, Birmingham or Tottenham and the lessons learned from them. However industrial disputes were a weekly occurrence throughout the UK and policing them was becoming more and more difficult. But our training wasn't taken that seriously by the instructors or their students. There was no shield training, no batton charges, no protective head gear other than our standard issue helmets and virtually no tactics involved. We learned how to link arms whilst an unruly mob tried to break through and once we had mastered that, we were introduced to 'trudging and wedging'. This was where most of the laughing took place. You lined up and linked arms with the two officers either side of you. Your line then moved forward in a V formation, side stepping in a forward motion whilst counting out loud "one-two, one-two, one-two...............". You just hoped that someone near you didn't get out of step because if they did that usually brought your line crashing to the ground like a stack of domino's! The idea was to break through a large mob of demonstrators and then once divided, the V would break open and the mob was split into two separate groups. I have no idea if it was ever used successfully but I suspect that if a V formation of gannex wearing coppers were trudging and wedging towards a hostile crowd that they would probably not be hostile for too much longer and would undoubtedly have been laying on the ground crying with laughter.

I was still struggling with my studies and dipped my week six exam. This time I got to see the Deputy Commandant, a Chief Inspector with the biggest ears I've ever seen. As I stood on the carpet in front of his desk I was transfixed by them. He probably gave me a right bollocking but I just didn't hear it, I was too busy wondering how two objects so large were able to stay affixed to the side of his head. But I was worried about my future. Would I make it to the final exam? Would I pass it? What if I didn't? Have I really got what it takes? I'd have plenty of time to think about it because this weekend I have to go home.

Up until now I hadn't bothered and chose to stay at Ashford during the weekends but at the halfway point of the course they closed the school for a long weekend and you had to leave. It was mid February and it was very cold. By Friday lunchtime it had started to snow. By mid afternoon it was settling and looked like a blizzard. I toyed with the idea of getting the train back to Portsmouth but in the end decided that I was made of sterner stuff and opted to ride my motorcycle instead. By 1600 hours when it was time to leave it was already dark and still snowing. We had been given reassurances that the main A20 and A25 roads through Kent were passable and so decision made I swung my legs over the Honda 750 and eased my way out of the car park. Indeed the A20 and A25 were reasonably OK. However the snow was getting heavier and it was getting to the stage where I could barely see more than about 50 feet ahead of me. The journey from Kent to Portsmouth should have taken about two and a half hours (there was no M25 in those days!) but by 1900 hours I was only in Surrey and still had over 50 miles to go. By the time I reached the A3 at Guildford to head south I was so cold I couldn't feel my feet or my hands at all. Pulling the clutch in with my left hand was excruciating. The road was now thick with snow and there was very little traffic about and I was now riding with both feet off the foot pegs and rubbing along the road surface as some kind of stabilisers. As I approached the Devils Punchbowl at Hindhead the snow was about six inches deep. The front wheel slid away and I fell off my bike. I got back on, travelled a few yards and fell off again. The snow was now a blizzard and I couldn't see more than about 10 feet in front of me. I suddenly realised that I was the only person out on the road and felt very lonely. I got back on and started to climb the hill towards Hindhead. The snow was now about a foot deep and covered the whole of the A3 except for a narrow path on the nearside just wide enough for my bike to get through. I fell off several times but managed to get back on and keep going. I was nearing the top of the hill when I fell off yet again. This time the bike fell on top of me. I laid there for ages completely exhausted and bitterly cold. I seriously considered just curling up and going to sleep right there but then mentally beat the crap out of myself for even considering something so stupid. I could barely move my legs and I was convinced my hands had frost bite and would just snap off because they were so cold. I heaved the bike back up yet again and slowly picked my way through the snow drifts, through Hindhead and south towards the coast. I'd convinced myself that by the time I got to Petersfield that the conditions would be a little more favourable. They weren't. I fell off again and again. I reached Portsmouth and the Isle of Wight ferry terminal just in time to catch the last car ferry at 2300. My journey had taken me almost seven hours. I shared the ferry with one lorry, the only other vehicle to have made it. I went upstairs to the bar desperate for some warmth. I knew the steward behind the bar, a bit of a camp individual; he had a lot of sympathy for me so I milked it for all it was worth. He let me sit on the Super Cer calor gas heater they had behind the bar to help thaw me out and he made me three cups of coffee and gave me two micro waved meat pies, all for free. I had just about started to get some feeling back into my bones when the ferry docked at Fishbourne almost an hour later. The journey from there to Cowes should take about 15 minutes. I was dreading getting back on the bike. The snow was just as bad here as it was everywhere else and that ride took me over an hour but at least I managed to stay on it for the entire journey. I got into bed and curled up into a ball.

I woke up the following morning and couldn't believe how bad the snow was. And listening to the radio the road from Cowes to

Newport was completely blocked with the Police making appeals for people not to venture out. I phoned Newport nick, which is where I had been stationed as a cadet to see if they needed any help. I was directed to the Cowes to Newport road to assist in checking the area for people trapped over night in their cars. I put my uniform on and managed to ride my bike, which looked even more battered and bruised than I was, towards the main road. The Cowes to Newport road is quite exposed and the snow drifts were over six feet deep in places. It completely transformed the landscape, it was weird. I met up with a few of the guys from my old Relief which was great and we spent the next few hours slowly making our way through the snow checking on abandoned cars to ensure that nobody had died in one overnight. The snow was so deep in places that the only way to determine if there was a car underneath you was to plunge your spade as deep as it would go. If it hit something metallic you started digging. Thankfully we didn't find an frozen corpses and I returned home in the late afternoon absolutely knackered. The studying will have to wait until tomorrow, but my brief rescue mission helped me understand why I had joined the job in the first place. As much as the study in law was important, doing what I did today was even more so.

We returned to Ashford the following Tuesday. Most of the snow had now melted away although it was still bitterly cold. We were now the senior course and we had a new intake to take the piss out of. Little did I realise that the biggest joke of all was about to be played on us. All the Hampshire recruits received a visit from a Hampshire Sergeant and he gathered us together to explain that it was time to sort out our postings for when we left Ashford. We were each given a photocopied slip of paper with the numbers 1, 2 and 3 on it. We had to place our name at the top of the paper and then in order of preference the station we would most like to be posted to, followed by the one we would choose as our second option. The third line was reserved for the station we would least like to be posted to. Simple really. I knew I wouldn't get the Isle of Wight because I had been there as a cadet and really, really didn't want to go there anyway. So I chose Southampton first, although I have no idea why, followed by

Aldershot, a town I'd never been to and Portsmouth as the place I'd least like to get posted to. I made that decision based on the stories I'd heard at school about fights at Portsmouth football ground and the fact that every time I rode through Portsmouth en route to the ferry it just looked like such a dump. Our slips were gathered up and we were told our postings would be sent to us by mail in a couple of week's time.

The social life at Ashford was pretty good and centred on the bar of course. All students were banned from the bar until at least 2100 hours to ensure you at least made some effort at studying before getting pissed every night. The drinks were heavily subsidised and incredibly cheap. The bar area was a large hall, with the actual bar at one end and at the other was the entrance to the solarium, a sort of Victorian conservatory that overlooked the parade square. And it was in here that most of us supplemented our diet with hot pies and pasties baked in the small kitchenette. Without these vital additions to our stomachs most of us would have probably starved because the food at Ashford was the stuff of legend and there were regular complaints about it. The bar also housed a sizeable stage where classes and individuals were encouraged to put on performances of their particular talents to amuse the rest of us. During my stay at Ashford a few of us formed a group, not to play on stage you understand but just to give us some light relief from studying especially at the weekends. I played drums, Malcolm 'Wolfie' Smith on bass guitar with Graham 'GT' Towersey on lead guitar. We were joined by a chap from Sussex who not only played guitar but could sing to, together with two of the girls from Kent who also sang. Over a period of weeks I have to say we got rather good and played everything from Ralf McTell's *Streets of London* to Status Quo's *Caroline*, which gave our guitar heroes the opportunity to extend that songs guitar solo to about 15 minutes in duration! Then we got spotted by one of the instructors over the weekend who insisted we play on stage during 'dining-in' night, which was traditionally held on the penultimate evening of the course and was a formal dinner, followed by speeches, awards and some light entertainment. We were to become the light entertainment.

When you've lived with a group of people for a number of weeks you invariably get to know them quite well, whether that be good or bad. Sometimes when its bad it can have a detrimental effect on the relationship no matter how many times you have tried being nice about it and perhaps dropped big hints about that persons behaviour. Well one such relationship deteriorated over a number of weeks to such an extent that revenge and public humiliation was the only option. Across the corridor from my room at Ashford were four room mates, one of whom was a chap from Sussex who happened to be the oldest officer on our course. Terry loved his drink. When he was drunk he was one of those really funny drunks, good stories, always laughing, lovable rogue types that eventually fall asleep and don't cause any trouble. Until it was time to get up the next morning that is. And no matter how hard they tried, his room mates could never rouse him. It cost them hours and hours in lost breakfasts, being late for parades, not getting their own acts together and getting bollockings of their own for being late. Terry merely shrugged his shoulders and laughed it off. So towards the end of the course they'd had enough. Terry had his usual Sunday night binge and staggered back to the residential block singing away and being everyone's best mate. He slept like a log and in the morning when his room mates couldn't wake him they put their plan into operation. They called in reinforcements from our room and others in our block and we carried Terry's bed and bedside table down the corridor, out of the block, through the grounds and gently placed him down in the middle of the parade square. We could hardly contain ourselves and were even more incredulous that he hadn't woken up. We all then went for breakfast convinced he would wake up shortly. We returned at 0800 to take part in the morning parade and there he was, still sleeping like a baby. Somebody had briefed Sgt Pond and I think he was as intrigued by it as the rest of us. We all lined up, the music started and out we marched. We were half way around the square when Terry suddenly sat up in bed. The look on his face was priceless; I think he thought he was in the middle of a bad dream. Needless to say our parade was a complete shambles with the entire course crying with laughter. Terry never lived it down and I heard later that he failed his probation, possibly because of his excessive alcohol consumption.

Week ten and our postings arrived. We nervously opened the envelopes. I got Southsea. Where the bloody hell is Southsea? Portsmouth, you muppet, quipped one of our number. But I put Portsmouth down as my number three I squealed. It became apparent as each of our postings was revealed that whatever we had put down as our least favoured choice was exactly what we got. Every single one of us had been shafted. There was no appeals system, no grievance procedure, it was take it or leave it. Howard got the Isle of Wight and he wasn't happy either. I learned from one of my former cadet colleagues that actually Southsea was quite a good nick to get posted to as it was busy and that Fratton Park, home of Portsmouth Football Club was on its patch. His enthusiasm for the place wasn't matched by mine I have to confess but I was quite pleased that GT had also been posted to Southsea, so at least there would be somebody there I actually knew.

The last two weeks of our twelve week course were the most frenetic, with preparations for our passing out parade mixed in with last minute panic attacks over certain definitions that had yet to be learned in time for the final exam on the last Wednesday of the course. The pressure was enormous and most of us could be seen pacing the corridors of our accommodation blocks, heads buried in law books, mumbling passages of definitions and quoting stated cases and getting horribly confused over Judges Rules. Never have I worried so much about a single exam, but then the rest of my life hasn't depended on one single exam before. And before we knew it that dreaded Wednesday had arrived. We filed silently into our classroom and with trepidation turned the exam paper over to begin. The pass mark was 80%. I struggled with some of it. After completing the paper it was time for lunch and the inevitable post mortem where certain clever-dicks ensured that you were even more convinced now than you were before you took the exam that you had failed miserably. And after lunch a second official post mortem with Messrs Standen and Johnson, who went through the paper question by question, which convinced me still further that I may as well just go and pack my bags right now to spare myself the inevitable humiliation. We then went for our afternoon tea break, after which the results would be announced. I think I smoked five fags in those 15 minutes. We filed back into class. Our two Sergeants marched in, ashen faced. They didn't look at us, their eyes fixed firmly at the floor. The signs weren't good and my heart was about to explode. To my horror Sgt Johnson started to read the results out aloud. My name was always close to the bottom of any register so the agony was prolonged still further. And then it came.

"PC Woodward"

"Yes Sgt"

"84%, well done"

I thought I was going to throw up. Two of my class failed and every one of us felt so incredibly sorry for them. However they had only dipped it by a couple of marks and were given the opportunity to take it again the next day. Both of them passed. The relief felt by all of us was incredible.

Dining-in night followed the next evening and after a splendid three course meal, served to us by professional waiters, the formalities and speeches over, it was time for the group with no name to get up on stage and strut their stuff. By the time we had got to this stage in the evening I have to confess that I was heavily under the influence of alcohol. We did a couple of numbers and to our surprise got rapturous applause and calls for more. So we obliged. And our audience obliged by buying us lots more alcohol. At one stage I had eight pints on a tray perched on the stool next to me. Being extremely drunk meant that the music we were playing sounded even better although I'm sure if somebody had recorded it and played it back to us when sober, we might have a slightly different opinion on our abilities.

I don't normally suffer from hang-overs but the next morning I really wasn't very well. I'd already thrown up out of my bedroom window a couple of times during the night and I was quite convinced it wouldn't be the last time today. But we had a passing out parade to take part in and I'm in the gymnastics display team after that. I'm never going to make it.

Parents, wives and other relatives started arriving around lunchtime, all wearing their Sunday best, with big hats and even bigger ties. We formed up in our usual spot out of sight in the alleyway, with last minute brushing down of each others uniforms. Boots were spit and polished so that the caps were like glass and our white gloves were as pure as snow. Then Sgt Pond gave us the order to line up in preparation for our passing out parade. He looked suitably impressed with us all and thanked Class 1/78 for being one of his best ever. I'm quite sure he said that to every intake at this exact point in time but it made us feel very proud and we stood another inch taller. Then that bloody music started up and we were off onto the parade square.

We did our lap and then halted in the centre and turned to face the crowds and the dignitaries. Our guest of honour and inspecting officer was to be the Lord Lieutenant of Kent no less, suitably dressed in full military uniform. As we were A Class it would be us he would inspect first. And as I was one of the taller officers it meant that I was at the front. And as it turned out I was the very first Hampshire officer he came across. Now it's at this point that you need to know that the helmet badge in Hampshire is completely different to any other Police force badge, in that it is basically a large square of laurel leaves that surround the Hampshire Rose. Most other force badges consist of a star surmounted by a crown. The Lord Lieutenant stopped in front of me. He looked like a horse, with huge stained teeth, a very pronounced jaw and a silver main of hair that was desperate to escape from the clutches of his military cap. He looked me up and down and then snorted out;

"I say, that's a natty hat badge, what"

"Yes sir" I replied "It's the Hampshire badge"

"Jolly good, jolly good" and with that he turned right and moved off to continue his inspection.

The entourage of Ashford's training staff followed behind him, the Chief Superintendent, the Chief Inspector, a couple of Inspectors, Sgt Standen, Sgt Johnson, Sgt Pond and bringing up the rear, our class leader PC Steve Smith, a former Guardsman. It just so happened that wherever our equine VIP had stopped further down the line meant that Smithy had stopped directly in front of me. He looked straight at me, winked then turned away from me. His hands were correctly placed behind his back and for some inexplicable reason I looked down at them. Big mistake. Because cupped in his hands was a piece of card with the words *"You snivelling shit"* written on it. Just like when you were a child in church or during some important school assembly where you were desperately trying not to laugh, but the more you tried the more you failed, I sniggered and snorted with tears running down my face. The guys either side of me plus a couple behind me had also caught a glimpse of the card and they too were fighting to control themselves. It was impossible and even half an hour later as we marched off to the strains of that infernal music we all burst out laughing. It was a great way to end the course.

CHAPTER 2

1978. Are you the new proby?

"The necessity of living in the midst of the diabolical citizens of Portsmouth" wrote General James Wolfe in 1758 **"is a real and unavoidable calamity. It is a doubt to me if there is such another collection of demons upon the whole earth".**

After leaving Ashford all the Hampshire recruits had to undertake a week long local procedure course at the old Cadet Training School at Bishops Waltham. This felt like home to those of us who had lived at the school for a year as cadets and on various courses in between. The monastery on which the school was built was located in superb grounds with excellent sporting facilities, although I wasn't particularly keen on the cross country course! The food was as bad as that at Ashford, but us ex-cadets knew how to get into the kitchens at night to raid the store cupboards to make sandwiches and coffee in order to supplement our meagre diet.

The local procedure course was exactly what it sounded like. It was all very well learning the law on a national basis but each force still had its own procedures and different types of paperwork and forms to master. This week long course was designed to teach us everything we needed to know about the way Hampshire went about its policing. It was pretty quick fire stuff and there was a lot to take in and I got the distinct impression that if you didn't grasp it first time, well it didn't really matter that much because you'd either learn it fast as soon as you got to your station, or more likely that older, much wiser officers would do things their own way anyway! We were strongly advised to keep away from such reprobates.

Whilst at CTS I took the opportunity to visit its small library and did what little research I could on Portsmouth, because up until this moment my entire knowledge of the place consisted of the route through the city on the A3 to the ferry terminal. I didn't learn that much to be fair other than finding out that the city was actually based on an island, referred to as Portsea, it was the home of the Royal Navy and Nelson's flag ship HMS Victory, most of which I already knew. Richard the Lionheart, King Richard 1st had granted the city a crescent of gold on a shade of azure with a blazing star of eight points as the city's coat of arms in 1194 and it had several famous sons including Charles Dickens, Sir Arthur Conan Doyle and Peter Sellers. It was home to one of the UK'S ugliest buildings in the Tricorn shopping centre which was almost as famous as its football club. It was also supposed to be the most densely populated city in Europe with some 180,000 residents crammed within its boundaries and had more pubs than anywhere else in the country. No doubt I'll get called to one or two of those I thought.

After passing yet another exam, we were allocated our lodgings address, details of the officers we were to report to at our respective stations together with our shifts for the next couple of weeks. This really was it then. So at the age of 19 years and weighing just 10 ½ stone I was about to be launched onto the people of Portsmouth to uphold the law. God help em!

I got Wolfie Smith to guide me through Portsmouth on our bikes to 84 Alverstone Road, Milton. We arrived in the early evening and Wolfie stopped outside the house, pointed at the door and then roared off. Did he know something I didn't? Number 84 was a small, mid terraced property that overlooked a rather run down looking factory that recycled rags, gathering by the mountains of material piled up inside the gates. And just at the end of the road, literally within spitting distance was Fratton Park, home of Portsmouth Football Club. It was the first time I'd ever seen it for real and some of the horror stories I'd heard from my school days came flooding back. It sent a shudder down my spine as I took the panniers off my bike. Anyway plenty of time to think about that later I thought, let's go and meet the new landlady.

The door was answered by a small woman in her mid 50s. She wore those terrifying looking horn rimmed glasses and had her greying, mousy hair tied back in a pony tail.

"You must be Steve?" she said with a nicotine stained smile.

She ushered me indoors where I was introduced to her husband Ted. He looked older than Eve and had one of those long suffering type faces. He struggled to get out of his arm chair next to the fire, folding his paper as he did so. He stuck out his hand to welcome me into his home and thoroughly pleasant as he was, I got the distinct impression that the idea of having a lodger was not his. As small as Eve was it was clear who wore the trousers.

We then went through the house formalities and two things were made abundantly clear. If I needed to use the phone I only needed to ask, but there was a lock on it to stop their 22 year old daughter Carol from using it. And when I come in from late turn could I please be very quiet because they all go to bed at nine! Here's your door key. Now what do you like to eat? Or rather is there anything you don't eat? Rhubarb and cooked apple was the reply, that's it really, apart from those two disciples of the devil I eat pretty much anything.

Carol and her boyfriend Steve then returned home from the cinema. She was a pale and pasty looking thing that tended to whine a bit when she talked. She was Ted and Eve's only child and it showed. When Carol and Steve went out into the kitchen Eve explained through gritted teeth that Carol was a bit of a hypochondriac.

I eventually got to see my room. It was a small affair at the rear of the house overlooking lots of other people's gardens. It was very basic, just a bed, an old wardrobe and dressing table with a cracked mirror and a small picture of Christ hanging on the wall. The décor was distinctly 1960s and there was a dank, musky sort of smell about the place. I had a big day tomorrow and needed to sort my uniform out and unpack all my stuff. I bid them all goodnight and retired.

I was woken in the early hours by a horrific screaming noise. It was coming from the room next door to mine and was like something from one of those old black and white B movies. I leapt out of bed thinking at the very least somebody was being murdered. I opened the bedroom door to see Eve scampering across the landing. She saw me standing there and said it was OK because it was probably just Carol having one of her nightmares again. After a couple of minutes she came back out and calmly explained to me that it was indeed Carol and that the man in the white suit was sat on the end of her bed playing the guitar again!

My first day's duty at Southsea nick started at a very reasonable 0900 and I was to report to the admin officer, one PC Ray Chudley. He was obviously in the twilight of his career and I suspected that he hadn't seen any front line action for many years. He was friendly and efficient enough but I got the impression that I was just another recruit fresh out of the box and that the sooner he had got me sorted and out of his cramped little office the sooner he could go to lunch. I bet he had ham and mustard sandwiches every day at bang on 1300 and woe betide anyone who prevented that from happening. After completing some paperwork and finding me a battered old metal locker to store all my uniform in he gave me a guided tour of my new work environment.

Southsea police station was old. Very old. In fact it was 1873 old. Although the original building had been replaced in 1956 the basic footprint and layout of the place had remained intact. It was positioned on the corner of Albert Road and Victoria Road South and was referred to by the locals as 'Albert Road' nick. It occupied a triangular plot on the junction and was just two stories high. It was a bit art deco in style I suppose with curved corners made from opaque glass blocks. On both sides of the station there were two red phone boxes and across the rear was a small service road, so the building was basically an island. There was another building tacked onto the rear corner and that was the public toilets and I remember thinking that it was a strange combination.

There were three entrances to the place; via the front door obviously that led to the front desk and was the only public entrance, whilst the other two were confined to those working there. One was adjacent to an area called 'the pad' that was a piece of tarmac on the west side of the station just large enough to accomodate three patrol cars on it. This was effectively Southsea's rear yard and so any other patrol cars were parked out on the street, where passing youths would quite often unscrew the lenses from the blue lights to keep as souvenirs! The third entrance was on the south side at the rear and consisted of a pedestrian gate that led to a very narrow alleyway between the main building and a single garage that apparently used to house the Superintendant's car in previous years. This alley led to a tiny little yard that housed an old fashioned bike shed, the sort you used to find in schools and the stations dog kennel, used to incarcerate the occasional mutt. Three concrete steps then led up to the doors on the east side of the station and these in turn led directly into one of the two locker rooms. That old garage was a dumping ground for anything that couldn't be stored properly elsewhere and included spare emergency and cleaning kit for the cars. In the middle of the floor was an old red fire bucket full of sand with the letters UXB painted on it. This is where unexploded mortars or hand grenades would be placed, when handed in by the public, until the Naval bomb disposal unit arrived! There were two items of note about 'the pad' in that one of the ground floor sash windows adjacent to it was always left slightly open so that the fire hose could be passed through the gap to facilitate the Sunday morning ritual of washing the patrol cars or the juvenile high pressure washing of colleagues! And the bushes beneath the first floor kitchen window were full of tea bags where policemen too idle to empty the tea pot into the bin would merely empty it out of the window.

The interior of the police station could best be described as homely I suppose. The hub of the whole building appeared to be the front office, complete with its wall mounted gas lamps. This was a large room that had several doors leading from it. The first and most important door led directly to the front desk, where the public came in to make their respective complaints, pleas for mercy or to dump their kids or livestock! Other doors led to the station sergeants office, the superintendents office, the charge desk and the only available interview room, which also doubled up as the fingerprint room, whilst the four others led to the telex room, the property cupboard, a detained persons room (a cell for holding juveniles and other vulnerable persons) and the main corridor. A set of stairs ran from the front office directly to the first floor where the wooden floors creaked and literally buckled under your weight. Up here was the parade room, typists office, chief inspector and inspectors offices, the CID office and most important of all the kitchen and canteen. The canteen was nothing more than a small room with a couple of old tables and plastic chairs in it. In the corner was another table with one of those really old valve radiogram sets that was used to listen to the one o'clock news by the likes of Ray Chudley and one or two others no doubt. Immediately above the radiogram was a cigarette vending machine made from wood with brass handled dispensing drawers where packets of Players No. 6, Guards or B&H could be purchased for 50p. Just outside the kitchen was a water boiler that dripped constantly into a battered old metal bucket that was full of tea bags that had been dumped there instead of the bin. This area was the focal point for every Relief to congregate before going to the parade room at the beginning of every shift. A million yarns have been spun over the work top area where that tea was brewed in one of those huge WRVS type metal tea pots. Just behind this area was access to the back stairs which led you down to the ground floor area and connected you back to the main corridor to the front office. As the stairs met the corridor you were greeted by a thick wall that divided the corridor in half and on either side of the divide was a cell. They were as old as the original part of the station and had had numerous amounts of graffiti and expletives scratched into the walls and doors by its inhabitants over the years. Each cell had a stainless steel toilet in the corner and there was a spy hole directly above it so that officers on gaoler duties could ensure that no misdemeanours were taking place out of sight of the main door. And those doors were incredibly heavy and were locked with a dual action barrel type key lock together with the added security of two sliding steel bolts, top and bottom. Once incarcerated in one of Southsea's guest suites there was no escape. There is a certain smell that accompanies all cell blocks, no matter how large or small, ancient or modern, they all smell the same and Albert Road's was no exception. It's a unique concoction of second hand alcohol fumes, urine, vomit, the smelliest of filthy socks, body odour and disinfectant. They have an aroma all their own and once tasted, never forgotten.

Southsea Police Station from the Albert Road side.

Ray was getting itchy feet as one o'clock got closer. He spotted PC 1960 Roger Wood and asked if he would be so kind as to take me out on patrol with him for the afternoon to show me part of the patch. I wouldn't be meeting my tutor constable or the rest of my Relief until next week, after they returned from rest days. Roger was an ex-military man, the Guards to be precise, but he was a gentle soul with a slight West Country accent. He was a big chap and did everything rather slowly and methodically. He didn't work with a Relief as he was one of four area beat bobbies, whose beats were their own. It was an old fashioned idea that was still being operated in Portsmouth and was a throw back to the Portsmouth City Police days, pre amalgamation in 1967 and it worked a treat.

Roger looked me up and down as if I were on a parade ground. He adjusted my helmet slightly and told me to stand up straight.

"Got any hand cuffs yet"? He inquired.

"No, not yet" I replied rather sheepishly.

Believe it or not but Hampshire coppers had to buy their own from 'somewhere' after they left Ashford. This caused much piss taking by officers from other forces at training school who were supplied with cuffs and who could blame them.

"Right then" said Roger "First stop Rothery's Gun Shop in Albert Road to get you some hand cuffs".

A gun shop I thought? Surely Pompey can't be that rough can it? All those stories I'd heard about the place whilst I was at school must be true then.

We stepped out of the back door of the station and out onto Albert Road. I immediately felt very self conscious. I was convinced my helmet was going to roll off my head and Roger looked like he was at least eight feet tall and dwarfed me considerably. I could feel my heart pounding through my tunic as we strode purposely along the pavement. It felt like everybody was looking in my direction and that they all knew this was my first time out. No sooner had I got into my stride than we stopped to enter Rothery's. It was like entering a small war museum. There were rifles and swords proudly displayed by hooks on the walls, whilst various cabinets housed military uniforms and headgear, with glass display cases housing medals, coins and hat badges adorning the window area. Behind the main counter were locked display cases that held all manner of firearms.

"Hello Roger" said Mr Rothery as we entered his domain "What's this then, another fresh one? Bloody hell they get younger every day, how old are you nipper, twelve?"

I was a bit taken aback by his in your face cheek.

"You know what you need to do son" he continued "and that's grow a moustache, it'll put years on ya. You have reached puberty haven't you?" He let out a huge laugh and I started to feel around my face with my hand and wondered what I might look like with face furniture.

Roger explained why we were there and as Mr Rothery dug out a brand new box of Hiatt hand cuffs for me to examine, he started to talk about all manner of officers from Southsea whom he obviously knew. He clearly enjoyed the name dropping exercise and I think it made him feel important. I don't think it was meant to impress me specifically as I got the distinct impression that had I gone in there everyday for a year he would be exactly the same and would moan about the same officers or the police force in general. I paid my £6 for the hand cuffs and hooked them onto my trouser belt. I immediately felt a little more secure as we left the shop to continue our patrol.

During the next couple of hours Roger taught me a lot of things about foot patrol. If you are patrolling with another officer always make sure you are both in step with each other, it looks so much smarter. There speaketh the military man. If anybody walks towards you, they move out of your way, not the other way around. He absolutely insisted on this and doubly so if it was a group of yobs. They walk around us, not through us. Understood? Understood. Shop awnings are the work of the devil and have a habit of knocking your helmet off when you least expect it. They also hold rain water for days after it has stopped raining, so never walk in front of one, always bypass them if possible. And talking of rain, a good copper never gets wet. This wasn't some great hint at making sure you always carried your rain coat even in mid July, but more that experienced coppers have a large number of tea stops on their beats and that they should be able to dive into one should the weather turn!

And we visited a couple of Rogers's tea stops that afternoon before returning to Albert Road in time for me to book off at 1700. It hadn't been an exciting introduction but I was very grateful to him for giving me some sound advice.

"And don't worry about what Mr Rothery said about looking so young. You'll just have to get used to it I'm afraid. But if you do fancy growing a moustache it might help".

I instinctively reached for my face again.

I returned to my digs and Eve was waiting for me like some excited school mum greeting her off spring at the school gates. She wanted to know everything and seemed rather disappointed that I hadn't solved any murders or been to a couple of bank jobs already.

"Well I did tell you last night that Portsmouth's a nice quiet place, I did say, yeeess".

And with that she whipped the paper out of Ted's hand, folded it up and told him to lay the table for dinner.

I suppose I was almost as disappointed as she was, I mean I'd been brought up on a diet of Starsky and Hutch and The Sweeney and I hadn't so much as heard a tyre squealing or anything like "get ya trousers on son, you're nicked".

After two days off I returned for my first proper late shift and time to meet my tutor and the rest of White Relief. I was definitely a lot more nervous this time, I mean these are the guys I'm going to be working with for the rest of my career so I'd better make the right impression I thought as I climbed the back stairs to the canteen.

"Are you the new proby"? Said one of them and after confirming their worst suspicions, that yes I was indeed their latest recruit, various introductions were made.

The friendly face that had greeted me first was in fact my tutor constable, PC 2141 Graham Norman. He was only in his mid twenties and seemed to have a permanent smile on his rather round face.

"We call him the Honey Monster" quipped one of the others and you could see why, the resemblance was uncanny.

One by one I was introduced to the others. Andy Kimber the area car driver, Adrian (Ado) Watts, Paul (Pecker) Wood, Nick (Ticket) Wood, Gary (GM) Martin, Norman Feerick, Paul (PD) Dawson and George Barker whom I already knew as we were cadets together and until today he had been the newest recruit. Seven out of the eight of them had a moustache.

"JB will be up here in a minute and I've no doubt he will give you one of his pep talks" smirked Graham.

"JB, who's that"? I inquired.

"John Batten, our patrol sergeant and we also have Laurie Terry, our station sergeant, but he will be downstairs. We call him Uncle Laurie but it might be a while before you are allowed to become that familiar".

As if on cue Sergeant Batten appeared in the canteen. He was a rather tall, well groomed and immaculately turned out man, who I estimated was in his mid thirties. He walked in as if he owned the place and it seemed as though the entire Relief had a very healthy respect for him. Graham introduced me and he shook me very firmly by the hand and said we would have a proper chat after parade. Graham gave me a knowing smile. With that we all filed down the corridor to the parade room. This was probably the most important and somewhat formal part of the day. It consisted of the entire Relief sitting around a large table with the sergeant at its head. He would read out various telex messages and other reports of interest, whether they be the registration numbers of cars stolen in the city over the last 24 hours, to the names of wanted villains or suspects. You were expected to make notes of these numbers and names on various different coloured index pages attached to your pocket book. As the names of suspects were read out, those more experienced officers would pipe up that they had seen so and so driving a red Cortina that morning and that he usually parks his motors in the car park behind the cinema. After all the reports had been read out the sergeant would then assign each officer his beat for the day. As we were on a late shift it meant that two officers would crew the van, whilst Pecker Wood crewed the area car with Andy Kimber. Two others were allocated a panda car each, whilst Graham and I got to walk Beat 9 which was the Palmerston Road shopping area.

After parade we all trooped down stairs to the front office. The first person I saw was GT. He'd been on early turn for a few days and I hadn't seen him since we left Bishops Waltham.

"What's that on your top lip Graham?"

"What's it look like? I got told on my first day that I looked like a girl so I thought I'd better grow a moustache as soon as I could. What do you think?" as he smoothed it down with a damp finger.

Before I could answer Sergeant Batten ushered me into an office. I was certainly treated to the pep talk and he made it quite clear what he expected of me. So long as I worked hard, produced results, looked the part, was keen and enthusiastic, we'd get along like a house on fire. There didn't seem to be much room for manoeuvre. The door opened and I was then introduced to Sergeant Terry, my Relief's station sergeant. He was a small, slim man in his late forties with swept back, wiry grey hair. He rolled his own tobacco and his hands shook as he did so. He was extremely pleasant and quite a comedian, in fact he had an incredibly quick wit. Both sergeants were ex-Portsmouth City men and weren't that keen on being amalgamated into Hampshire and even less keen that both of them were former CID officers who now found themselves back in uniform. I didn't feel brave enough to ask them why!

It was raining outside and Graham checked to see if I'd got all my wet weather gear with me. This meant donning my three-quarter length gannex rain coat together with water proof trousers. Except they weren't trousers at all. They were actually two separate legs with a strap at the front that fastened to a special button on the inside belt loop of your trousers, very similar to a pair of stockings. I reckon these were designed by somebody who hated coppers and it gave them some kind of perverse pleasure every time it rained knowing that policemen everywhere were dressed to thrill. Graham and I ventured out on foot patrol and we spent a couple of hours getting to know each other. He was very laid back and easy to get along with and gave me chapter and verse on all the personalities both on White Relief and at Southsea nick in general. As far as actual work was concerned, in-between being sent to jobs by the station or the control room we would be expected to generate our own and that meant stopping offenders and dealing with them accordingly. He reassured me that we would start off with some easy bread and butter type traffic offences and work our way up.

He then gave me a brief history and geography lesson on policing Portsmouth which was really useful. The city used to have its own independent force until April 1967 when it was amalgamated into the Hampshire Constabulary. He went on to explain that older officers like our two sergeants were still firmly entrenched in the 'city days' and that being part of Hampshire was definitely second best. Graham continued to explain that the hierarchy within Hampshire hated the old Portsmouth force or K Division as it was now known. He said I would soon learn that if you worked in K Division and went up to HQ at Winchester or worse to F Division, which was Southampton, then be on your guard because there might be some who will give you serious grief because of it. And I thought we were all on the same side! He further explained that there were in fact three stations within K Division, with Southsea (Kilo Sierra) policing the southern and eastern area, Kingston Crescent (Kilo Foxtrot) or Fratton as it was often referred to policing the north of the city and Portsmouth Central (Kilo Charlie), as the name suggests got the bit in between. The local control room (Kilo) was based in a small room on the first floor at Central whilst the main county control room was at HQ in Winchester. The only time I would have dealings with them would be if I ever got to go in the area car as that was the only vehicle we had fitted with a VHF radio set. All our other transmissions were made on UHF personal radio sets.

Before I knew it we had been out on patrol for a couple of hours already and were heading back to the station as we were due to do an hours patrol in a panda car whilst that officer took his meal break. It meant we could take our gannex coats off and as it had stopped raining I happily got rid of my waterproof stockings! As I was about to climb into the blue and white Austin 850 Mini Graham advised me to check the underneath of the hinged passenger seat before sitting in it.

"Why"? I asked.

"Because certain individuals on this Relief have a habit of leaving glass stink bombs under the frame so that when you sit in the seat you smash it and I'm not driving around with the bloody window open all day" laughed Graham.

He went on to explain that it was highly likely that I would be the target of some kind of initiation ceremony as my official welcome to the Relief. As green as I was I had expected this and knew that whatever it was I had to laugh with them and at myself or suffer for a long time to come. I probably wouldn't get it today, but it could be tomorrow, next week or even next month, you just don't know. After giving me a good guided tour of the entire patch we drove down to Queen Street and to the Royal Sailors Home Club, which was basically a Naval hotel to collect a couple of prisoners meals from the kitchens out the back. The meals looked disgusting and could well have been scraped out from the slop bucket. After being plated up they were covered with aluminium dish covers and we drove back to Southsea with them sat on my lap. I then had the job of delivering them to the prisoners currently occupying our guest suites. They didn't look too impressed. Then it was upstairs to our own canteen where apart from eating the main sport was cards. It was almost a religion for certain individuals and although no money was involved, pride was at stake. There was no abstaining either.

After grub we went back out on foot patrol and within seconds we had our first customers, two young lads riding two-up on a pedal cycle on the pavement and with no lights on. It wasn't exactly the crime of the century but it gave me the opportunity to show Graham what I was made of. And by all accounts I wasn't made of much as I made a complete hash of all of it. He was very nice about it but I think he was probably already wondering what it was he had done to deserve a probationer like me. It didn't help when an hour or so later we stopped another lad riding a moped which had a number of minor faults on it. I bumbled my way through the offences, cocked up the caution and forgot to get the boys date of birth. Never mind, there's always tomorrow.

As work finished at 10 pm a second religion kicked in; the pub. Most of the Relief walked the short distance out the back door of the nick to the Lord John Russell, or the LJR as it was known. Week day closing time in those days was 10.30 pm (11 pm Friday and Saturdays) so downing as much alcohol as possible was the order of the day. As we approached the door the sounds of Gerry Rafferty's *Baker Street* pierced the night air from the juke box and as we entered we were greeted by a favourable buzz from the place. Mine hosts were Dave and Diane who were the archetypal husband and wife pub landlords, very caring and knowledgeable about their clientele and they ran an extremely orderly house. They knew straight away that I was the new boy and they made me feel very welcome. By the time I got back to my lodgings it was just past eleven and sure enough the house was in complete darkness and they were all in bed!

The following Saturday was my first football duty and I was frankly terrified. As a youngster I'd never had the opportunity to go to a major football match despite being an avid football fan, but I doubt I would have chosen to see Pompey anyway. Living on the Isle of Wight didn't help obviously and like a lot of young lads growing up in the 1970s I was a Leeds United fan, just like many kids in the 1990s and beyond are Manchester United fans. Graham seemed quite put out that I liked football because he loathed it.

We spent the morning patrolling the city and the area surrounding Fratton Park in the van to ensure that there were no trouble makers in the area. Then it was back to the nick and across the road to the Victory Restaurant for our meal. Within minutes the place was full with about 100 police officers all filling their faces with either sausage and chips or pie and chips. Most of the conversation centred on Pompey having to win today to stand any chance of surviving in the third division. Lose or draw and they got relegated to the fourth division. Some of those present were obviously Pompey fans who were adamant that they would survive but this was tempered by those who were clearly relishing the prospect of seeing them go down.

Then it was back in the van to the ground. I sat in the back of the Bedford CF with several other officers and it seemed that all of us smoked. It wasn't long before you couldn't see the person sat opposite you. In fact the smoke was so thick that every couple of minutes the rear doors needed to be opened to let some of it out!

After arriving at Fratton Park we filed in via the Frogmore Road entrance. Graham showed me around part of the ground, starting at the Fratton End, home of its fervent supporters. Beneath the stand was the bar which was heavily policed before, during and after the match. Pints of alcohol were served in plastic glasses for obvious reasons and fans were even allowed to drink them up on the terraces. Next door to the bar was the gent's toilet. It was a large place and the whole of the far wall consisted of a concrete and tiled trough urinal. It looked and smelt more like a cesspit, it absolutely reeked of urine, much of which was spread all over the floor and it was vile. Mind you they were luxurious in comparison to those at the Milton End for the visiting supporters. A sort of brick built shed housed another trough urinal that was permanently blocked with toilet paper, fag butts and chewing gum and that in turn ensured that the black painted floor was an inch deep in urine. You had to wade through the stuff to get to the urinal which seemed like a rather pointless exercise when all you needed to do really was just piss on the floor! I'd been told earlier in the day that if you spelt Fratton Park backwards it would say NOTTARF KRAP which just about summed up the place!

My knees were quite literally knocking together and I could feel my legs shaking and yet the ground was still empty at this stage! Today's opponents were Carlisle United who themselves were struggling to survive. The ground started to fill but not by much. In fact the official figures showed that less than 6000 spectators bothered to attend. Just before kick-off about 30 of us made our way up the steps to the back of the Fratton End, which was an old wooden and concrete two-tiered terrace, with standing room only. There were about

2000 fans there I suppose and there were huge gaps everywhere. One of my colleagues mentioned that he had never seen such a low turnout before. The Carlisle supporters numbered about a dozen but I suppose they could be forgiven as Carlisle is just about as far away from Portsmouth as you can possibly get without climbing over Hadrian's Wall.

I was intrigued by the number of older officers who seemed to be wearing the old fashioned capes instead of a gannex. Graham simply said "They're all smokers" and then told me to watch them more closely. I was fascinated to see that you could actually smoke a fag and in between drags you could hide the cigarette under the cape to prevent a senior officer from spotting you having a crafty one. Ingenious. I'll have to get myself one of those I thought.

By half time Pompey were leading three nil. As soon as the half time whistle went we all trooped off to the St. John's Ambulance room positioned beneath the Fratton End for a cuppa and another cigarette. This small room was packed with every copper in the ground and another smoke screen filled the air. The tea was delivered by ladies from the WRVS and served in those really flimsy plastic cups that you usually get orange squash in. Just after the second half got under way we went back upstairs again. I was a lot more relaxed by this time and actually quite enjoying myself.

No sooner had we got back into our positions then Carlisle scored. A few of the Pompey fans actually cheered which I found quite amusing. A few minutes later Carlisle scored again and the cheer from the home supporters was even louder. Then some of them started actively encouraging the away team to score again. I found this bizarre. Some of them started dancing around in groups as if they had won the league. And then I noticed a young lad aged about 17 who appeared to be egging the others on. Unfortunately for him I took an instant dislike to him because he was the spitting image of a boy I hated at school. I was to learn later that this youth was Robin 'Fish' Potter and he and I would cross paths several times in years to come. A small fire was started by those within his group and they all danced around it. Carlisle then equalised and a huge roar went up from the Fratton End. I couldn't comprehend this at all. Potter then took off his shirt, waved it around his head for a bit and then threw it onto the small fire. As it erupted into flame two officers grabbed him by the arms and led him away to eject him from the ground. This was met by loud cheers from his mates as Potter laughed out loud in a display of complete contempt for anything resembling normal behaviour. The match finished 3-3 and that meant Pompey would be playing in division 4 next season. As we lined the pitch and faced the crowd in the Fratton End there despondent shouts from one or two but in general most of them seemed resigned to their fate and slowly trudged away from the ground.

It wasn't anywhere near as bad as I feared, although to be fair it wasn't the biggest crowd in the world and they were somewhat pre-occupied. But I did learn that some of Portsmouth's youth had a twisted sense of humour that I might find hard to understand.

I'd started to feel like the odd one out because I didn't have a moustache. Graham advised me that should I wish to start sprouting facial hair that I had to do it at a certain time and according to Force Standing Orders which believe it or not actually covered such subjects. FSO's clearly stated that officers could only grow a beard or moustache whilst on annual leave or during a period of extended sickness, having obtained written permission from a senior officer first! However Graham assured me that you could in fact grow it whilst on nights so that by the time you got back onto day shifts ten days later it should be fully grown and no-one would take any notice. So over my weekend off and before the start of my first set of nights I started to allow my top lip to become furry. Trouble is it looked just like fair coloured bum fluff and didn't seem to resemble a moustache at all. I'll get used to it I suppose.

The following week and it was time for my first set of nights. I was as nervous about doing nights as I was about going to Fratton Park, not because I was frightened of the dark or anything but more because most violent incidents take place at night. I entered the nick via the back door which leads straight into the locker room. This in turn was right opposite the wall to the charge room and as I was getting my kit out of my locker there was a horrendous racket coming from the other side of that wall. It was obvious even from my lack of service that there was a violent struggle going on, with lots of shouting, screaming, swearing and shouts of "get him on the ground". I was naturally rather intrigued and made my way through the lockers to the corridor. As soon as I arrived the volume increased significantly and then to my horror there was an almighty bang as a head came through the stud wall right opposite me. The head was upside down and about a foot from the ground. There was plaster dust everywhere as the head spat out a mouthful of the stuff before screaming out loud. And in an instant it was whisked back inside the charge room to more howls and screams. A shudder went down my spine and a couple of seconds later the plaster ridden head, plus its body was being unceremoniously carried by four officers, one in each corner down the corridor towards the cells. The prisoner was kicking, spitting and screaming as he continued to resist. Oh shit, this is exactly what I thought it might be like. That hole was later patched over with a piece of plasterboard that was still there ten years later. I looked at it everyday.

Graham and I were on foot patrol in Palmerston Road precinct. It was just past midnight and it was pouring with rain. We stood in the doorway to Knight and Lees department store trying to stay dry when John Travolta walked passed us. OK so it wasn't actually John Travolta but he was doing a fine impersonation of him dressed in a three piece white suit with black shirt undone to reveal a couple of gold chains. He was in his mid 30s and he was so drunk he could barely walk and passed within six feet of us and didn't even notice. At first we chuckled about him being the oldest swinger in town and then Graham noticed that he had a set of car keys in his hands. We followed him around the corner into Stanley Street. We were so close to him that we could almost touch him but he still didn't realise we were there. He stopped beside an MG Midget sports car and tried unlocking it. It was pathetic to watch as time and time again he failed to connect key with lock. Then he dropped them and ended up scrabbling around on his hands and knees, in the rain, in his nice white suit trying to find them. It took him more than five minutes to actually open the door and get in. He tried starting it but it failed. Graham had seen enough by then and we approached the car. Straight away he denied driving it or even trying to start it and in fact he was waiting for a friend to give him a lift home. I had my first arrest for being drunk in charge of a motor vehicle and as we conveyed him back to Kilo Sierra I felt quite chuffed that I hadn't made a cock up with this one.

The procedure in 1978 involved calling your Sgt back in to obtain a breath specimen using the old bag and tube method. These were the first breathalysers ever used and had been in existence since 1968. The kit consisted of a small plastic bag with a tube insert at one end. You then took out a sealed glass tube from the little green box this lot was all housed in and by using the razor blade edging installed along one side of the box you rubbed both the sealed ends of the tube along the blade until you had sawn the things off. You then inserted the tube into the bag and placed a plastic mouth piece over the other end of the tube. You then offered the bag to the suspect who blew into it until the bag was fully inflated, during which the yellow crystals inside the tube changed colour. If they went green your suspect had alcohol in him and if those green crystals went over the red line, half way along the tube then your suspect was very probably over the prescribed drink drive limit and was therefore arrested. Once back at the station your Sgt had to offer the suspect a second test so that the Sgt was sure your suspect was over the limit. If he agreed then you called out the Police Surgeon who took a blood specimen which was sent away for analysis and only when you had the result back from the lab in a couple of weeks were you entirely sure whether or not your boy would go to court or not.

John Travolta meantime was in no mood to cooperate and refused point blank to take a breath test. Instead he insisted on making a written statement. I was somewhat confused by what might happen next but it was a pleasure to watch JB in action. He obliged by giving our still rather sodden guest the necessary statement forms to fill in. Like a school child he leant over the desk with his arm across the paper trying to hide it from prying eyes. The stench from second hand alcohol fumes was over whelming and Graham opened the window. After about ten minutes our literary friend sat up and demanded another piece of paper as he had made an error on this one. JB said he could but only after he had signed the one he had just written. After much argument he agreed and then handed over the paper. He was obviously so inebriated that he couldn't see the lines he was writing on because each line of writing took up three lines on the paper. It was all over the place and completely incomprehensible reading. JB stalled him further by requesting a breath test again. He refused. A second statement form was placed in front of him. He seemed to take more time over this one, in fact after half an hour JB asked him if he had finished. The man stated he wasn't satisfied with what he had written and asked us to help him! JB told him that it was his statement and we couldn't possibly assist him, besides which we weren't entirely sure what he wanted to say anyway. He signed it and refused a breath test for the third time. He was then given a third statement form and a warning that this would be his last. Another half hour went by as our man scribbled out a string of words that simply made no sense at all. He refused to sign it and JB then requested a sample of his blood to be taken by a Doctor. Again he refused and by now JB had lost his patience and John Travolta spent the rest of night dancing in a cell.

But those three statements he had written eventually convicted him because you could clearly see that they were written by somebody under the influence but the biggest lesson for me was just how bloody awkward people who are drunk can be. By the end of that first week of nights I'd had a further two arrests and my new moustache was still looking decidedly sparse in the actual facial hair department.

Being on nights meant that I got to see the city in a completely different light (no pun intended) and more importantly my colleagues and the police force in general in a different light. I had been intrigued for a couple of days that certain individuals would disappear for some considerable time during the early hours. I was also intrigued by the large number of freshly baked loaves of bread that would mysteriously appear on the table in the middle of the front office. But then one night Laurie Terry asked if I was busy and as it happened it wouldn't have made the slightest difference if I had been because it was my turn to go and make the bread. Make the bread? I was instructed to walk to the bakers on Albert Road, just next door to Tesco's and assist the two bakers inside to quite literally help them bake. I was sure this was a wind-up. It wasn't. So there I was at 4 am loading up trays of rolls, buns and assorted loaves into ovens, making these two chirpy bakers cups of tea, whilst all the time wondering what the hell I was doing there. Prior to being sent on my latest probationer attachment I had been given an order list and came out of the shop at 0530 with a large bag of rolls and loaves, still warm and smelling fabulous stuffed under my gannex. I never found out how it started or why but gathered from the two bakers that it was almost a tradition that the new boy gives them a hand from time to time.

Another tradition was reserved for Sunday night. In the early hours, just so long as it was quiet, the whole Relief would gather down at Billy Mannings funfair on the seafront, which was actually on Central's patch. The van was parked at the rear of the premises and one by one we would climb up onto the roof of the van and then hop over the wall and into the funfair, where we would grab some mats and spend a childish half hour or so sliding down the astro-slide.

Even though we had left Ashford a few weeks before it wasn't the end of our academic training, far from it. In fact we had to attend monthly training days with an exam at the beginning of each on last months work. In between you were expected to study that month's subject matter. K Division probationers plus a few from the likes of neighbouring J and H Divisions had to attend Byculla House in Queens Crescent, Southsea. This truly magnificent building was the former headquarters of the old Portsmouth City Police. It was now part of the Training Department and even housed the vehicle workshops within its grounds. The building dated back to 1890 and had seen many uses over the years including that of a Red Cross military hospital just after the First World War and then as a residential school for girls. The exterior of the house saw it clad with ornate, carved wooden beams with white mottled rendering in between. The interior was even more impressive with a beautiful wooden staircase and galleried landing that complemented the wood panelled walls throughout.

Our trainers were Inspector Bob Allen and his 'gorilla' Sgt Dave Morgan, both ex-city men. Bob Allen was a Pompey boy through and through. Born and bred within the city walls he was in his early 50s and spoke with a true Portsmouth accent. Not only did he know his stuff but he knew exactly how to teach it and it was always with an accompanying true life story mixed in with a touch of bad language and plenty of comic delivery. It was a pleasure to be taught by him. Likewise his gorilla. A quieter man, complete with full beard he did actually walk like he had just descended from the trees. Between them they made training quite a laugh and to start off with I took a lot of notice. But it wasn't to last.

Riding my bike whilst off duty was what I lived for. Together with a couple of old cadet mates we would ride all over the country to race meetings or other motorcycle events. And being 19 of course we thought we were bullet proof. In June I found out I wasn't. Whilst riding sedately through the city one morning a cigar smoking, Jaguar driving blind man pulled out in front of me. After colliding with the front end of his car and bouncing off his windscreen I ended up laying in the road, looking up at him as he casually rolled the window down and uttered those immortal words "sorry mate I didn't see you".

My bike was carted off to a repair shop and I had to walk everywhere with a limp. Two weeks later and still bike-less I managed to blagg a ride on Chris Cox's Honda 500 to go down to Bognor Regis for the evening. Chris and I were great mates, having joined the cadets together and he had been posted to Ringwood of all places. His bike was incredibly smooth and as I rode through Emsworth towards the Sussex border I saw a policeman standing in the road with his arm in the air ushering me into a lay-by. I'd just been checked by the Traffic Division radar team at 52 mph in a 30 limit. PC Bob Scorey who I had never met before was somewhat legendary in that he hadn't been presented with any discretion when he joined up because he was last in the queue and they had run out. He was going through the formalities whilst filling out a form HORT/1 with name, address, date of birth etc and then he asked the very question I was rather hoping he wouldn't ask. Occupation? I very sheepishly told him that I was a police officer.

"Are you still a probationer"? He asked.

"Yes at Southsea" I replied.

"Hmm, hard world isn't it, you should have known better" and with that he reported me for speeding. My heart sank.

"And don't forget to tell Superintendent Neville in the morning will you" and with that he turned and walked away.

My heart sank even further. Tell the Superintendent, oh shit, no. As a proby you don't even look at the Superintendent let alone confess any wrong doings. But Bob Scorey was right, it is a hard world and yes, I really should have known better.

To make things worse I was late for early turn the next morning! And it wasn't the first time either, in fact it was becoming a bit too regular but I just didn't hear the alarm clock going off at 0515 in the morning. It wasn't that I was too lazy to get out of bed, I genuinely didn't hear it go off. So I came into work about 15 minutes late and was greeted by both JB and Laurie Terry. I got yet another bollocking for being late and got told to get my hair cut. Could it get any worse? Well yes because I now had to summon up the courage to tell them about last night. I blurted it out and the pair of them sat there in disbelief. I was told to do a duty report and submit it to Mr Neville immediately. I then got told to buck my ideas up and quick.

As some kind of punishment I got told I would be doing station duty for a week or two. This was no easy option and I hated doing station duty, having previously had spells of it whilst a cadet and by doing the odd hour here and there since arriving at Southsea. A good station duty officer was worth his weight in gold and Southsea had two such masters in Jack Day and Horace Evans, both long since retired police officers and now undertaking this thankless task during the day as civilian employees. Apart from answering queries at the front counter the station duty officer during the 1970s was also responsible for taking outside phone calls, including some redirected 999 calls from the control room, internal phone calls, dispatching units to various calls via the radio system and answering their calls for advice or assistance, monitoring the alarm board, sending and receiving telex's, gaoler duties, including checking on prisoners every half an hour plus feeding them, dog kennel duties, including the feeding of any incarcerated mutts and a whole lot more besides. It could be quiet for a couple of hours and then all of a sudden everything would happen at once and you needed the coordination skills of an octopus.

It was during my second morning that I got tasked with what I thought was my long overdue initiation ceremony, in that at 11 am I had to fire up the air raid siren located outside the station. Are you serious? This is a wind-up right? But Laurie Terry seemed serious enough and handed me a key and an instruction manual. He was most insistent that it was to be started at bang on 11 am and was to last exactly 30 seconds. I read the manual and it seemed simple enough, open door at base of siren poll, insert key into slot, turn to the right and press the red button. To end, turn key back to off position. I still wasn't convinced but in view of my previous misdemeanour's I wasn't exactly in a position to push things too much. So just before 11 am there I was armed with a key and the instruction manual. After clearing away various weeds and cobwebs I opened up the rusty door and inserted the key. I kept looking behind me to see if everyone was looking at me through the windows. They weren't. So at precisely 11 am I turned the key and hit the button to release a quite deafening and truly frightening sound from above me. Everybody in Albert Road stopped and stared. I recall thinking how terrifying the war years must have been with this thing going off all the time. It was a long 30 seconds and even after I had switched it off the siren continued for another 30 seconds before dying away. It transpired that this was a bi-annual test of all the air raid sirens in the city and I had to sign a special log book that the test had been conducted in a proper manner and that the siren appeared to be in good working order.

After serving my two week penance it was time for me to go solo without the back-up of my tutor constable. It was now mid summer and the 1978 World Cup was coming to a climax with the final between Holland and West Germany. An old black and white telly was lifted out of the crime property store and heaved upstairs to the canteen so that White Relief could watch it live. After all the rest of the population would be doing the same, so why not us? The match had literally only just kicked off when a report of a sudden death came in. Away you go then young Steve, seemed to be the general consensus. Bloody marvellous I thought as I trudged off towards nearby Chelsea Road. Why me? Stupid question really. Upon my arrival a few minutes later I was greeted by the GP who had called us. He explained that the elderly gent had a long history of illness and that he would be issuing a death certificate. It just needed me to sort out the undertaker and secure the house. The body is behind the settee. With that he left. I entered the house which was in a bit of a state with a pungent smell about it. I'd been to several deaths before and was reasonably used to seeing dead bodies but nothing could ever relieve the anxiety you feel whilst searching for one in a house. Even though I knew it was behind the settee, it was still somewhat unnerving. It was even worse if you didn't know whether there was a body or not whilst conducting a search. I entered the lounge and sure enough there he was laying on his back behind the settee. I called the control room to arrange for the undertaker to attend. A few minutes later I got my reply.

Kilo to 2113, the undertakers are busy at the moment, they will be out to you in about an hour and a half.

An hour and a half? Oh that just happens to be 90 minutes doesn't it? Busy my arse. Nothing else for it really and with that I switched the TV on in the lounge. And it was in colour. Bonus! With that I pulled up a chair and made my myself comfortable. I had no idea whether my temporary companion had been a football fan before he passed away so I assumed out of respect for him that he had been and therefore gave him a running commentary on the match. And funnily enough the two undertakers arrived about 15 minutes after the final whistle, bloody comedians.

"They'll nick anything around here" said Graham "Even if it's nailed down the bastards will take the nails instead".

He was absolutely right of course; it did seem that if you left something unattended for more than two seconds it would be lifted. This was proved to me beyond all reasonable doubt one afternoon when I got sent to a report of a theft from a motor vehicle in Carlisle Road, which was a pretty run down area on the point of being demolished to make way for a new road and roundabout. The victim was a young mum who had gone to visit her friend in Carlisle Road. In mid afternoon she had parked her MK2 Ford Cortina right outside her friends mid terrace house. It was a typical Portsmouth terrace property where the door opens straight out onto the street with no forecourt or garden. After an hour or so it was time for her to leave. After placing her young child in the back she went to start the car but it just wouldn't fire. So her friend called for her husband to come out and take a look. He opened the bonnet and to his utter amazement found that somebody had nicked the carburettor! They'd even locked the car afterwards!

I was soon back on nights and patrolling the seafront area for the first time on my own. Southsea seafront could be an incredibly busy place both during the day and especially at night with a number of night clubs and pubs on the front itself or in the immediate area. The main hub of activity centred on an area less than 100 yards long that housed the Esplanade Bars pub, The Intrepid Bun burger joint, Nero's nightclub, Tiberius Casino, the Glitter Bay amusement arcade and the world famous Joanna's night club. World famous for two reasons; one because it was frequented by sailors from every foreign navy that had ever visited the UK and secondly because your feet stuck to the carpet every where you went! There was also a large plastic tree in one corner that was kept alive by large numbers of people either pissing into its pot or throwing up all over it. Whenever the American fleet docked large numbers of prostitutes would arrive from London and elsewhere which rather annoyed our local girls! Across the road was

South Parade Pier which housed two establishments, the Albert Tavern and the Gaiety Show Bar. All of these places closed at 2 am and they all kicked out their drunken clientele at the same time and on really busy nights it wouldn't be unusual to have some 2000 people in the area, most of whom seemed to want the same taxi. The taxi rank was actually positioned in the middle of the carriageway and was a favourite spot for fighting to break out when the taxis eventually turned up or for some to get run over by passing traffic.

Getting to know the staff at these places was essential as we both relied on each other a great deal at times. Two of the bouncers at Joanna's in particular were great and I had a lot of respect for them. Chris Wilson and Ray Harwood were true professionals and had great communication skills and could defuse most situations. You knew that if things had got out of hand when those two were on the door then there really was little hope of resolving things by talking. Both men were in their 30s I suppose and wore black and white hounds tooth patterned jackets, black ties and black trousers. Chris walked with a pronounced limp and Ray and I spent most of our time talking about his Range Rover. Part of their job was to protect the cashier who sat inside a room not much bigger than a broom cupboard with metal bars on the door. The other part of their job was to quickly open the doors if other bouncers like Chalkie White or the clubs manager Leo, came tumbling down the stairs with a violent drunk that they needed to eject and then bolt it firmly behind them again afterwards as that same drunk then attacked the doors by either head butting them, kicking them or punching them, or sometimes all three!

Some of the female clientele were so regular that Chris and Ray knew their names and they were usually allowed in for free because they kept the sailors happy. One by one you would see them leave with a drunken matelot on their arm to take them around the corner into the darkness of Alhambra Road or into the car park beneath the Royal Beach Hotel where they would give them a quick shag or a blow job before returning 15 minutes later to start the process all over again. Some of them would do this four or five times an evening. One girl in particular was known as the bow-legged dwarf and she was legendary and always the busiest. As her name suggests she was of dwarf like proportions and her deformed legs were completely bowed outwards and I often wondered just how much alcohol you would need to consume to have gone anywhere near her. Chris and Ray would always chuckle as she came down the stairs holding the hand of her next client, looking for all the world like a fully dressed chimpanzee from a circus act.

The world famous Joanna's nightclub.

I was standing inside the doorway talking to Ray whilst Chris had the front door ajar and was talking to two lads just outside. After a while Chris calmly closed the door and asked if I had overheard any of the conversation he'd had with them. I hadn't and he went on to explain that this pair had tried entering the club for free by waving an ID card under Chris's nose and purporting to be from the Police drugs squad. Chris said it was quite obvious to him that they weren't from the drugs squad because the ID card was from

Southern Gas! Once I'd stopped laughing I went outside to see the pair of them hovering around outside Nero's. As I approached they were nearing the front of the queue and I stood behind them as they repeated their cheeky request. The door staff weren't quite as switched on as Chris and allowed them entry. I stopped them as soon as they entered and arrested them both for impersonating a police officer. I was feeling rather pleased with myself and arranged transport back to Kilo Sierra and presented them both to Sgt Terry who duly booked them both in and locked them up in a cell.

"I suppose you're feeling quite chuffed with yourself, aren't you young Stephen?" said a slightly sarcastic Laurie Terry returning from the cells.

"Yes sarge, a bit" I replied.

"You do know there is no power of arrest for impersonating a police officer don't you?" he said with a wry smile as he started to roll a fag. My jaw obviously fell wide open.

"Been in the job five minutes and he's already making up his own fucking laws" he continued.

I was speechless. I'm in the shit again. But to my surprise I wasn't, it was an honest mistake and Sgt Terry sorted it out for me. Both men were later charged with attempt deception and the impersonation offence.

It wasn't too long before I got to find out exactly how dangerous being a Police officer could be. I was out in the van with Graham and had been assisting him with a minor enquiry, after which he thought it might be an idea to just stop off on the seafront to ensure that all was quiet. We'd been there for a few minutes when we heard a lot of shouting and screaming coming over the radio. There were several voices, including that of a female that could be heard screaming "stop it, stop it". Then silence. The control room asked the last unit to respond. Silence. And again, silence. Then one by one they called every single officer on duty by number and name to respond. The only one that didn't was Ado Watts. They kept calling him and got no reply. No-one knew where he was because he hadn't been deployed to anything recently. We started an area search for him. The control room kept calling him but again there was no reply. A few minutes passed and then we got directed to Goldsmith Avenue where a passing taxi driver had found Ado unconscious on the pavement with his panda parked across the road. The whole Relief and every other unit in the city seemed to arrive at the same time. Ado was out cold with blood streaming from his face. His radio was missing. He slowly came to as the ambulance arrived. He briefly told us that he had seen a couple coming out of the Rainbow Club in Goldsmith Avenue and they were having a raging domestic dispute. He was getting physical with her which is just when Ado was driving passed. He got out to calm things down and instantly became the target himself. He was trying to call for assistance when his radio was snatched out of his hand and that was the last thing he could recall. The radio was later found in a litter bin and following extensive enquiries a couple were arrested and charged.

I have to confess that at the age of 19 I was somewhat naïve in the ways of the world, particularly where females were concerned, because I thought they were all sugar and spice and all things nice. Graham and I were in a panda for an hour during meal break relief when we volunteered to help out just across the border on Central's patch at a place called The Bistro Club in Osborne Road. There had been a fight inside and the officers attending needed some back up. It was about 1 am as we pulled up on the other side of the road and as we walked towards the club Graham said "I hate this place, it's a dump. They don't call it Beasties for nothing".

It was little more than a standard sized shop front with a single door that opened inwards to reveal a dark and rather sinister looking establishment with a long L-shaped bar and a dance floor towards the rear of the premises. It was run by a rather portly gentleman called Charlie Dyke who constantly puffed on cigars. We could just about see two officers at the back hanging onto a prisoner and all they really wanted was a van to attend. The music blared and as I looked around it appeared that this wasn't a club for the youngsters, because it was full of thirty-something's, most of whom seemed to be extremely pissed. On the corner section of the bar were two rather large females who kept looking towards us and laughing. They were sat on bar stools that made their already very short skirts ride up even further, revealing rather too much of their fat upper thighs, whilst their over sized stomachs ballooned from the top of their skirts making them look like a couple of Pilsbury Dough Boys. They both had short hair, one peroxide blonde the other jet black and as they puffed away on their fags and sipped on their Martini's I'm sure they thought that they looked wonderful. Suddenly the prisoner started to struggle and Graham moved towards the rear of the club and I followed him. As I walked past the two women so one of them leant back slightly and grabbed me by the testicles and shrieked out "Phwoar, you're a bit of alright".

Both of them let out a huge, deep roar of laughter that made them sound like a couple of old witches. I moved swiftly past them and was somewhat taken aback and asked Graham if he saw what happened. He said he hadn't but suggested I watch my back because the place was full of Toms. It wasn't my back I was worried about.

"Full of Toms?" I enquired "What are they?"

"Toms, prostitutes, prossies" he laughed.

Prostitutes? What, I've just had my nuts squeezed by a prostitute? I kept looking at them and a shudder went down my spine. They really were quite revolting. The trouble was I had to walk back past them in order to get out again. The van arrived outside and the four of us moved towards the door. The two witches winked at me as I deliberately made sure that I had one of the Central officers between me and them. They shrieked out loud again as one of them said "Ah leave him alone, he's only a baby".

Now I know why it's called Beasties!

The following week and the older members of White Relief had arranged a night out, commencing at the LJR and then onwards to the Playboy Club in Osborne Road. In comparison to The Bistro the Playboy Club was at the opposite end of the spectrum. You had to wear a jacket and tie for a start and the drinks were double the price of anywhere else. It was rather plush inside, with typical 1970s décor complete with lava lamps. We sat down on comfy sofas and arm chairs and were waited on by the Bunny Girls, complete with fluffy tails, fishnets and black ears. They were utterly charming towards their guests and had to put up with all sorts of rather lewd comments and innuendo from some who should have known better. I found it rather embarrassing I have to say and felt sorry for them, although they smiled sweetly and acted in a very professional manner. In truth the place was way beyond us financially and after just one drink we were already talking about where we were headed next.

"How's about Beasties?" was one suggestion.

Graham burst out laughing and said "I don't think Steve would fancy that would you mate?" He was absolutely right on that one.

We ended up walking the short distance to Palmerston Road where we entered the Pomme D'or Club, which was a big place but a bit spartan in comparison with the likes of Nero's and others. On this particular night it was virtually empty to and as I sat down at a beer sticky table with an over flowing ash tray in the middle of it so my eye was caught by two girls on the dance floor. They were smooching to a slow number with their arms slung across each others shoulders and they were almost nose to nose. Then to my utter amazement they started kissing. Not just a peck or two but full on snogging! I'd never seen a lesbian before, let alone two of them cavorting in public. I was fascinated.

"I wish I was a lesbian" said Nick Wood "I quite fancy the blonde one".

The following week saw the entire Relief and about 150 other officers gather at the Police club at Kingston Crescent nick for a night of food, cheap beer, a couple of stand-up comics with the high light of the evening being two strippers. The comedians were about as blue and politically incorrect as it was possible to be, being racist, sexist, homophobic, blasphemous and everything else-ist, which made them all the funnier of course. By the time the first stripper hit the stage the testosterone was in full flow and like baying animals we shouted our encouragement towards her. No sooner had she stripped off than it was exit stage left and she was out of sight. Back came one of the comedians and after another half hour or so we got the second stripper who did some highly unusual things with a live Boa Constrictor which had my eyes popping out on stalks! She got a standing ovation and calls for more, but I don't think it was for her artistic merit.

So within a matter of weeks I'd had my balls grabbed by a fat prostitute, been served beer by a Bunny Girl, seen my first two lesbians locked by the lips and watched in fascination as a stripper reached a simulated orgasm with a snake! Sugar and spice? I don't think so.

By July the relationship between me and my landlady appeared to be on a very slippery slope downhill. In truth I don't think I had done much wrong but they had clearly not found having a lodger much to their liking. Before I knew it I'd been given two weeks notice to quit. By sheer coincidence my best mate at the time, Andy Goward had also been having a bad time at his lodgings. He and I had been room mates for a year as cadets and shared a love for riding our bikes. It made sense therefore to look for a flat together and we found what we thought might be suitable at number No. 1 Campbell Road, Southsea, which was only a two minute walk from the nick. We arranged to meet the landlady there at 6pm one evening. Christine was a smart looking lady in her 40s with gold dripping from every finger, her wrists and her neck. As she opened the front door to the three storey Victorian house she explained that she didn't actually have the keys to the ground floor flat that we were interested in and that one of the other tenants was looking after them, as she rang his door bell. We stood in the hallway as a door at the top of the stairs opened and the tenant started to walk down the stairs holding out a set of keys. I looked at him and thought 'oh fuck what have we done'. He was a thirty something hippy, with a full beard and unkempt hair down past his shoulders. He had torn jeans on and bare feet. There was a strange smell coming from his room to. Well we haven't got to sleep with him I suppose and the flat was reasonable and at a fair price, so we took it. The bearded hippy went back upstairs and we took the keys.

No.1 Campbell Road, Southsea became home for the next three years.

The next day I had to submit a report requesting permission to reside at Campbell Road. It meant that Inspector O'Flaherty would need to come and inspect the premises before deeming it suitable for a junior officer to live in. As his name suggests Mr O was of Irish descent and quite often said things that left his subordinates slightly bemused and that's if they actually understood what he had said in the first place. And so I proudly presented my humble new abode to him and he granted permission for us to stay there, but on one condition, that I PNC'd the other occupants of the building first to ensure that they were suitable neighbours! What? You want me to go and knock on the doors of four complete strangers and demand their full names and dates of birth to ensure they don't have a criminal record before you'll rubber stamp my application? Basically, yes. Needless to say I didn't do it and he didn't chase me up on it either. Andy and I moved in a few days later and not having to creep about the place after 9 pm was rather liberating.

In celebration we went and watched the film Grease that everyone was raving about. Like lots of other young males we stepped out of the Salon cinema in Highland Road afterwards with our leather jackets on, walking in a certain manner but thankfully not attempting to sing the final note from *Summer Nights* like most of the girls seemed to be doing!

I got a summons to appear in court for the speeding offence. I pleaded guilty by letter and got fined £35 and had three points put on my licence. In the same week I was walking down the corridor when I saw PC 1188 Mick Smith approaching me. He was quite simply a legend at Southsea. He was the beat bobby for the Eastney area and had been for many years. He was immaculately turned out with bulled boots and not a hair out of place from his silver beard. He commanded huge respect from his colleagues both old and young, but even more so from the public, everybody, and I do mean everybody on his beat either knew him as Mick, Mr Smith or PC Smith, which is the way it was supposed to be. He smiled at me and asked if I was PC Woodward. No sooner had I confirmed it then his expression changed completely and he grabbed me by the lapels and threw me up against the wall so hard it winded me. My feet were barely touching the floor as he screamed in my face about seeing me and another motorcyclist tearing along the seafront last weekend. Mine was the only registration number he could get because we were going so fast and he was incensed when he found out it belonged to a copper. I apologised profusely to him and he left me in a crumpled heap by the door. I was really upset by his understandable reaction and it played on my mind for days. I was starting to wonder if I was made of the right stuff to be a police officer.

It didn't help my mind set that JB was starting to put pressure on me for some results. Ever since I'd gone solo my self initiated work rate had dipped considerably. But I found it difficult to just step out into the road and stop vehicles for no other reason than to merely check them and their occupants out to ensure they were legal. It was purely a confidence thing on my part and what little I had was evaporating fast. I wasn't what you might call 'street-wise' either which didn't help. JB went onto state that he was further concerned that my studies were suffering since I moved into the flat with Andy and that my exam results were also starting to slide. In a rather fatherly manner he told me to buck up or face the consequences.

In September I got some light relief in that I was sent to Farnborough in the north of the county to help police the Farnborough International Airshow. It wasn't quite as glamorous as it might sound as I spent seven whole days on a roundabout waving my arms like a windmill, directing traffic. I didn't even get to see the Red Arrows! We spent 12 hours a day in the same spot and lived in the same Bedford CF van in between our stints on the roundabout. It was knackering and laborious work. We were billeted at the Aldershot Army Barracks but we couldn't socialise there because of security issues and therefore had to walk a mile or so to Aldershot nick to use their bar in the evenings. To gain access to the station you had to take your warrant card out and hold it up the camera before the control room could open the door. Taking it in and out of your wallet every time became a bit tedious so I kept mine loose in my pocket.

Several weeks later I realised my warrant card wasn't in my wallet. I couldn't find it anywhere and couldn't remember the last time I'd seen it, until the penny dropped and I recalled using it at Aldershot. I turned the flat upside down, I searched every possession I had but couldn't find it. This time I really was in the shit, losing your warrant card was a hanging offence. But I didn't have the bottle to confess so I left it another couple of weeks. Then one evening Andy and I were in a pub in Bognor and my wallet fell out of my jacket pocket and under the chair I was sitting on. After my initial panic was over I had a sudden brain wave that now would be the right time to report my wallet and warrant card as lost or stolen.

So the next day on early turn I did just that. I thought that once I had submitted my report that it would merely be a case of arranging for a new warrant card to be sent to me. But no, it wasn't that simple. First I had to write a statement, then a duty report, then it got telexed to every police force in the country, then it got crimed and sent to Sussex Police for them to investigate and then I had to arrange for a new photo to be taken and only then would I get a new card. In between times I got called a 'wanker' by both my Sgts and a 'fucking wanker' by one of the Inspectors. Fair enough.

Three days later I got called into Mr Neville's office. He said he had a copy of the report concerning the loss of my warrant card. He said it was very interesting and would I care to go over the loss again so that he had a first hand account of it. By now I'd told the story so many times that I actually believed it myself. As I concluded my fairy tale he leant back in his chair and said.

"That's very interesting PC Woodward, are you sure that's right?"

"Yes sir" I replied confidently.

With that he opened the drawer to his desk, took out my warrant card and placed it in front of me.

"Is that your warrant card PC Woodward?"

"Er..........yes sir" I squeaked.

"It's been in my drawer for several weeks now waiting to see if you would ever report it as lost" he said with his eyes brows firmly raised.

I was speechless. What could I say? He went on to explain that almost immediately after Farnborough the Bedford van we had been living in went to workshops to be decommissioned and sold off. Whilst in the process of stripping it out one of the workshops staff had found my warrant card and kindly handed it in. Mr Neville was clearly about to burst with anger. He threw the card in my face and bellowed.

"DON'T YOU EVER LIE TO ME AGAIN, NOW GET OUT OF MY FUCKING OFFICE".

I couldn't get out of there quick enough.

It took a while for those on my Relief to stop looking at me as if I were public enemy number one. Even Graham's usually sympathetic attitude towards me seemed to have gone cold. But I was due to start my two week area car attachment and I was determined to prove a few people wrong. At least being mobile meant that I would get to deal with some more interesting jobs rather than stopping errant youths riding on the pavement all the time.

PC Andy Kimber had the best job in the world as far as I was concerned. He got to drive Kilo Sierra 51, our MK4 Ford Cortina 2.0S with blue light and two-tone horns blaring everyday and even better than that, as an area car driver he got to wear a Belstaff jacket complete with red lining. OK, so it doesn't sound much but this was the first departure from the traditional tunic that us mere mortals wore and that red lining was like a badge of high office to the rest of us.

And I thoroughly enjoyed myself. Andy was very laid back and insisted I deal with everything. I'm quite sure JB had told him that was the way it was going to be and that I was being tested once again. We attended several RTA's, a couple of fires, got involved in a brief pursuit and stopped some half decent local villains. I certainly seemed to have got enough work out of it to keep JB off my back for a while.

We'd done a set of lates and earlies and were on the final night in a week of nights. It had been a very quiet Sunday evening and Andy was feeling particularly tired after grub. As we slowly cruised around the streets Andy started to nod off. Eventually he pulled over and asked if I'd like to drive? Only slowly though, nothing stupid. And if we get a shout, let him know and he'll take over. I jumped at the chance to drive the nicest car I'd ever been in. Within seconds Andy was knocking out the zeds with the passenger seat fully reclined and I set off to patrol the mean streets of Southsea at four in the morning. It felt great and I was in my element. About half an hour later I drove up Festing Road and stopped at the T junction with Highland Road. Hmmn, which way shall I go now, as Andy started snoring. Then from the shadows of the doorway to the Salon cinema I saw the silhouette of a policeman coming towards the car. Hello I thought, whose that? Oh shit, its JB. He crouched down beside the passenger door and did a double take on me in the drivers seat and Andy in the passenger seat.

"And just what the fuck are you doing driving this?" he exclaimed.

"Er........Andy wasn't feeling too good sarge, so I was just driving him back to the nick"

With that Andy came to and looked bad enough to have made my story look feasible. JB made me get in the back whilst he drove the car back to Kilo Sierra and Andy got sent home! That was the end of my two week long area car attachment which had certainly whetted my appetite for more.

CHAPTER 3

1979. Training days with the gorilla

The Christmas and New Year period were marked by two things, an IRA Christmas bombing campaign, which meant we patrolled all our shopping areas virtually non stop plus the awful weather. It was absolutely freezing cold for what seemed like months on end in what was later to become known as 'the winter of discontent'. We had lots of snow and our flat was like the inside of a freezer. It was a damp building anyway with no central heating and our only warmth was supplied by a paltry gas fire, fed via a 50p gas meter that devoured money like a nest of hungry Starling chicks.

The winter of discontent was the culmination of a series of industrial disputes at the likes of Ford and British Leyland, which inevitably led to other workers demanding ever higher pay. Some dustbin men went on strike in many areas resulting in mountains of rubbish stacked high on the streets and then the fuel tanker drivers walked out, threatening supplies of petrol to filling stations the length and breadth of the country. It didn't help the situation when the Prime Minister, James Callaghan, a Pompey boy by the way, when challenged by the press is alleged to have said "Crisis, what crisis?"

In the meantime Andy and I weren't that bothered about the collection or otherwise of our rubbish, just so long as there was enough four star petrol to fill our bike tanks with, we were happy. We took a ride out to Bognor and shortly after arriving there I discovered that I had virtually no fuel left in my tank, having forgotten to switch back the reserve tank the last time I ran short. After asking around it transpired that the only petrol station open after 6 pm between Bognor and Portsmouth was in Kingston Road, Portsmouth some

20 miles from where we were. I don't think Andy was too pleased with me because that meant he would have to take me back to Pompey to get some fuel. So off we went leaving my bike in Bognor. We filled a plastic can in Kingston Road, put it in his quick-release panniers and sped off east, back towards Bognor. Now I'm not the greatest passenger in the world I must confess, but Andy always scared the crap out of me, he rode like a thing possessed at times, especially if he was in a bad mood. And tonight he wasn't too happy. We rode along the old A27 and entered the small village of Bosham. There is a decent sized roundabout there with the White Swan pub adjacent to the left. We approached at some mind boggling speed and as we scraped every item of foot wear on the road surface we saw some people outside the pub start pointing at us. Andy instantly thought they were impressed by his biking prowess and on the exit from the roundabout he gave it a huge handful of throttle making the Kawasaki Z1000 howl in protest. It must have looked very impressive! But I wasn't convinced. As we roared away I looked down to my right. There was smoke billowing out from under the bike, in fact it looked like it was coming from the rear wheel. I beat Andy on his back as we entered a sharp left hand bend. I looked down again and could now see flames. I hit him again and told him to pull over and stop just as we entered a right hand bend. He pulled over and I leapt off the bike. The rear brake calliper was well alight and flames were now licking the underside of the pannier where the fuel can was. His quick-release panniers were anything but and after several seconds we gave up trying and I merely opened the box, took out the fuel can and hurled it across the road into a ditch. Meanwhile Andy was desperately trying to dampen the flames using the brand new, lime green leather gloves he had only purchased earlier that day. They did the trick but were blackened and melted in the process. But so was the brake calliper and the plastic shroud that covered it. We needed to get the back wheel off and remove the calliper straight away so that we could at least continue our journey, even if we only had the front brakes. Tool kits on Japanese bikes weren't exactly comprehensive and we were struggling to get the wheel off, when a Sussex Police panda car stopped behind us, just off the apex of the bend. On went the blue light and the hazard lights as a smart looking young Sussex PC got out.

"Need a hand lads?" the PC asked "I've got a full tool kit in the car if you need it" he continued enthusiastically.

It was very handy and as Andy got to work on removing the wheel and the calliper so I chatted away to our new best friend. He was very proud of his new panda, a Talbot Sunbeam 1.3 LS which he had only picked up yesterday and it was so much better than the old Hillman Avenger he used to have. He'd only done about 200 miles in it so far but he fully intended to look after it as best he could. He was clearly very proud of it and kept looking back towards it in a loving sort of way.

I think we all heard it coming, but Andy was too busy and I was in full flow with the officer, but approaching us from Bosham was a car that was seemingly accelerating very hard. An MG Midget suddenly appeared being driven by a young woman, with a friend in the front seat and another sat on the rear deck. She didn't see us until the last second and despite braking hard and swerving she hit the back of the panda really hard. The MG ricocheted across the road and went straight into the ditch, flinging the rear passenger over the hedge and into the field. The panda got shunted about 20 feet past us and looked a complete mess, possibly a write off.

"Is now a good time to tell you we're both in the job?" I said.

"I should have bloody guessed" our exasperated Sussex PC replied.

Since our arrival at Campbell Road I'd made friends with two of its other occupants including the hippy. To say I'd misjudged Steve first time around would be a huge understatement. He was a worldly-wise bloke with a great sense of humour who lived in the tiniest bed sit imaginable. But what a fascinating place it was. In the middle of his floor was a mattress that doubled as a settee if he had visitors. The walls were shelved, floor to ceiling and housed the biggest record and cassette tape collection I had ever seen. He had something like 3000 albums, over 5000 singles and had recorded every single program from the John Peel Sessions and the Tommy Vance Saturday Night Rock Show and had them meticulously catalogued with coloured spine labels. He had a large book collection and also dug up and collected Victorian medicine bottles and he hand painted white metal military figurines. His room invariably smelt of joss sticks although I was still too naive to understand why! The whole room was painted dark blue and there was a poster of Jimmy Hendrix on the back of the door. I'd sit in his room for hours just chatting or learning how to play Back Gammon and as he opened up to me I learned that he had lived in every room in the house over the last ten years and had some hilarious stories to tell about some of its previous occupants. But he also gave me an insight into the Portsmouth psyche and the people that lived there, which proved invaluable.

The other resident I got to know was Mike, who lived in the bed sit on the top floor. Mike was a forty-something, pipe smoking gay man, typically very camp whose bed sit was at the opposite end of the spectrum to Steve's. It was immaculately kept and everything in it had its place. Mike too liked his music although it wasn't always to the same taste as Steve's who lived directly below him and so on occasions when both of them were playing it out loud it got a bit confusing.

Chris, Andy and I all have our birthdays in March, within 10 days of each other and this year was particularly special as we would all turn 20. No longer teenagers, we decided this momentous occasion should be celebrated. After starting at the LJR we looked in on a couple of other pubs in the area before getting a taxi to Granny's night club at the Tricorn Centre. Granny's started off as *the* place to be seen at during the weekends and it was usually packed out, even though it was slightly more expensive than most of the others. You had to get the lift from the ground floor up to the second floor of what was basically little more than a concrete multi storey car park. But it was quite plush inside and your feet didn't stick to the carpet like they did at Joanna's. It had two dance floors inter-connected by the bar and there were velvet covered booths to sit at. The disco lighting was state of the art although the general atmosphere always seemed a bit dark. The three of us strutted in already half cut. It didn't cost us anything to get in as it was accepted practice that you merely flashed your warrant card to the door staff if they didn't already know you. In return it was understood that they would call upon you if they needed assistance in the event that fighting broke out. As the evening wore on Chris and Andy started on the whisky chasers which I refused to join in with purely because I hated the stuff, it always made me ill. But I knew I was heading that way anyway and eventually ended up cradling the big white telephone in the gents, calling out for God. I vaguely recall being lifted to my feet by a couple of bouncers and being dumped in the lift. Andy and Chris were already in there slumped on the floor. We were virtually unconscious. The doors closed and I was aware the lift was going down. It stopped and the doors opened. A police van had reversed right up to the lift door and both the rear doors to the van were open. A voice then called out.

"Woodward, Goward and Cox, I might have fucking guessed". It was Adrian Prangnell. We'd all joined the cadets together and he was now at Central.

"You're all nicked" he laughed.

"But Praggers we love you" Coxy spurted out.

He poured the three of us into the back of the van and took us back to Campbell Road shaking his head as he did so. Welcome to adulthood!

Patrolling Southsea seafront was never dull but occasionally I would get taken completely by surprise. Whilst standing outside Nero's about 11 pm one Friday night watching all the taxi's arrive to disgorge their fares into the clubs I became aware of a rather strange noise. It grew louder and louder. Then people outside of The Intrepid Bun burger bar on the corner to my right started pointing down Clarendon Road. Some were laughing, some just stared in disbelief whilst a lot of the girls put their hands over their mouths and gasped. A couple of cars turning the corner from the seafront were forced to stop. As I arrived at the corner the noise became even louder and I knew now what it was. But it couldn't be, surely? It sounded like hob nail boots that were marching. And it was. For there, marching down the road, four abreast and about 30 in number was a group of skin heads! Dressed in skin tight, ankle high jeans, black lace up boots, white tee shirts and braces, they looked terrifying. Their cropped hair and menacing looking faces made them look like commandos on a day trip to the seaside. They were being given orders by one of their number who ordered them to a halt and as one, they did. It looked as impressive as it did aggressive. He then ordered them to 'right turn' and 'fall out' and as they did so they let out a huge roar and then went on the rampage, punching and kicking everybody in sight. It was mayhem. Every unit in the city was dispatched to assist and the seafront was awash with police cars and the air was a haze of blue lights. It took us more than an hour to take control again.

But that pales into insignificance for what happened the following evening. I was on foot patrol with George Barker, who was a cocky git who reckoned he was a big hit with the ladies and used the uniform as a weapon to impress. It had been a fairly quiet evening and at some point we got split up to deal with separate minor issues and didn't meet up again for some reason. It was about 1 am, that quiet time before they start kicking out at two and I was walking slowly passed Nero's, when I looked up and saw a large group had gathered near to the entrance to Joanna's. When I say a large group I do mean over a hundred or so people and they were gathered in a circle and seemed very excitable, just like you see in a school play ground when there is a fight in progress. I feared the worst obviously and quickened my pace towards it. As I got closer I could hear the crowd cheering and clapping above the sound of Silvester's *You Make Me Feel, Mighty Real* coming from the upstairs open windows to Joanna's. I pushed through the crowd expecting to see a couple of matelot's having a scrap but was confronted by George Barker, in full Police uniform break dancing! Yep, there he was spinning on his back before doing some kind of flip onto his shoulder and then landing on his heels and then majestically falling onto his front and moving forwards in a worm like motion before leaping back to his feet to milk the applause. How he loved it, especially when it earned him a kiss from the young lady that had been holding onto his helmet whilst he performed.

Having completed my two week area car attachment meant that every now and then I'd get the occasional shift as the observer and I always looked forward to that, especially if it was on nights. One Friday night about 2330 hours, just as things were hotting up;

Kilo to Kilo Sierra 51

Kilo Sierra 51, go ahead

Make Outram Road, two men seen loading a large motorcycle into the back of an old green van

Kilo Sierra 51, 10/4 making towards

Andy Kimber laughed out loud and said "I bet that's yours" because Outram Road was just across the road from my flat and although I laughed with him I was a bit worried. We weren't that far away when we got the call and as we raced up Lawrence Road we saw an old green Transit van emerge from Campbell Road. We followed it, doing various radio checks on the registration number before we stopped it. It came back as 'no current keeper' but intelligence reports suggested it was being used by a well known Hells Angels Chapter from Southampton. We pulled it over and in the cab were two males and a female, all wearing black leather jackets with denim cut-off's with Hells Angel regalia on the back. They said they had only borrowed the van and had no idea what was in the back. We asked them to open it up and as I did so I took a step backwards in shock. It wasn't my bike in the back, it was Andy Gowards! His Kawasaki Z1000 had been unceremoniously lobbed in the back and was now laying forlorn on its side with the fairing all cracked and scuffed. All three of them were arrested and carted off to custody. I then went back to the flat and woke Andy up. I dragged the grumpy git outside dressed only in his pants and asked him if he noticed anything unusual about Campbell Road? It took him five minutes to realise his bike was missing and even then he thought I'd hidden it in some kind of wind up. Our informant turned out to be a neighbour from across the road and Ed Brown and his family became very good friends of ours because of their public spirited actions and from then on we were allowed to keep our bikes in their garden, which was much safer.

Walking the beat did mean that you got to meet and talk with some real local characters and they didn't come much more characteristic than Alan, the Albert Road street cleaner. He was a small man in his mid 60s although he hid it well. He walked with a very pronounced limp having been involved in a bad accident many years before. Most of his front teeth were missing and those that were left were brown and nicotine stained. He hand rolled his own cigarettes and always seemed to have one in his mouth. He would smoke them down as far as he possibly could and even tried relighting them with his Zippo lighter when there was virtually nothing to hold, quite often burning his face and browned fingers in the process. He was a very simple man who hadn't asked for much in life and sadly it didn't seem to have delivered him much in return. He always wore a grubby old grey blazer that was covered in metal bus enthusiasts badges from his days when he worked for the Portsmouth Bus Corporation. He would start work at 2 am six days a week and could be seen with his little yellow hand cart sweeping up the days rubbish and shovelling it by hand into his cart. Albert Road and Fawcett Road were his beat and they were kept clean and bright and by 6 am he would be finished and the rest of the day was his. I would always stop for a chat if I could. He would laugh and joke about the daftest things as we hid in a shop doorway so that I could enjoy a quick fag with him. I'd always give him one of mine rather than see him burn his fingers again. He was a mine of interesting information about some of the things that went on in and around the area. He saw everything that went on and could often be called upon to guide us in the right direction if we were looking for somebody or give us descriptions of offenders he had seen doing something criminal.

Every now and then I'd get collared into doing spells of station duty either for an hour or two or sometimes all day. As I grew in confidence over what needed to be done I actually started to enjoy it a bit more, in fact the busier it got the more I relished it. It became a challenge from within to be able to cope with everything that got thrown in my direction. I particularly enjoyed it when Laurie Terry was on duty. Not only did he provide constant comic moments but his advice, if needed was always sound. On one occasion I heard frantic ringing of the bell from the front counter. I went out to see what all the din was about to be greeted by a small man in his 50s, wearing a very sharp pin stripe suit, carrying a walking cane and wearing a large Panama hat. He looked like a miniature version of George Melly.

"The Russians are coming, the Russians are coming" he banged on the counter. "What?" I retorted.

He insisted they were landing on Southsea beach right now and what were the Police going to do about it? I said I'd go and ask the Sergeant for his advice, which is exactly what I did! Uncle Laurie smiled and went straight out to the counter to investigate.

"Hello Peter" he said

"The Russians are coming, they're landing on Southsea beach right now" he insisted.

"Yes we had heard" said Laurie "Now what I need you to do for us is to draw me a map of exactly where they are so we can pass it onto the army for them to deal with. Can you do that for us"?

Peter agreed immediately and so Laurie handed him some paper and a pen and he started to scribble away. We left him to it and after half an hour or so he'd vanished, leaving his maps spread all over the counter. He was obviously a regular customer.

Very little seemed to faze Sgt Terry especially if he was dealing with any prisoners. He always greeted them with a smile, put them at ease and rarely had much trouble in return. However every now and then he'd get one that was a complete arsehole. I was on station duty relief for an hour and went to check on a prisoner who had been brought in a couple of hours earlier. As I approached his cell I could see a large puddle of urine all over the floor coming from under the cell door. This was despite the fact that each cell had its own toilet.

I went back and informed Laurie Terry who grabbed the cell keys and we went to speak with the prisoner. As we opened the cell door the man, in his mid 30s I suppose was casually sat on the edge of the bench reading a magazine. Laurie asked him politely if he would be prepared to mop it up.

"Nah mate, that's your job" he said with a smirk.

Laurie calmly shut the cell door and instructed me to get the bucket and mop from the cleaners cupboard. I thought I was going to have to clean it up. As I returned to the cell door Laurie returned from the charge room carrying a very expensive looking, shiny brown leather jacket. He unlocked the cell door, threw the jacket into the puddle of urine, grabbed the mop, rubbed the jacket all over the floor and the puddle and then flicked the jacket up and into the arms of its flabbergasted owner!

"Next time use the facilities provided you filthy little bastard" said Laurie calmly, as he shut the cell door. "Cup of tea Stephen?"

I think so, yes.

On the 3rd May 1979 there was a General Election and I and many of my colleagues were drafted in to man various Polling Stations. This was obviously a first for me and I was stationed in the church hall on the corner of Francis Avenue and Albert Road from 1500 hours to 2300 hours when the Polling Stations closed. My job was to ensure that all the rules and regulations concerning voting procedures were complied with in conjunction with the actual Polling Station administrator. In truth it was an extremely boring duty. Members of the public filed in throughout the day to cast their votes but tended to whisper as if they were in a library or church. A couple of times during the day I got a visit from an Inspector whom I didn't know and later on a welcome visit from Sgt John 'Cruncher' Taylor, who was as mad as a hatter. He was anything but quiet and could usually be relied upon to tell you some bizarre story of an incident he had just been involved in or more likely provoked. At 2300 hours sharp the doors were closed and the voting boxes sealed in my presence.

I had to stand guard over it whilst the Polling Station staff closed everything else down. Then the box was carried out to the chief administrator's car and I escorted him and the box to the Guildhall where it was handed over to the Presiding Officer and his staff. After signing the necessary paperwork I met up with several colleagues in a side room where we had a cup of tea and swapped various tales about our day. But most of the talk centred on who might win the most important election in years. Would the current Prime Minister Jim Callaghan be returned to office or would Britain elect its first woman Prime Minister? By the next morning of course we all knew that history had been made and Margaret Thatcher was duly elected. Within weeks she had kept one of her election promises and awarded the Police a 30% pay rise in line with the recommendations of the Edmund Davies Report which took many police officers off the bread line and at last gave them a half decent wage.

Over the next few months I was still getting myself into trouble both at the station and on training days. JB just wasn't satisfied with my performance in general because I failed to generate enough self initiated work. Our weekly sessions would invariably end with him saying.

"There ain't no substitute for experience in this job son, now go out and fucking find some".

He eventually insisted that I couldn't return to the station at the end of each shift unless I had at least five new names in the back of my pocket book. He was most insistent on this. It really didn't matter what it was for just so long as I had five names. I have to confess that on days when I struggled to obtain those names that I'd sneak back in via the rear door and hide in the toilets adding the names of people I used to go to school with just to make up the numbers!

Meanwhile at Queens Crescent I had to face Inspector Allen and his gorilla on a monthly basis because I just wasn't attaining the right level of results in my exams. It came to a head when, having done no study at all that month I recorded the lowest ever exam result of just 2% and that, according to Bob Allen was only because "you spelt your fucking name right, you fucking little wanker" and with that he hit me around the back of the head.

He then sat back behind his desk and told me that unless I got 100% in the last four monthly exams plus 100% in my final exam then he would have no choice but to recommend that I be dismissed from the force. He meant it to.

I went home and spoke to Andy about it. He was in similar trouble himself and we knew we had no-one to blame but ourselves. So it was no more bike rides, no more pub or clubbing, this was serious, or we would both be out on our ears.

The following week I was on nights and back out on foot patrol. I was being frustrated by a lack of work, due in part because of the weather; it hadn't stopped raining all week. But I had high hopes for the weekend, at least I'd be on the seafront and guaranteed a couple of drunk and disorderly's at least. Come Friday night and we were short on manpower and yet JB stuck me on foot patrol in Albert Road with no-one on the seafront at all. I was livid and somewhat convinced now that he wanted rid of me and was making it as difficult for me as possible to reach the targets he had set. In a huff I walked straight back to the flat which was just off the Albert Road beat. Andy was out and so I sat there in the dark, on my own with my head in my hands, close to tears. In a fit of temper I picked up a wooden chair we had by the table and threw it against the lounge wall, where it smashed into several pieces. I sat back down again. What the hell have they reduced me to? I was visibly shaking. I'd never felt so low in my life. I wanted to be a police officer, it's what I was put on the planet to be. Ever since I can remember it's all I've ever wanted to do. But it wasn't a right. I had to earn it. And neither JB nor Bob Allen are going to have the pleasure of seeing me fail, I thought to myself. I *won't* let them beat me.

I went back out and stopped everything that moved, but again I got frustrated because I didn't come across any offences. About two hours later Andy Kimber stopped in the area car and offered me a lift for a while because it was still pouring with rain. I welcomed the chance to dry out a bit. Within seconds of getting in we received an attention drawn to a hot stolen Triumph 2.5 and within seconds of that it passed us going the other way. The Triumph accelerated away north along Fawcett Road, turned left at Fratton Bridge and headed south along Victoria Road North. It then mounted the footpath and drove across it into Rugby Road. Fortunately for us Rugby Road is made up of cobble stones which are very slippery when wet. The Triumph slid sideways and crashed into a lamp post. The driver got out and leapt over a wall into the back gardens of Brittania Road North. Still wearing my sodden gannex I gave chase. He was one garden ahead of me all the way. We entered 42 gardens in total, demolishing four garden walls and one of those glass cucumber shelters. And twice I almost strangled myself on washing lines. During all this I kept saying to myself.

"If I don't get this bloke JB's gonna kill me, if I don't get this bloke........."

As I jumped over the last wall I entered a brightly lit wood yard and my car thief was no-where to be seen. I couldn't believe it. Then I heard a noise behind a dustbin. I pulled it away and there he was crouched down behind it, panting like a dog. I told him to stay exactly where he was. He said he wasn't going anywhere and promptly threw up. Large amounts of alcohol, an Indian meal and a 200 yard hurdle sprint don't mix, especially when you are up against Hampshire's finest cross country runner! I took him back to Kilo Sierra and presented him to Laurie Terry in a positive manner.

"Nice one young Stephen" he said after locking my man up in a cell "A few more like that and we'll make a copper out of you yet".

I was elated, at last a bit of praise. I felt ten feet tall.

Andy decided to move out and into a new place with his girlfriend Sue. It came at a time when the upstairs single flat had become vacant and so I moved in up there. It was a huge single room with a sort of lounge, bedroom and kitchen merged into one. It was great having my own place and Mike and I spent the whole weekend redecorating it a very tasteful shade of dark brown and magnolia! Whilst covered in paint and dust we listened to Mikes latest album; Geoff Waynes *War of the Worlds* which I have to say was perfect decorating music when played loud. In between tracks you could hear Steve shouting up the stairs "Turn that fucking shit off".

Steve's taste in music was hugely varied and he was something of an aficionado on the subject but without being a complete bore about it. We both shared a common love for punk rock music and he frequently introduced me to new groups or artists that the rest of the world were yet to hear on mainstream radio. Groups like The Clash, The Jam and some freak called Frank Zappa, who I never really took to I have to be honest. Later he introduced me to the sounds of Ska with the likes of The Specials, Selector and Madness being our favourites. We'd sit in his room for hours talking and listening to the latest track. He came and knocked on my door once and insisted I come and listen to something. He was giggling away as he put on a cassette of a new program he had taped from the radio. The program was Douglas Adam's *The Hitch Hikers Guide to the Galaxy* and we sat there laughing out loud at it. We couldn't wait for next week's episode and it became cult listening for us, much like Monty Python was to others. When we eventually found out that the meaning of life, the universe and everything was 42 it solved many of life's little mysteries for us!

Music became an important companion to me. Although living on my own was great it did get lonely at times, especially if I'd had a bad shift and I had returned home to an empty flat with no-one to talk to and off-load. So I'd play music, lots of it. I bought albums and singles like they were going out of fashion. And before I went to work on nights, but especially on Friday and Saturday nights, I'd play one particular 12 inch single from The Clash that contained two tracks, *London Calling* and *Armagideon Time*. And I played them at full volume because it quite literally psyched me up for what I might have to face that night. *London Calling* would help me put my suit of armour on whilst the opening words to *Armagideon Time* I found to be rather ironic given my line of work;

A lot of people won't get no supper tonight,
A lot of people won't get no justice tonight,
The battle is getting harder.

It sounds strange I know but I found it the best way of coping, to relieve the anxiety I felt prior to hitting the streets at the weekend. Those two tracks are still favourites of mine even now and conjure up all manner of memories.

The early hours of a night shift can be a killer if it's quiet. And anything you can do to keep yourself awake and perked up has to be good. I was on foot patrol with PC 1179 Dave Sigournay, a slightly built chap of Italian descent, he was a bit of a chancer who was somewhat unorthodox in his ways and in some of the things he did in life. I mean he is the only person I've ever known to have owned a Wartburg estate car for goodness sake! We were both wearing capes to conceal our fags as we plodded our way up Highland Road towards Eastney. As we got to the mini roundabout at the junction with Henderson Road Dave spotted an abandoned pedal cycle in the middle of the roundabout. It was an old Raleigh Chopper bike, just like the one my parents refused to let me have as a child because they were dangerous! This one was a bit of a rat though because it had been hand painted black and had no brakes or lights fitted. On checking the frame number it turned out to be stolen. It was nearing 4 am which meant it was cup of tea time and what better way to get back but by bike? So there we were, dressed in capes, me on the back, Dave up front giggling like a couple of kids as we headed back towards the nick. Over the radio came a call for a silent alarm at the Liberal Club in Duncan Road, which was about half a mile away from us. Dave answered it by stating that we were 'mobile' and en route. We laughed even louder as he peddled furiously and I made nee-nah noises! We were going much too fast as we turned left into Duncan Road and as Dave lost control of the bike we both crashed to the ground and rolled into the gutter. It was only funny until we saw that Inspector O'Flaherty had arrived just before we had and was standing in the doorway to the Liberal Club and had seen everything.

In the late summer of 1979 I was due to go on my Area Beat attachment and I was lucky enough to get it with PC 1188 Mick Smith. I think he'd forgiven me for my previous misdemeanours and I was quite looking forward to seeing how he went about his business. Mick's beat was at Eastney, the boundary of which was about a half hours walk from the nick. That's half an hour if you weren't with Mick Smith that is, because if you were with him it took two hours just to get there. Why? Because everybody wanted to talk to him; old, young, rich, poor, business man or unemployed youth, they all stopped to talk, to pass information, to thank him for something he had done for them or just for being there. And whilst he was talking to one person a passing car would toot its horn and a waving hand would be thrust out the window or somebody else would call out his name from the other side of the street. Mick would always wave back and the most unbelievable bit of all was that he knew all of them by name and where they lived or worked, which school they went to, who the kids parents were and which pubs they drank in. And he didn't write any of it down either. It was truly amazing. He was the absolute epitomisation of what a beat bobby was all about. His communication skills were something to behold and he had a great sense of humour. I learned more in my two weeks with Mick about basic coppering, humility, compassion and a sense of fair play than I could ever have imagined possible. It was a real privilege.

Whilst out on Mick's beat one day we had to call into a second hand store on the corner of Albert Road and Old Fawcett Road to speak to the owner about some property from a burglary. The shop was run by a Caribbean man in his 30s known locally as Sambo Betts. I'd heard his name on a number occasions together with another black male by the name of Sambo Meredue. To my surprise they were apparently the only two black people to live in Portsmouth at this time and were known to everybody, not just the Police, as Sambo or Sammy. We entered the shop which housed a mixture of old black and white TVs and racks of second hand clothes. Mick greeted Sambo like a long lost friend and then introduced me to him. He was pleasant enough but you could tell that he was being quite guarded about what he said simply because we were police officers. But that all changed when Mick made comment about Sambo's beard, then all hell broke lose. Sambo's beard was jet black Afro hair which matched his long dread locked and braided hair. Mick's beard was silver, neatly trimmed and covered more of his face than his head of hair did because he was three quarters bald. And shiny with it! The banter between them was intense and lasted without pause for more than five minutes. They were an even match and shook hands at the end and we all left laughing.

Being able to laugh at yourself when things go wrong is vital and let's face it, so far in my Police career I've had plenty of things go wrong, although not too much to smile about. As a cadet one of our instructors favourite sayings was "If you can't take a joke you shouldn't have joined" although that was usually accompanied by us being on the other end of something painful like circuit training, log carrying or cross country.

I was on foot patrol one night heading down Clarendon Road towards the seafront. I was passing the Captains Table pub, a small but very noisy establishment on the other side of the road. There were about 20 youths gathered on the pavement outside, all drinking and in high spirits. I started getting cat calls and sarcastic whistling. It wasn't worth any form of confrontation as it was generally good natured, but just so that they knew I wasn't ignoring it completely and that 'yes' I could hear it, I gave them my best stare. This continued as I walked passed the pub, so that my head was now looking over my right shoulder. And then I walked straight into a lamp post and my helmet fell off and rolled into the road. Bollocks, I didn't need that I thought, as I grabbed my helmet out of the road before a car compounded my misery by running it over! There were howls of laughter from the assembled youths. So I took my helmet, put it back on my head, faced them and then took it off again in a big sweeping motion whilst giving them the deepest bow possible. The laughter changed to applause and I continued on my way.

One of Graham's favourite sayings was "Never do today what you can put off until tomorrow" which always referred to us doing paperwork. He wasn't a great lover of it and would rather go out and police the streets than sit down writing statements or putting crime files together. And like much of what he taught me as my tutor it rubbed off and stuck. And it invariably got me into yet more bother. Depending on the type of file or report would depend on the time limits on you submitting it. All reports were hand written whilst court files required typing up, but they were mostly copied from your original hand written statements. Only the biggest of files were first dictated onto tape and then handed to one of our two typists, Pat and Sally. Part of JBs job was to go through our paperwork on a regular basis, doubly so when it came to mine! I would dread him doing it because it meant I'd get a bollocking first and then I'd have to stay in and get it sorted. Which usually meant me paying a visit to the typist's office, armed with a wad of paper and a pathetic look on my face? I'd look at Sally and she knew the look.

"When do you need it by?" she'd sigh.

"Er………….yesterday" I'd reply sheepishly.

"Are you in trouble with John Batten again?" she'd ask.

"Aren't I always?"

"When are you going to learn? Give me an hour and I'll have it done for you"

What a star she was. She saved my life so many times but I'm ashamed to say that although I did improve things a little over the coming years, Graham's philosophy on all matters relating to paperwork stuck with me and I always put it off until tomorrow.

I still had a problem getting up for early turn and now had three alarm clocks to wake me up from my nightly coma. JB was getting so worked up about it that he was now threatening to stick me on for neglect of duty. I had to do something about it, especially on quick swings, where we would finish at 2200 hours one night and start at 0600 the following morning. We did two of those a month and they were killers, nobody liked them and there was no reprieve if you were late off the previous evening either. After paying our nightly homage to the LJR and getting home about half eleven I came up with the perfect solution. If I stay up all night and clean the flat, then I won't be late. Simple. So I commenced a huge spring cleaning operation. Nothing was left untouched; if I didn't hoover it I polished it instead. I even did some ironing! By 0430 I was feeling very pleased with myself and the flat was spotless. But it was getting cold, so I made myself a cup of coffee and sat down in front of the fire. My door bell rang at 0615. I looked like a sack of shit and JB took great delight in telling me so. But at least he accepted my totally original story and he didn't stick me on.

Amongst the many attachments you had to undertake as a probationer was a two week stint with the CID, the Criminal Investigation Department or depending on your viewpoint the Creeping Insect Department. Southsea CID office was right opposite the canteen and was a regular haunt for most of us because they ran the chocolate cupboard, the profits from which funded most of their Christmas piss up. It was a busy place with Detective Inspector Jack Rogers as its head and Detective Sgts Derek Rowles and Pete Spencer, who were like chalk and cheese when it came to the methods they employed, running a number of Detective Constables. DS Spencer had a bit of a reputation, not all of it good and he tended to bend the rules somewhat. This often brought him into conflict with uniformed Station Sgts, especially when he would bring a suspect in on a Friday afternoon, book him in, chuck him in a cell and leave him with the words "You have a think about what I said and we'll talk some more on Monday".

I have to say that being cooped up in an office all day wasn't my cup of tea and I'd had previous experience of CID work as a cadet when I had to do a similar attachment, so I wasn't exactly looking forward to this one. I got passed from pillar to post for the first three or four days but then got taken out by DC Bob Tompkin. He was a very knowledgeable chap with a relaxed air about him, but once he had a bee in his bonnet about something, that was it, he wouldn't let go.

The hotels on the seafront had suffered a number of burglaries and

Bob was in the middle of the investigation. It was really interesting to see how he worked and built up a picture of who he thought might be responsible. I helped him by taking a number of witness and victim statements, which made me feel slightly more useful than if I'd stayed in the office making the tea. Sadly for me the enquiries didn't result in any arrests before I finished my attachment but Bob had the decency to come and find me a few weeks later to tell me that he had two in custody and had retrieved some of the stolen property. But I knew that CID work wasn't really for me, even though I was getting a taste for dealing with criminals I wanted to be out on the streets dealing with them rather than doing the follow up enquiries.

I was somewhat put out by the fact that my next training day was to be at Hulse Road in Southampton. It was the first time I'd been to F Division and I was reminded of the advice Graham had given me all those months ago. And sure enough the three of us from K Division were made to feel like lepers by Inspector Snook who was neither witty nor knowledgeable in his delivery. And they had a uniform inspection which we didn't do at Queens Crescent. Oh how he loved picking us up on every little item, telling us that he really wasn't surprised that K Division officers were the scruffiest, dirtiest officers in the county and that if he ever came to Portsmouth on promotion he'd really kick some arse. My biggest concern though was my exam. I was convinced that I would probably lose 20% just because I was from K Division. I really sweated on it but to my huge relief I hit the 100% mark. I cannot tell you how that felt but I had a long way to go yet.

One of my biggest attributes (in my humble opinion) is that I'm not squeamish. I don't know why but the sight of blood, guts, vomit and most other bodily fluids and functions just doesn't bother me the way it does many other people. I can even do post mortems without any bother. I do know police officers who are squeamish and who simply cannot stand the sight of blood and will turn the other way if they can. But there is one thing I really can't deal with and that's stomach pumps. I think it has something to do with the gagging sound that accompanies such operations combined with the smell of someone's stomach contents and I have quite often found myself joining in with the gagging.

On far too many occasions for my liking I found myself in the casualty department at the old Royal Portsmouth Hospital with a semi conscious teenager who'd taken a drugs overdose, which was usually valium or sleeping tablets of some description and usually because they'd been dumped by a boyfriend or girlfriend. Some of them were regulars at it and for the life of me I cannot see why, given what the treatment was. The patient was laid on a trolley and a one inch wide plastic tube was thrust down the throat and into the stomach. A funnel was then attached to the tube and large metal jugs filled with water were brought in. The funnel was then held aloft whilst several pints of water were poured in. Once it had travelled down the tube and into the stomach the funnel was lowered below the height of the body and gravity took over and brought the contents of the stomach up and into a bucket. This was done three or four times to ensure that any drugs had been cleansed from the system and I have to say that some of the nursing staff were none too sympathetic and were quite rough in their handling. Myself and colleagues were often called upon to hold the patient down as they struggled. It was barbaric and the gagging and that smell will stay with me forever.

My confidence levels were on the up and JB was right, there was no substitute for experience and that you learned from your mistakes. Well mostly anyway. I was on foot patrol with PC 603 Ray Harbour, who had arrived on the Relief almost a year after me, but he was quite self assured as a probationer. We were on the seafront and had received several complaints about two youths causing a disturbance on South Parade pier. We located them, a couple of 19 year old students, slightly under the influence but not actually drunk. A bit gobby but not using any foul language. They were banging on the windows of the Albert Tavern although even they couldn't explain why. So we asked them to leave the pier and go elsewhere. They refused. We then demanded they go. They refused and merely laughed at us. So after several warnings they were arrested for obstructing the highway and conveyed back to Kilo Sierra and Uncle Laurie, who duly booked them in and locked them up. Ray and I were pouring out a cup of tea in the front office when Laurie returned from the cells.

"Well that's a new one on me" he said.

"What do you mean sarge?" said Ray.

"Since when has South Parade pier been a fucking highway?"

Ray and I just looked at each other blankly.

"Tossers" I think was the last thing Sgt Terry said to us. He some how talked our two miscreants into pleading guilty to a common law breach of the peace offence instead.

October's training day was back at Queens Crescent and I did it again, I scored 100% and for the next two training days I somehow managed to achieve the seemingly impossible and yet Bob Allen didn't say a word to me. All I had to do now was pass the final exam on the same score. I studied and revised like I'd never done before; everything I had worked for over the last two years now seemed to hinge on one more exam. In the meantime I continued to go up in JBs estimation with a series of half decent arrests and a constant stream of traffic process. But it was the exam that would seal things one way or another. To my utter relief I got 100%.

One by one we had to line up outside Inspector Allen's office for our final interview. His door opened and I was beckoned in. I sat down as he closed the door behind me. He smacked me hard across the back of the head and shouted out.

"You fucking little wanker".

I was completely taken aback, I wasn't expecting that at all.

"I knew you had it in you and you've put me through hell this last couple of years" he continued.

I've put you through hell? You ought to try being me I thought.

With that he shook me by the hand, as did his gorilla who smiled at me for the first time ever. He went on to say that he really didn't think I was going to make it but was thankful that I had proved them all wrong, but not to sit back on my laurels and to get out there and be the good copper he knew I could now be.

I've never been so relieved in all my life. And to cap it all JB wrote on my final probationary appraisal that he was now proud to have me on his Relief and that he could rely on me to get results a lot more than he could some other more senior members of the Relief. Praise indeed.

A couple of weeks later and Class 1/78 were summoned to HQ at Winchester to be confirmed by the Chief Constable, Mr John Duke. We were no longer probationers, we'd made it.

CHAPTER 4

1980. Blue and white pandas

Having been confirmed meant that I was now free to start moulding my career which meant that I needed to start driving as soon as I could. So in March 1980 I started my two week Improver Driving Course and if I was successful it qualified me to drive panda cars.
My instructor was a retired Traffic PC by the name of Ron Anderson, a tall gentleman, for that's exactly what he was, who was calmness personified. I loved driving in general, even though I didn't own a car at this stage and my biking experiences, both good and bad put me in good stead for my course. I couldn't wait to learn the basics of the Police 'System of Car Control' and was a very willing student and in return I think Ron enjoyed himself to. The book on which the 'System' is based was called Road Craft and it became my bible. The improver driving course was just that, it was designed to improve your driving skills to just above that required to pass your DOT test. There was no speed involved, no pursuit training obviously, but you did learn how to steer and change gear properly, how to double de-clutch and make better use of the brakes. We spent the first week just driving around housing estates in a driving school MK4 Cortina 1.6L, but I loved it. On the second Friday afternoon I got tested by the head of the Driving School, Sgt Ron Shepherd and passed. Now I could really start policing because I would get sent to a much wider range of jobs which in turn will increase my knowledge and experience.

I was on lates the following Monday and JB and Laurie Terry called me into their office. I must be in the shit again, but what for? They congratulated me on passing my driving course and in the next breath said that White Relief was already over burdened with panda car drivers and that it was highly likely that I might only get to drive once a week if I was lucky. I was gutted, I really didn't fancy plodding the beat any longer. However, there was an alternative in that Green Relief only had two other drivers and they were desperate for a couple more, so that's your choice young Stephen, either stay with us or move on. Would I like some time to think about it? Yes please.

I went upstairs to the parade room feeling really dejected. Graham and Pecker Wood were there and like a couple of old uncles they strongly advised me to jump ship and join Green Relief. I knew it made sense but I'd grown up with White Relief and JB, although he had been an absolute bastard towards me at times, I was actually very grateful to him for kicking my arse as hard as he had done, because I needed it. I went back downstairs and told them I'd made my decision and that it was time for me to move on. I knew I was welling up as I said it and JB made it worse by telling me he would rather I stayed but fully understood my decision. I would have to wait until my driving permit arrived but it was likely that I would start on Green Relief next Monday, on nights.

I felt like the brand new boy again as I was welcomed by my new Relief. My new patrol Sgt was Dave Martin, a slightly built man who had a great sense of humour. He had a completely different style to JB but nonetheless still commanded the respect of the PCs. Our station Sgt was Dave Fryer, who was from Lancashire and spoke with a very broad accent. He was nearing the end of his career and like many in his position he couldn't wait to leave, which I found rather sad. He didn't have a great deal of time for senior officers especially if they were "wet behind the ears having only just finished their fookin paper round".

There were some interesting characters on the Relief including Gary King who was waiting for his posting onto CID. Gary was famous for having been stabbed in the face a couple of years earlier. He was attending a domestic dispute at a house that held regular such incidents for the entertainment of their neighbours. It was so regular in fact that Gary's crew mate stayed in the car whilst he stood by the front door waiting for a reply. When it came it was shocking.

The door opened and the male occupant just came straight out and plunged a large kitchen knife straight into Gary's face, just beneath his eye. The knife penetrated his skull and stopped just short of his brain. When I spoke to him about it later he said the most terrifying part of the whole incident was being driven in the Mini panda up to the Royal hospital, at stupidly fast speeds on the pavement and anywhere else his partner could drive just to get him there and that all he could see was the handle of the knife bobbing up and down in front of him. He was given a local anaesthetic and the surgeon then got onto the trolley, knelt over him and just pulled the knife out. But Gary was still suffering black outs every now and then which is why he couldn't drive at this time.

The Relief had two area car drivers in Ken Munson and Craig McIntosh who had transferred down from Glasgow Central a couple of years before, after he nearly died having been carried on the bonnet of a stolen car that then deliberately crashed into a lamp post causing him serious injuries. Roger Hogben was a quiet individual and a thoroughly decent chap in his late 20s and the other two I knew very well already, Dave Brown and Steve Moore had been part of my cadet intake and they made me feel really welcome. I felt quite at home with this lot and was satisfied that maybe I had made the right decision.

We were half way through parade when the phone rang. Could we turn out for a 10/10 shout in Osborne Road. A 10/10 shout was an officer requiring urgent assistance and it was just about the most urgent call you could get. When one of your colleagues was in serious trouble everybody went. We ran downstairs and I grabbed the keys to a panda, a MK2 Ford Escort 1.1. These blue and white cars were fitted with a blue light and two-tone horns and even though I hadn't been trained to respond to such incidents it was all going on anyway. I jumped into the driver's seat and four others piled in. My heart was pounding as we raced off along Elm Grove with two-tones blaring. At the cross roads I needed to turn left. Having never driven an Escort before, especially five-up and at speed I wasn't at all sure how it was going to react. I got the turn into Grove Road South completely wrong and the rear nearside wheel hit the kerb and the car went right over on two wheels. It seemed to hang there forever before crashing back down again. A huge cheer went up from the back seat, more out of relief than anything else I would imagine. We thankfully arrived in Osborne Road a minute or so later in one piece and the officer who had called for help was fine and was placing his hand cuffed prisoner into the back of the van. I'd learned a valuable lesson very early on though.

Southsea Ford Escort MK2 'Panda 9'

Over the next few weeks my work load increased significantly because I was being deployed to a lot more jobs and as a result my confidence was now at an all time high. But I was about to be tested like never before. I was on early turn about 0830 at a burglary in Locksway Road when I got a call from the control room.

Kilo to Panda 9

Panda 9 receiving

Kilo to Panda 9, once you've finished at the burglary can you go to 42

Wisborough Road for a Misper enquiry. Apparently the adult male Misper has returned after two days so can you go and do the necessary and make sure he is OK?

Panda 9, 10/4

By the time I'd finished at the burglary and driven half way across the patch to Wisborough Road it was almost three quarters of an hour since I had received the call. I parked right outside the house which was a typical mid terrace house where the door opened out onto the street. I knocked on the door and a male in his early 30s I'd say opened it, thanked me for coming, beckoned me in and said.

"He's through here".

I was ushered down the hallway to the rear lounge. It was a cramped two-up, two-down house that was a bit dark and dingy. I entered the lounge and saw two women standing in the middle of it, together with three young kids aged between 4 and 7. It transpired that the man who had answered the door was the best mate of the missing person and that one of the women was his wife as were two of the kids and that the other woman and child were the mispers wife and daughter.

Sitting in an arm chair just inside the door was a male also in his 30s. He was slumped in the chair wearing a blue anorak done up to his neck. He had a bottle of whisky in one hand and a glass in the other. It was obvious that he had been crying. His mate introduced me to him as Mark Clare.

I stood in front of him and asked if he was alright? He looked up at me through tear stained eyes. Then he let go of the glass and the bottle, stood up and at the same time unzipped his anorak and pulled out a sawn-off shot gun. He stuck it straight in my face. I could feel myself go boss-eyed as I stared down the end of the twin barrels which were less than six inches from my nose.

"Get out of my house or I'll blow your fucking head off" he growled.

He meant it to. I instinctively raised my hands in a submissive manner as I backed away from him. The nearest door was into the kitchen and I very slowly and quietly ushered everyone else into the kitchen whilst not taking my eyes off the gun. The gun followed us around the room to the kitchen door and he was still pointing it at me when I closed it. I felt quite calm until his mate said.

"I'm sorry about that officer; I've been trying to get that thing off him for more than an hour".

"What? You knew he had it?" I screeched.

I was incensed by his complete stupidity. Not only did he not tell the control room when he phoned but he didn't tell me when I arrived at the door. The kitchen had a second door that led outside into the garden and I took them all outside and locked the door behind me. I needed some assistance and quick. I called Kilo Sierra and asked to speak to Sgt Martin. I was told he was busy at the moment and I'd have to wait a few seconds. By now all three kids were sobbing and the adults were quietly arguing amongst themselves.

Sgt Martin came onto the radio. I very briefly told him where I was and what had happened and finished it off by saying.

"………so have you got any advice please?" as soon as I said it I thought 'you wanker, any advice, what kind of a question was that?'

I had to get the family out of the garden and so looked over the fence and saw that it led out onto the Waverley Road Bowling Club grounds. I got everybody over the fence and was half way across the green when the grounds man saw us. He let out a huge scream as if I'd just cut his heart out. I told him to shut up and mind his own business as we scampered out of the grounds and into Waverley Road which felt like relative safety. I made them wait there whilst I ran back into Wisborough Road. I crawled beneath the front room window to number 42 and met up with Sgt Martin and Inspector Dave Watson a hundred yards or so down the street. We were joined shortly thereafter by our new Superintendent Mr Bob West. I briefed them on exactly what had happened. A unit was dispatched to Waverley Road to collect the family and take them to Kilo Sierra as Dave Watson asked Mr West if he should arrange for the ARV to be brought in. He agreed and whilst Mr Watson spoke to the control room on his radio I was stunned to see Mr West lean to his left and quietly ask Dave Martin what the ARV was.

"The armed response vehicle sir" he replied in disbelief.

"Oh yes, quite right, quite right"

The front door of the house then opened. Clare stood in the doorway with the shotgun in his left hand and now had a revolver in his right hand. He shouted out that he wanted to talk to Ace Mapplebeck, who was a detective based at Southsea. He then shut the door.

The ARV arrived a few minutes later. The Rover SD1 V8 looked like it was about to burst into flames, there was smoke coming from every orifice. Two officers, each armed with a revolver got themselves kitted up.

The front door opened again and Clare demanded the keys to my panda, which was parked immediately outside the premises. You're not having that I thought, I've only just started driving it, I'm not giving it away now! His demand was refused by the Inspector.

About half an hour later Ace Mapplebeck arrived and it transpired that he knew Clare very well having been at school with him many years before. He mentioned that Clare's mother was a cleaner at Central. Within minutes she had been brought to the scene.

The door opened again. Rather dramatically Ace had to take his jacket off and prove he wasn't armed and then to my utter amazement both he and the man's mother were invited inside. I remember thinking that maybe this was all some kind of a trap to lure Ace into the house and that maybe Clare had hated him since school and wanted to shoot him or his mother, as son's quite often do.

Thankfully I was wrong and about half an hour later the front door opened again and Ace had both weapons plus a huge commando knife that had been strapped to Clare's leg, safely in his hands. He was driven away to Kingston Crescent nick.

With that we all went back to Kilo Sierra for a nice cup of tea. There was no de-brief, no trauma counselling, no pat on the back from the Superintendent and no Chief Constables commendation either. Dave Martin asked if I was alright and would I like to go home, which I didn't and that just about summed up the forces response to my first really serious incident. At the end of that shift I went back to my little flat, on my own and sat there all evening playing the scenario over and over in my head. I didn't get a lot of sleep that night.

A few months later and Mark Clare appeared at Winchester Crown Court where he pleaded guilty to threats to kill, unlawful possession of various firearms and several other offences. It transpired that both weapons had been fully loaded on the day and that he had been taking the shotgun into work at the dockyard on a daily basis for more than two years! I expect the people of Portsmouth were as relieved as I was when Clare was given two years probation for committing these offences!

Being mobile meant you could and would get sent to anything, even full blown emergencies. If the area car was tucked up with something else then a panda car was obviously the next in line. This suited me down to the ground, I absolutely loved it. I'd be lying if I said I didn't get a real kick out of driving fast with two-tone horns and blue light on. Isn't that everybody's idea of a great time? And most of us thought we looked really cool at the time if we didn't wear a seat belt, had our tunics undone and had a fag hanging out of our mouths whilst on a shout, even if we were driving a Mini. Mind you I wouldn't have done that if JB had been watching! We were on nights when I got a call.

Kilo to Panda 9

Panda 9 go ahead

Kilo to Panda 9 can you assist Fratton units with an RTA in Fratton Road, just over the bridge, car into a lamp post

Panda 9, 10/4

It was about 0430 in the morning. I arrived at the same time as a Fratton panda. A Hillman Minx had left the road and demolished a lamp post. The driver, who was a senior naval officer was extremely drunk, hadn't been wearing a seat belt and had head butted the top of the exposed steel windscreen frame. He was a mess, there was blood everywhere, all of it coming from his face. He was unconscious but stunk of booze. Thankfully the ambulance arrived shortly after we did and as they wiped away the blood from his face we were all shocked to see that he had lost his eyes. It was a gruesome sight. The ambulance crew were very concerned for him and got him out of the car as quickly as they could. They placed him on a stretcher and as they were getting him into the ambulance they called back to ask us to look for his eyes.

The patrol Sgt from Fratton, one Ray Smout had recently arrived. Ray was a scouser and one of the funniest people I had ever met. The seats on a Hillman Minx are plastic and impervious so the blood hadn't seeped through the material and was at least an inch deep. It was the really thick stuff and we weren't issued with plastic gloves in those days, so I dived in with both hands to search for two eye balls, with Ray Smout insisting I find them otherwise our man wouldn't be able to read his charge sheet in the morning!

I couldn't find them and we were starting to panic. The ambulance crew then discovered why we couldn't find them. He had quite literally split his head open from ear to ear across his forehead. The wound was so deep that his face had actually slipped down more than an inch leaving two exposed holes where his eyes should have been. When they pulled the skin back up his face, hey presto there were his eyes! Inspector O'Flaherty arrived as he was the night duty Inspector. He asked Ray Smout for an update on the man's condition.

"Well sir, he'll never play the piano again"

"Oh, pianist was he?"

Football duties were a regular affair obviously with Fratton Park on our patch. However as football violence increased so did the necessity for the force to send extra officers to certain games if the potential for trouble was increased because of the calibre of the visiting supporters or because of the historical background. Hampshire also had Southampton Football Club to contend with and at this time they were in the top flight of the English league, which meant the likes of Manchester United and Liverpool paying regular visits. So occasionally officers from K Division were sent to police 'The Dell' Southampton's flea pit of a football ground. And just as at training days as a proby we weren't exactly treated like royalty. We would arrive at Hulse Road training school and were inexplicably always last to get fed, got the crappest of pre-match areas to patrol, always got the away supporters pen to look after, to avoid us upsetting the local Southampton supporters and were always the first to be stood down to ensure we didn't get as much overtime as those from F Division and elsewhere. It was quite deliberate and only seemed to strengthen the underlying hostility between both Divisions. It was always fuelled by those senior officers who were perhaps former Southampton City Police prior to amalgamation and I often wondered quite what the difference was between them and a football hooligan whose territorial boundaries were so strong that to even speak on level terms with an opponent wouldn't enter their narrow minded brains.

I came in for earlies on time for once. There was a buzz about the place, even at 0545. Dave Martin put me in the area car with Ken Munson and we were to take up a static position at Rudmore roundabout immediately. The other two city area cars were placed in similar positions in strategic locations and there was even an early turn Traffic motorcyclist available to assist, which was unheard of. We were briefed that the Regional Crime Squad (RCS) had been keeping obs on a red MK4 Cortina parked outside the Queens Hotel in Osborne Road and that the two occupants were armed, highly dangerous and had committed an armed robbery in Brighton the previous day and were likely to return to London later this morning. Between us, our job was to stop the car and then allow armed officers from the RCS to carry out the arrests.

Our own Cortina had recently been replaced by a brand new Volvo 240 and this was my first tour of duty in it. Ken and I headed up to Rudmore which was on the northern exit from the city and leads directly onto the M275 and ultimately towards London. However we had convinced ourselves that they would probably take the Eastern Road out of town and we'd miss out on the action. By 0830 the rush hour was in full swing and we heard that the car was on the move and that it was heading our way. Kilo Charlie 51 soon picked it up but was advised to hang back until it reached Rudmore. A few minutes later there it was driving passed us. My heart was now in my mouth. Kilo Charlie 51 passed us, we tucked in behind it and as soon as we did the Cortina took off. We were joined by the Traffic motorcyclist as we hit 100 mph travelling north up the M275. The Cortina forced cars out of its way as it then headed east onto the A27. The motorcycle, ridden by PC Chris Hill pulled up beside the Cortina at 100 mph and indicated to them to pull over, which seemed unlikely given the circumstances. The Cortina tried ramming Chris into the central barrier and very nearly succeeded. Chris came straight back at them and kicked the drivers door really hard. In a flash the Cortina moved across three lanes of traffic and took the slip road towards the Eastern Road. The slip road was full of stationary rush hour traffic. The Cortina drove straight down the off-side grass verge at 80 plus, with Kilo Charlie 51 directly behind it. Ahead was a very busy roundabout. The Cortina had to be stopped and it had to be right now. Charlie 51 rammed it hard from behind. The Cortina spun out of control, backwards out onto the roundabout where it collided with another car, both of them coming to an immediate halt.

The doors on the Cortina opened and out jumped two males. They ran off in separate directions. Ken and I went after the driver who headed towards the Pall Europe building. As he scaled the wire fencing hundreds of bank notes fell from his jacket pockets. He was half way up the fence as Ken and I grabbed his legs. He kicked us several times but we managed to pull him down. Punches were exchanged as we got him on the ground and cuffed him. There was money everywhere and it was just like a scene from one of those old spaghetti westerns! Other units started arriving and we saw that PC Nick Pugh, the driver from Kilo Charlie 51 had also got his prisoner. Mind you the area car was a write off. We looked inside the Cortina and there on the back seat were two hand guns, both loaded.

And then somebody asked the obvious question.

"Er...........where's the RCS boys then?"

It took a while to find out but apparently they went home at 0600 because they'd been up all night!

I wasn't that keen on Ken Munson, he was a bit too full of himself for my liking, rather too self assured and full of his own importance. He was a reasonably good copper though and he did sometimes make me laugh.

Kilo to Kilo Sierra 51

Kilo Sierra 51 go ahead

Embassy Court, Fawcett Road please, elderly lady is having problems with some local kids

Kilo Sierra 51, 10/4

The block was a fairly new establishment with smart apartments that catered for mainly elderly residents. We rang the bell on the intercom and the lady buzzed us through and we took the lift to the third floor. On the way up Ken and I discussed the fact that this was an unusual type of call to receive from an establishment like this, especially as the complainant lived on the third floor. We were greeted by a small lady in her late 60s I would guess. She was immaculately dressed and so very grateful that we had arrived so quickly. She asked us in and as she did so she started to explain that she was having real problems with half a dozen kids and that they were making her life a misery. We stood in the hallway as she went on to say that they would come to her flat everyday and would drink all her orange squash and eat all her cake and biscuits and that she couldn't stand it any more. Today they have eaten all her food and were now sat in the lounge watching TV and were refusing to leave. OK we said, let's have a word with them. The lady opened the door to the lounge and showed us in. She pointed at the settee and said.

"There they are look".

The only thing on the settee was five neatly laid out cushions. I quickly glanced around the rest of the room. The TV was on but there were certainly no kids. She was still pointing at the cushions and said.

"I want them to leave, they've eaten all my biscuits and I want them to go".

Without hesitating Ken opened the lounge door again, looked at the cushions and shouted out.

"Right, you heard the lady, everybody out, out, out, left, right, left, right, left, right" and then slammed the door shut again.

"Oh thank you officers, you are kind. Can I offer you a cup of tea?" our host cooed.

We politely declined but only because she didn't have any biscuits left for us to dunk.

My new Relief didn't frequent the LJR like my old one did, but that didn't mean they were anti social, far from it. They tended to frequent the Police club at Kingston Crescent nick. It was safe and above all cheaper than your average pub. After closing time, if we felt so inclined some of us would either go down to the Tiberius Casino or to a private club called the Calross Club in Clarendon Road. It was the strangest establishment I've ever been to. For a start it was located in the basement of a large Victorian house and was run by the campest man in the city. Aubrey was in his 60s and always wore a brightly coloured silk cravat under his shirt. He dripped gold and bore a striking resemblance to Larry Grayson. To gain entry you walked down the stone steps to the basement and knocked on the door. Aubrey would slide back a small viewing door, just like the ones you see at prison gates and you had to announce yourself. Police officers were always welcome. I think it made Aubrey feel safe because most of his other guests were Portsmouth's hardest and most prolific criminals. Not the street thugs or football hooligans but the antique knockers like the Ashes and the Stanley's, mixed in with other big Portsmouth families like the Deck's and the Madgewick's. It was a bizarre combination but somehow it worked. The bar seemed to be the demarcation zone, with a large group of the aforementioned hoodlums at one end and half of Southsea nick at the other. We all kept ourselves to ourselves whilst Aubrey fussed over us all like some great aunt. There was a small dance floor adjacent to the dining area where you could obtain superb food, but at some rather high prices, so it was the steak sandwich for me and most of the other coppers. And it didn't close until the last person left the club!

I met an amazing girl called Tricia.

Pompey started to play well and crept up the Division 4 table and were eventually promoted this season. As they improved so the numbers attending each match increased and so did the need to send more officers. Football violence on a weekly basis was now the scourge of the whole country and seemed to be getting worse. Portsmouth was no exception; in fact it was starting to get a reputation for serious disorder especially away from home.

We also started to see a marked increase in the number of larger public order incidents out on the streets at weekends, either on the seafront, in Palmerston Road or in Commercial Road outside the Mecca Ballroom. We were seeing the same group of youths at the same type of incident every week. They seemed oblivious to the consequences of their actions and some of them were openly challenging the police to come and take them on. This was new and quite disturbing.

The first time I can recall seeing them in action as an organised group was in the Osborne Road area one Friday night. A local motorcycle club called 'The White Ace' was holding its annual bikers ball at the Cambridge Hotel in Portland Road. The bikers were a friendly, no hassle bunch unless you touched their bikes! There were more than a hundred superb looking machines gathered in the car park, when a group of 50 males all chanting Pompey songs exited a nearby pub and systematically destroyed several of the bikes. A large fight broke out and there were several nasty injuries on both sides, with a handful of arrests made. Even the rumour of one of the bikers going home to fetch his sawn-off shot gun to wreak his revenge didn't appear to worry them, in fact if anything it goaded them into even greater bravado. One of the youths who appeared to be orchestrating this group was Fish Potter, the lad I'd seen on my first ever visit to Fratton Park. He positively revelled in his role and as I caught his eye he smiled at me as if to say "I'm really enjoying this".

I knew several of the bikers personally and when I spoke to them they referred to these youths as "dressers" or "casuals" which was a term I hadn't heard before. But it did make a bit of sense, for most of them were smartly dressed in V necked jumpers with diamond patterns on them from the likes of Pringle and La Coste with casual trousers to match. Their hair styles were typical early 1980s with Simon LeBon type flicks and some of them even wore mascara and eye shadow! As they committed public order offences of breach of the peace, drunk and disorderly, obscene language, obstructing the highway and assaults, so they would get picked off and thrown into police vans. This invariably caused some of them to rush to their mate's aid and in an effort to rescue them so they too got detained. Some of them ran away and were only brave enough to shout obscenities towards us from a hundred yards away. Nonetheless there was definite tension growing and they seemed totally oblivious to the consequences. The country and in particular its youth, seemed to be on the brink of some kind of anarchic precipice and although Portsmouth didn't have any of the racial tensions other big cities seemed to be suffering from, there was a disturbing rise in the mass orchestrated violence now being used not just against the police but against its own citizens.

Death in all its forms can sometimes be grotesque especially if it was a violent one. And even though I've said previously that I'm not squeamish there have been times when the nature of the death has made me really think afterwards how awful it must have been for the poor individual concerned.

Kilo to Panda 9

Panda 9 go ahead

Can you attend 57 St. Ronan's Road, report of a possible sudden death

Panda 9, 10/4

Bloody great, I thought, just before breakfast, thanks. St. Ronan's Road was mainly bed sits and sure enough this house was split into several small rooms over three floors. I was greeted by a couple of builder types who couldn't get a reply from the room that their mate lived in. He was in his 50s and was in poor health and they were worried about him. I knocked on the door several times, calling out his name. No reply. Nothing else for it then but to put the door in. The second shoulder barge popped the door open. I think all three of us uttered the same thing at the same time.

"Faarkin ell" and they both then turned on their heels and ran.

I wasn't afforded such luxuries! He was indeed dead.

His bed sit was a tiny triangular shaped room with just enough space for a bed and a chair. He was laying face down beside the bed and was cradling a metal bucket in his hands. There was blood everywhere; on the walls, on the window, on the curtains, all over the floor and it was literally dripping from the ceiling. The bucket was half full of his guts, the entrails of which were hanging out of his mouth. I had to fully check him to ensure he was actually dead of course and everywhere I went and everything I touched meant I got covered in more of his blood. It was truly awful.

Whilst waiting for a GP to turn up to medically confirm death I went and found his two mates. One of them did mention they'd heard him coughing a bit during the night. Coughing a bit? That must have been the understatement of the year because this poor man had literally coughed his guts up. I was to learn later that in fact he had a burst stomach ulcer. This one played on my mind for quite a long time afterwards.

Some sudden deaths provided other challenges, either gaining access or difficulty in removing the body from the premises. I attended a terraced house one morning where the neighbour, who looked in on the elderly lady everyday could see her laying on the floor of the lounge. For some reason the front door was double locked and so we couldn't use the spare key the neighbour possessed. But that wasn't the real problem. The German Shepherd was the real problem. He was in the front room with his owner and was clearly on the defensive as he barked and growled at us through the window. Now I like dogs, but a fully grown and angry Alsation might take some befriending. I thought that if I could at least get in I might be able to bribe him with some food and so I hopped over the back garden wall, removed the burglar's favourite louvre windows from the kitchen and climbed in. The dog was going ape-shit behind the lounge door. Not only did he know that his owner was in trouble but he now had an intruder to contend with. I searched the cupboards for dog food. Nothing. Bugger. I talked to him through the door but it didn't seem to calm him too much. Nothing else for it, I'll have to front him up. I took out my truncheon just in case I needed to whack him with it. I opened the door very slightly and fed my truncheon through it. He grabbed it in his mouth and refused to let go. But his demeanour had changed and he thought this was some kind of a game, so we had a pretend tussle over it as I led him into the kitchen and shut the door behind him. I went back to the lounge to confirm that the lady was sadly dead, whilst Muttly ate the rest of my stick.

Hampshire Police suddenly got fashion conscious and ditched the traditional tunic for a Nato style jumper and short style weather proof nylon jackets. They were so much more comfortable than the tunic, especially when driving. They were certainly a lot more practical to and it was a lot easier to grab items like truncheon or hand cuffs if required. The wooden truncheon slid into an extra long additional pocket located on the right side of your trousers. The leather strap attached to it was supposed to be secreted, out of sight, tucked into the standard trouser pocket. However, most of us left the strap exposed, in readiness for a rapid draw and left it dangling for all to see in a sort of threatening posture, which our senior officers were always telling us not to do.

I was still dining out on the theft of the carburettor from the Cortina almost two years previously when I got sent to a job that surpassed even that.

Kilo to Panda 9

Panda 9 go ahead

Can you attend Craneswater Park please, report of a high value burglary

Panda 9, 10/4

The Craneswater area of Southsea was the posh end of town, full of very expensive detached properties at over inflated prices, only a stones throw away from the bed sit areas, that were themselves big expensive houses in a previous era.

Upon my arrival I wasn't surprised to find that this was one of the bigger detached properties, fully enclosed with high walls, fencing and lots of trees and shrubbery. I rang the door bell several times before eventually a side gate opened and a lady in her late 50s looked out and apologised for not answering the door but everybody was in the back garden. It wasn't exactly garden weather, but hey, who am I to judge? But there was a very good reason why the lady, her husband and several neighbours were in the garden. They were admiring the point of entry into their house, a huge four foot wide hole in the side wall of the house straight into the dining room. A pneumatic drill and compressor had been used to literally cut a hole through the side of the building to bypass the alarm system that secured the doors and windows. They were only after one thing and that was the gentleman's extremely valuable coin collection. And they had cleared the lot. They had also caused thousands of pounds worth of damage to the house and to the furniture inside, which was now completely covered in a fine layer of brick dust. All I could really offer this couple were words of sympathy, I mean the usual patter about house security and marking your valuables with a UV pen seemed rather inappropriate right now! We just kept staring at the burglars handy work. It just proved the point that if they really want, they'll have it no matter what you do to protect yourself.

In complete contrast to the Craneswater houses were The Keswick and The Strand Hotels. Both were located close to the seafront and housed a mixture of DHS residents and those who had seemingly given up on life. To call them hotels was nothing short of a gross insult to the hotel trade. I wouldn't have kept a pet mouse in there, although I suspect that had I actually owned a pet mouse at the time it would have made plenty of friends in either establishment. Both places were huge and housed about 200 residents each. They were squalid, damp, dark and hostile environments. Everyday we would get called to one or both establishments because one of the residents had been assaulted by another or a number of rooms had been screwed, again by other residents. The Strand in particular was a death trap. It was a maze of dark corridors and stair wells. To illuminate your passage you had to press those timed lighting switches that automatically switched off again just a few seconds later, leaving you scrabbling around looking for the next one. There were bikes and push chairs strategically placed for you to walk into or trip over and even if you found the hovel you were looking for, trying to find your way out again was even worse. I often thought about using a guide line upon entry to The Strand so I could find my way out but thought better of it, knowing that one of the residents would probably nick the line! By some miracle there was never a major fire in the place but had there been, it would have been a disaster.

I arrived there one morning to serve a summons. The door to the room I needed was thankfully on the ground floor, so no guide line was required. The door was answered by a fat moose, her hair pulled upwards into what is locally referred to as a 'Pompey pineapple' where it is tied on top of the head with a rubber band and the remaining hair is allowed to just stick straight up in a rather untidy manner. She was wearing grubby, stained white leggings that revealed every lump and bump of cellulite beneath. Why is it that fat, ugly women insist on wearing such figure hugging leggings? Don't they have friends that say.

"..........er, no love, you can't wear them, you might frighten the children".

She also wore a black V necked top that revealed far too much of her huge breasts, the left one of which had a tattoo of a rose on it. The fag that was hanging out her mouth had dropped ash all down her cleavage. She was a class act.

As she was explaining to me that "her fella" was out somewhere, but she didn't know where, so a young girl, aged four appeared behind her mother. She had blonde hair and looked rather cute, even if she was even grubbier than the leggings she was swinging from.

"You're a pig aren't you?" she uttered.

I looked down at her and before I could say anything back she spoke again.

"You can fuck off then, we don't want you here" she said.

"That's not a nice thing for a young lady of your age to be saying" I retorted.

"I don't care, go on fuck off, my daddy told me to say that to pigs" she said with an angelic smile.

I looked at the mother for a bit of support. She merely pushed the child back into the bed sit. I served the summons and walked away shaking my head and thinking what hope was there if four year olds were now being taught such things by their parents.

I'd been to a number of fires, both in buildings and in cars and had seen the full aftermath of what a fire can do. Even a relatively small house fire can wreak havoc with smoke damage and I had a very healthy respect for it. In truth it scared the crap out of me. Being trapped by fire or worse dying in one must be truly awful.

Kilo to Panda 9

Panda 9 go ahead

Can you make towards Cannock Lawn, Somers Town report of a first floor maisonette on fire. Hampshire Fire Brigade on route.

Panda 9, 10/4

It was mid morning and I had Hampshire's last ever Police cadet, Phil Marsh with me. He had been on our relief for several weeks now and was going to make a good Police officer. We arrived a short time later and there were two fire engines already in attendance which was a welcome sight. I looked up and could see activity on the outside balcony on the first floor. There were faint whiffs of smoke coming from the doorway. We entered the block and followed a line of fire hoses up the vomit stained concrete stair well and out onto the balcony. The fire appeared to be coming from the third maisonette along and there were a couple of firemen stood outside. I'd reached the halfway point between the stair well and the fire when one of the firemen told me to stay where I was. I didn't fancy going much closer anyway. He came over to us and explained that the occupant had left the flat when the fire started and was safely downstairs in the warden's office and that he hoped that they would soon have it under control. At this point there was no need to evacuate the entire block. He turned and started to walk back to his colleague when there was an almighty explosion. I saw the big lounge window literally bow outwards before giving way, with glass flying everywhere, as a cloud of thick, black smoke enveloped the balcony. It took less than two seconds to reach us. It was hot. My lungs filled with the stuff and in an instant I was on all fours gasping for clean air. My lungs refused to open and panic set in straight away. I couldn't see a thing. I thought I was going to die right there and then. But survival instinct kicked in and I turned and crawled as fast as I could back towards the stair well. Being blind meant that my senses weren't functioning as they should and this in turn led me to panic still further. I had found the wall to the building on my left and then, oh thank God a door. I pulled down on the handle and it opened. I rolled through the door and slammed it shut behind me. I laid against the door coughing and gasping. As I opened my eyes I could see a little old lady at the other end of the hallway staring at me. I wasn't in the stair well; I was in somebody's flat. She looked mightily surprised to see a policeman spread-eagled on her floor! I could hear voices outside and so I got up and opened the door again. The smoke had cleared and there were firemen running everywhere. My thoughts turned to Phil. Where was he? What had happened to him? I went back outside to the stair well, dodging more firemen as I did so. There he was, crouched over, with an oxygen mask on his face together with the firemen I'd just been talking to. Instead of falling to the ground like I had they had just run straight back to the relative safety of the stair well. The rest of the block was then hurriedly evacuated, starting with the lady I'd frightened to death only a few moments before. The explosion was apparently caused by a large television set which was positioned right next to the window.

There was an area of waste ground at the far eastern end of the patch called The Glory Hole. It wasn't a hole at all, although I suspect it may have been many years before. It was an area about two acres in size and I think may have been used as an amenity tip or a site to dispose of war time debris cleared from many of Portsmouth's bombed streets. Amongst the grass and small shrubs was always an assortment of brick rubble and jagged lumps of metal sticking out of the ground. It was triangular in shape and on one side was the shoreline to Langstone Harbour whilst on the other was a barbed wire fence that surrounded Fort Cumberland which was a secret MOD testing site. At the pointed end of The Glory Hole was a single track lane that led to a peninsular overlooking the southern tip of Hayling Island. We would patrol this area several times a day and especially at night because it was a dumping ground for stolen cars and a haven for perverts and other ne'er-do-wells. It was also an unofficial site for gypsies, tinkers, pikies, did's, travellers, call them what you will, to stop at overnight, or for a week, a month or even more. If they ever arrived in town that's where they got directed to by the Police and that's where they stayed, no if's, no but's.

Most of them, it has to be said kept themselves to themselves but occasionally we would get a group that were nothing but trouble. You could usually tell in advance. If their caravans were the big twin axle models from German manufacturers like Hobby, complete with engraved windows and posh net curtains then they would invariably be decent enough. If they turned up in a fleet of knackered Transit pick-ups towing a hardboard replica of a shed then it was almost inevitable that they were about to increase our workload.

The Glory Hole was really busy and had over 50 caravans on site together with large numbers of pick-up trucks, horse boxes and a multitude of wild dogs running free. These were a deliberate ploy to keep outsiders firmly out, especially the Police. Meanwhile back in civilisation the latest 'must have' toy in Margaret Thatcher's brave new Yuppie world was the Ford Escort XR3i. The new sports hatchback came with previously unseen goodies on a standard car like smart alloy wheels, colour matched door mirrors, a boot spoiler and sports interior. Every red blooded male wanted one. I think Portsmouth had less than a dozen at the time and we had six stolen in less than a week. This was highly unusual. Most of our local car thieves were only just about bright enough to pick the locks on an old Cortina or a Mini, they certainly didn't have the nous to TWC brand new motors.

Then in the early hours one of our Relief stopped an Escort van. He requested some back-up because he wasn't happy with the vehicle or its occupants. When I arrived I could see why straight away. Two big males, covered in tattoos and holding onto a couple of even bigger dogs were being about as non communicative as you can possibly be. The dogs were doing more talking than they were. The van looked really good though. It had smart looking alloy wheels, colour matched door mirrors and a lovely sports interior. When we opened the bonnet we found that it was powered by a fuel injected 1.6 litre engine, not the usual 1100cc lump. A quick PNC check on the engine number revealed it to be from one of our stolen XR3i's. Both men were arrested and we took a gamble on their current residence because they had refused to say where they lived. An unmarked car was then sent to do a quick reccie at The Glory Hole. There were several other good looking Escort vans on the site. Every unit in the city was brought in and at day break we surrounded the site and moved in. To our surprise there was no resistance. What wasn't a surprise was that nobody there knew who these vans belonged to. All five had been customised with the stolen engines and accessories from the cars we had lost during the previous week. It wasn't long before the shells of those cars were found submerged in the harbour. By the next evening the site was deserted and they had all moved on.

Being able to drive panda cars afforded you the occasional perk in that you might get dispatched to a foreign force in order to collect a prisoner arrested on behalf of Hampshire who needed transporting back to the motherland for incarceration. It was a good excuse for a day out from the norm. I was on late turn and was asked to go to Exeter Police Station to collect a prisoner with GT, who still looked like a girl even with his well groomed moustache.

It was a Saturday lunchtime as we headed west in our blue and white MK2 Ford Escort panda. Neither of us had ever been to Exeter before and armed with just an ordnance survey map we beat a path along the A31 and A35, arriving in the town by mid afternoon. Everywhere in Exeter is sign posted. The railway station, the library, the local hospital, the town hall, the fire station, the bus station, places of historical interest, everywhere that is but the police station. We drove around for ages looking for it. We couldn't ask anyone for Christ's sake, we were policemen! How stupid would that look? We got lost and ended up in the back yard of the library. Nothing else for it but to look stupid and ask for directions. We must have picked on the only man in Devon without a sense of humour, he didn't bat an eye lid when we asked. He gave us a long complicated list of directions and I knew we would be lost again within thirty seconds of leaving him. Just as I was driving away he banged on the roof of the car. He said there was a much quicker way that all the local Police used. If we go to the end of the road here, look across the junction, we'll see the pedestrian precinct. If we drive down the precinct the police station is at the far end. You can't miss it. Now that sounded like a much better idea. So off we went to Exeter precinct, which was just like any other precinct, full of Saturday afternoon shoppers, who glared at us as we drove slowly through the slalom course of trees, benches and push chairs! We smiled and waved like royalty and in return the local butcher shook his head as we passed by his window and an old man armed with a walking stick looked horrified as we crawled on by. Sure enough at the far end of the precinct on the other side of the junction was Exeter nick. We were greeted by the station duty man who showed us into the cell block where we met the custody sergeant. He kindly welcomed us to Exeter, offered us a cup of tea and then asked if we had had a trouble free trip down. GT said it was fine until we reached Exeter itself and that we'd had to ask for directions which was somewhat embarrassing. And then he let the cat out of the bag by telling the good Sgt that we had driven through the precinct. It was if the entire station had taken a simultaneous deep breath inwards.

"You did what?" the Sgt exhaled "The superintendent here only issued a memo last week banning all marked police cars from driving through the precinct after the number of complaints he had received from the shop keepers and locals. He gave his word to them that it would never happen again. Oh my Gawd, he's going to go bananas over this".

We were only there for about half an hour but in that time every single person who worked in that station seemed to know exactly who we were, where we had come from and every detail of the heinous crime we had committed. Even the prisoner we had come to collect came out with a smart arsed comment about which route we were taking home. He got told to sit in the back of the car and to be very quiet.

Palmerston Road was the dividing line between Southsea and Central's patch. One end of Palmerston Road had been partly pedestrianised, but a narrow roadway had been left running right through the middle to allow buses to continue using it as they had done for years. There are shops and department stores located on both sides of the road and above many of these shops there are flats, so the area was both commercial and residential. Because the buses stopped running after midnight, the bus only route was a suitable place to sit up in, out of the way of the traffic, to watch the world go by and spot anything worth stopping.

About 0430 one night I was sat there making up my pocket book for the evenings events so far, when out of the shadows on Central's patch came Andy. I hadn't seen him for a while because since he had moved out with Sue we seemed to have lost touch a bit. He wanted a crafty fag, which I had to supply him with because the tight bastard never bought his own, and so I opened the driver's door to the panda and he crouched down beside me whilst he puffed away and we caught up on all the gossip. Then he stood up, said his goodbyes and then without warning he deliberately whacked the switch that operated the two-tone horns on. He hit it so hard that the toggle switch broke off completely. The two-tones were blaring out into the stillness of the night as I watched him sprint down Osborne Road and out of sight. I couldn't for the life of me switch the damned things off until I took a pen from my pocket and stuffed the nib into the hole and lifted up the remaining stump from the switch.

"You tosser Goward" I thought, as I very quickly started the car and drove off before any of the residents copped my registration number.

In October Tricia and I got engaged. We threw a big party at my prospective new parents-in-law house. White Relief and Green Relief turned out in force as did a few other reprobates. I had to tell Tricia that I actually had to obtain written permission from the job to marry her, so she better not have any skeletons hidden in her closet. I think she hit me.

The following week we were back on nights. I spent Friday evening pumping myself up in the usual manner with lots of loud music and then trotted into work. Sometimes you can just tell, the atmosphere is so thick it's tangible. I don't know what it is or how it's created or even how you know, but every now and then it just feels bad. And tonight it felt really bad. It started half way through parade. We got turned out to the Mighty Fine pub in Arundel Street to help out

Central units with a big fight. Then it was across to the Cumberland Tavern at Eastney for a stabbing, then back to Palmerston Road and the Some Place Else Club for a fight, then down to the Esplanade Bars on the seafront for another fight and so it went on and on. And it wasn't even pub closing time yet. I was crewed up with PC 2376 Geoff Tarvin and I was moaning at him to get us back to the nick so I could get my fags because I'd left them behind when we got turned out.

Kilo to Panda 9

Panda 9 go ahead

Make the Akash restaurant, Albert Road, plenty trouble inside.

Panda 9, 10/4

The Akash was a large Indian restaurant run by a jovial Indian chap by the name of George. We entered the restaurant and saw George standing beside the big table at the front. There were about a dozen or so males in their early 20s, obviously in high spirits sat at the table. George explained that they didn't want anything to eat and were just mucking about throwing salt and sugar at each other and that he wanted them to please leave. I repeated the request and beckoned them towards the door. They all got up making stupid comments, which we smiled at, but at least they were heading for the exit. Except three of them, who made their way to the bar just behind where they had been sitting. Whilst Geoff ushered the others outside I went to the bar and said.

"Come on lads, you've had your fun, time to leave".

Two of them turned and laughed and said.

"Yeah awright mate, we're just going".

With that the two of them headed for the door, but the third one completely ignored me and walked to the rear of the restaurant and stopped at another table to talk to a couple he obviously knew. There's always one. I walked up behind him and waited for half a minute or so. I then leant forward and asked him to join his mates outside. He didn't reply but turned and headed towards the door.

We were half way through the restaurant when he suddenly launched himself upwards, turned 180 degrees and screaming like a banshee he punched me hard in the face. As I hit the floor I grabbed his clothing and pulled him down with me. In an instant his mates came crashing back into the restaurant and straight away I could feel the boots raining in on my body. I took several direct hits to my chest and back. I had hold of him with one hand and whilst curled up like a foetus on the floor I screamed 10/10 down the radio. He struggled free and ran to the back of the restaurant again. Women were screaming, glass was being smashed and there was a huge amount of noise. When he got to the back wall he put his fist straight through the front of a fruit machine and then turned to face me. I grabbed him again and as we struggled he fell to his right straight into the toilet cubicles.

By now the two men that had been with him at the bar had come to his rescue and were trying to get me away from him. I had hold of his jacket and there was no way I was going to let go. One of them literally got in between us and my arm was now bent backwards over his shoulder. He was screaming in my face to let his mate go and I was screaming back that there was no way that was going to happen.

The noise at the front of the restaurant suddenly grew louder as I saw Craig McIntosh burst in. He was exactly who I wanted to see. He came straight to my location and heaved the other two out of the way. He then helped me get the other male to his feet and after cuffing him Craig led him outside. More officers arrived and the other two males were arrested. The restaurant had been completely wrecked, there were tables laying on their sides, chairs upside down and glasses smashed everywhere.

I went outside and felt a searing pain in my ribs and that's the last thing I remember. I woke up in the back on an ambulance en route to hospital. I was in a lot of pain and all I wanted was a cigarette.

One of the ambulance men kindly gave me one but every drag hurt like hell. After arriving at the QA Hospital I was x-rayed all over and whilst awaiting the results I could hear Tricia walking down the corridor.

"I hope you've got clean underwear on" which made me laugh, but that hurt to.

We'd been engaged for less than a week and so this wasn't the best introduction to life with a police officer. She was particularly incensed by the boot prints that had been left on my torso. My results showed I had three fractured ribs, a broken nose, torn ligaments on my right thumb where I wouldn't let go of the male, plus all the trimmings like cuts and bruising. I was kept in hospital overnight and was off-sick for six weeks.

It had been the busiest night in the city for years and was headline news in the local papers the following day. I only saw the first couple of hours and it apparently got even worse after midnight with units being brought in from as far away as Winchester and Southampton, with all the cells completely full. When it came to court proceedings all three of them pleaded guilty to assaulting me and causing an affray. Unfortunately there was a prison officers strike on at the time and they were refusing to take new inmates and so the magistrates were under severe pressure not to jail people. In the end Tony Swan, who had done most of the damage was sentenced to three months whilst Wayne Gissing and Stuart Bavistock were sentenced to 30 days, all of it in Police custody cells at Basingstoke.

By the time I had returned to work winter had set in and although us southern softies don't suffer the worst of the winter elements too often, we do still enjoy the snow if and when we get any. The winter of 1980/81 saw us suffer a particularly bad week of weather, with several inches of snow that froze solid over the next couple of days rather than thawing away into slush. All the main roads were kept passable but the minor side roads were left with compacted snow that now resembled an ice rink. Of course being on nights meant that the temperatures were particularly cold and accordingly most sensible people were wrapped up indoors, meaning that it was particularly quiet after midnight. Still, it allowed us the time to practice our skid avoidance techniques in local car parks! But perhaps I didn't practice quite enough. About 1.30 am I saw a MK1 Ford Escort with a couple of young lads in it doing power slides around various junctions, doing their best to get the car to go sideways on the ice. I smiled and thought that would be me if the roles were reversed! However I really shouldn't ignore it because they were after all on a public road. I took the decision to merely follow them for a while so that they got the message to behave themselves. We got to Bradford Junction and it was obvious that they had seen me and were now being sensible. They turned off the roundabout into Cumberland Road, an old residential street with terraced housing and a newish block of flats at the far end by the T junction. I thought I'd follow them to the end of the road and then leave them to it as they had taken the hint.

The road was particularly icy but the Escort driver was driving at a reasonable pace and I stayed a good distance behind him. I saw his brake lights come on as he approached the T junction. The Escort spun 180 degrees, slid straight across the junction, over the pavement and straight through the fencing into Somers Town Junior School. As I watched in amazement, I too started to slide. I was powerless to prevent my car turning 90 degrees to the right as I slid across the same junction and came to a halt against the far kerb. I leapt out of the car to check on the occupants of the Escort. Straight away I could hear cheering and clapping coming from behind me. I looked back towards the flats on the corner and to my astonishment about a dozen residents on the second floor were all out on their balconies holding up pieces of card with 5.7, 5.8, 5.5 scrawled on them. We had clearly been the highlight of their evening's entertainment and had been judged according to our artistic and technical ability. I was somewhat aggrieved that we hadn't scored a single six and told them so!

CHAPTER 5

1981. You don't belong here

Public order training was the new order of the day. Following the riots that had occurred in Bristol the previous year, where Avon and Somerset Police were found in the embarrassing position of having to defend themselves with dustbin lids and plastic milk crates, there was a ground swell of support from the ACPO ranks that Britain's Police needed some serious retraining and a modicum of new equipment, including shields and protective helmets. Whilst the Bristol race riots were something that took everybody by surprise the now weekly brawls inside and outside our football stadiums was not. Mass organised violence was now headline news and it seemed that it was also spilling out onto the streets at pub kick out times on a regular basis.

Hampshire Police decided to form the Regional Support Group (RSG) which required fit, keen and enthusiastic volunteers that would be the first units called upon to attend any violent situations throughout the county or beyond. I decided this sounded like a lot of fun and promptly put my name forward. Our training was based at the old Cadet Training School at Bishops Waltham. We gathered in the car park under the direction of Chief Inspector Don Emery together with his two main instructors, Sgt Kelvin Thorne and his brother Sgt Gerry Thorne. They were quite an act and between them they really put us through the mill. We cowered behind our shiny new long shields as wooden bricks were hurled at us, whilst Don Emery barked out his orders. We ran bloody miles with those shields in a sort of cross country hike but without the cow pats and stinging nettles! We learned new tactics on how to clear road junctions, to lock shields together to form an impenetrable wall and spent hours learning how to get in and out of a Transit minibus in a system called 'em-bussing and de-bussing'. The idea was to get 12 coppers into a Transit in rapid time and I think the record was something like four seconds. Every single one of us banged our heads either on the way in or on the way out. Just when we were starting to question the validity of doing so much training so Brixton erupted into a ball of fire with further race riots, that were firmly blamed on over zealous policing by the Met, but were in truth a combination of underlying tensions caused by unemployment, degradation, poor housing and racial tension. Although we were never called up to assist the Met Police it was a bit of a wake up call that maybe Bristol a few months earlier wasn't a one-off and that there might be more to come.

Every now and then I would have to endure my fair share of station duty relief, either because of sickness or leave or even just to fill in for an hour during the SDO's meal break. I took over one evening from Horace Evans and he said it had been particularly busy. He wasn't kidding either. There were several people at the front counter, all driving document productions or those needing to sign on in the bail book. Both external and internal phones were ringing, the telex machine was spewing out miles and miles of ticker tape and a prisoner in the detained person's cell was banging on the door because he wanted a drink.

The prisoner was a very well known local youth called Gary Saunders, a huge brute of a young man who used his size and strength to intimidate people, especially women and those obviously smaller and meeker than him. He was an out and out bully. His father was just as bad. He was known locally as Loopy Saunders and it was easy to see why. He could be seen most days riding his bike along Albert Road cursing and swearing at everything that moved.

I shouted at Gary through the door that I was extremely busy but I'd get to him just as soon as I could. It didn't make the slightest bit of difference; he continued to bang on the door demanding a drink of water. I'd just finished clearing the front counter and was about to attend to his desires when the phone rang. I picked up the phone and knelt on a chair as I listened to the call. Saunders was now really giving it his best against the door and then there was a huge crash as the entire door and frame came out of the wall and fell to the floor in a large cloud of dust. Saunders filled the void where the door used to be and bellowed at me.

"I said I wants a fuckin drink mush"

"And I said you'll have to fucking wait, now go and sit down" I bellowed back.

I apologised to the lady on the other end of the phone and told her I would phone her back in a minute. To my surprise Gary went and sat on the bench whilst I ran upstairs as fast as Wily Coyote chasing the Road Runner and returned in less than 30 seconds with a cup of water, convinced he would have legged it. But no, there he was sitting on the bench staring at the door.

"I suppose I'll get charged with that will I?" he asked mournfully.

"Yep I think there's every chance you might Gary" and with that I transferred him to a proper cell.

For several months myself and many of my colleagues had started to notice a significant increase in the amount of graffiti daubed on walls throughout the city. It wasn't any of the fancy artwork type you might associate with the London underground or on some remote motorway bridge somewhere. This was a mixture of the letters PFC and the numbers 6.57 scrawled in white aerosol paint. It was everywhere; on walls, bus shelters, on those green telephone junction boxes, fences, hoardings, road signs, everywhere you looked, everyday, more of it had been added somewhere. But what on earth did it mean? The PFC bit was obvious but 6.57 baffled us for ages. Occasionally the numbers 6.57 came with the word 'Crew' written underneath or alongside. It transpired that this had become the name associated with Portsmouth's football hooligan element; they now had themselves a name, the 6.57 Crew, so called because they caught the 6.57 am train from Fratton station to away games.

But who were they really? Although hundreds of youths who travelled on that train quickly latched onto the idea that they were part of the 6.57 Crew, in reality they were nothing more than pawns, foot soldiers, minions to be guided to where the next big scrap was going to be. The real members, the original cast, were far more sinister and had a far bigger agenda than even they realised when they first started out.

Without question there was a hierarchy within the crew. Although effectively leaderless, there were definitely those who ran the outfit as some kind of exclusive club. A nucleus of about a dozen hardened criminals, whose reputations had been built as juveniles in schools throughout the city, who had progressed to assaults at pubs and clubs and now found themselves revered by slightly younger, more impressionable youths. This second tier of males would be at the fore front of any fighting in order to prove themselves to those above them, perhaps in the vain hope of promotion? There was a third tier and these were the pathetic sheep of the outfit, the graffiti sprayers, those that helped swell the ranks from the rear and would be the first to run away at the first sign of any real trouble!

The main players included the likes of Ian 'Froggy' Ford, Robin 'Fish' Potter, Robert Sylvia, Paul Van Clerk, Graham Murphy, Jason Estuary and several others. At the start of it all they were aged 19 to 20 years old and most were very handy when it came to the physical stuff and at first it was all a bit of fun, the yob element having gained themselves a name. But the name wasn't enough, it had to have notoriety to gain the respect of other such organisations like the Chelsea 'Head Hunters', West Ham's 'Intercity Firm' or Millwalls 'Bushwhackers'. The 6.57 Crew built much of their reputation upon the violence and damage they inflicted on those towns and cities they visited on away matches. They would rampage through city centres, smashing shop windows, steaming through supermarkets on massive hit and run shop lifting sprees to grab food and alcohol and once refuelled would seek out the opposing team's mob to wage their pathetic war of brutality.

But it wasn't always away from home that they inflicted damage.

They were quite partial to attacking their own citizens or would use intimidation tactics that bred a feeling of fear throughout the community. We were on nights and had been called to Wilmcote House in Somers Town. This 20 storey block of flats was one of several on the estate and it was a breeding ground of crime and poverty. There was never any peace there either. If you happened to find yourself there in the dead of night there was always a shouting match going on in one flat, with loud music blaring from another, whilst the sound of unsprung fire doors banging against their door frames at the entrance to the concrete stairwells would echo as if they were located in the Swiss Alps! Those same stair wells stunk of urine and vomit. They were littered with fast food wrappers and soiled nappies, whilst the walls proudly displayed the latest 6.57 slogan.

There was a big party in full swing on the 15th floor. Except this was no ordinary party. It had started out that way, a few locals had invited along some friends and they in turn had invited the 6.57 Crew. About 100 of them. It very quickly got out of hand and the owners of the flat were forced to leave. As more and more Police units arrived so the volume upstairs increased. Then to howls of laughter came the fridge, hurled from the kitchen window towards a patrol car beneath. It missed its target but smashed into a thousand pieces. The washing machine followed as did a couple of chairs and the toilet seat. These were followed by glasses, bottles, clothing and food, in fact anything they could lay their hands on. The reactions from the locals outside were a mixture of laughter from some, anger from the older generation and tears from the occupants of the flat who could do nothing but watch their possessions take a swallow dive from the window. We stormed the flat. I have to confess that I was crapping myself. There were less than 20 of us and apart from the fact they outnumbered us they were in a highly agitated and excitable state whilst high on lots of alcohol. To the blaring sound of The Specials *'Too Much, Too Young'* we arrested a handful of the ring leaders whilst the others were pushed outside and downstairs where there was a brief stand off, before they filtered out through the side streets. The flat was left an empty shell, what few possessions this couple owned were now splattered across the concrete below. This wasn't a one-off incident either. Every weekend would be the same, some poor resident was subjected to the same treatment and we found it increasingly difficult to deal with because by the time we got called, most of the damage had been done and the intimidation was so bad that obtaining witness statements was next to impossible.

Whilst herding a group away from another gate crashed party one night I took a youth to one side to search him for weapons. He thought the whole thing was one "big larf mate" and this was typical of their attitude. He was the archetypal foot soldier with self inflicted tattoos on his knuckles, with PFC on his left fist, 6.57 on his right fist and Pompey dots on the back of every finger. These dots were blue and were exactly as described, just self inflicted dots about 2mm across. No self respecting Portsmuff yoof would be without them. Whilst searching him he asked me a question.

"Where you from then mush?"

"London originally" I replied.

"What farkin right you got to come and police us then, you ain't from ere, you ain't got no farkin rights ere" he snarled.

"I don't really see it makes a lot of difference do you?" I retorted as I patted him down.

"It makes every difference, if you was a Pompey boy I'd ave some respect for ya but you ain't, you don't belong ere mush" he laughed.

His words reverberated around my head all night. In fact they haunted me beyond belief. I was born and bred in south west London and at the age of nine my parents moved us to the Isle of Wight because my father, a prison officer, had been promoted and posted to Parkhurst. We hated the place; it was like being thrown back in time 20 years. We arrived in 1969, a month or so before the first big riot inside the prison where several officers sustained serious injury. Then we had to put up with further rioting and fires inside Albany Prison caused by the dozens of IRA prisoners housed there, followed by the IRA hunger strikes and the subsequent funeral of Michael Gaughan. We had armed Police in our junior school and a night time curfew for weeks on our estate. We put up with all of that because we had to. But it was the attitude of some of the islanders that got to me the most. At school and at scouts, myself and my younger brother were treated as complete outsiders. We were from the mainland and worse still we were labelled as prison kids, as all the kids on my estate were. Because we weren't born and bred on the island we didn't belong, pure and simple.

So it dawned on me tonight that both communities are very similar in their attitudes. Both are islands and many of their respective residents have an island mentality. Everybody born there seems to know everybody else who was born there and outsiders are viewed with a degree of suspicion and held at arms length. In the football hooligans mind if you weren't born and bred on Portsea island then you were fair game. Now I understood that mentality I could deal with them a lot more effectively because I'd had to in the past.

It was 10.30 on a Saturday morning and I was sat on the seafront admiring the view across The Solent.

Kilo to Panda 9

Panda 9 go ahead

Can you back up KC units at Portsmouth and Southsea railway station, we've had reports that some Millwall fans are on board having arrived early for this afternoons match. The train is due in 10 minutes.

Panda 9, 10/4

Oh great. Pompey at home to the notorious Millwall for the first time in several years. I'm not even on football duty today. Mind you, those that are won't be ready for another hour or so yet. As I arrived at the station I parked my panda out the front with a couple of others and we walked inside onto the main concourse. There were only four of us as the train pulled in. You could hear the noise from inside the train before it had even stopped. The doors opened and out poured over 200 of them, chanting Millwall songs like;

We are Millwall, we are Millwall,
No one likes us, we don't care,
We are Millwall, fucking Millwall
No one likes us, we don't care.

You could instantly see why nobody liked them. Most had retained the old skin head, boot boy look, with shaven heads, Doc Martin boots, jeans, braces and black Harrington jackets. They just ran straight at us whilst letting out this huge roar. It was terrifying. They steamed past us and out the front of the station. They ran across the road towards the City Arms pub, which was often frequented by the 6.57 Crew. It was too early for it to be open and as they ran past so all the windows got smashed. We needed reinforcements and quick. They ran through the Guildhall Square and I decided to go back and get my panda, I certainly had no intention of doing a cross country run today! I rejoined them at the end of Guildhall Walk as they crossed the dual carriageway at Winston Churchill Avenue. They were heading straight for Somers Town. As quickly as we corralled them in one direction, so others broke away in another. We were hopelessly out numbered. Then like rats from the sewer, Pompey's finest emerged from nowhere. Running street battles went on for more than two hours before we had enough man power to split them all up and march the Millwall fans to Fratton Park more than two hours before kick-off. As we progressed down Goldsmith Avenue so the Pompey idiots would appear from a side street in an effort to ambush us. Bricks and bottles flew through the air towards us as Millwall sang and roared their loudest. We pushed them into the Milton End of the ground and I parked my panda outside at the end of Specks Lane. We were all ordered to continue policing this lot until after the game.

By the time 3 o'clock arrived the atmosphere inside the ground was the most hostile I had ever experienced with the Milton End now heaving under the weight of 3000 Millwall fans, barracked inside the steel cage erected after trouble during several of last seasons games. At half time both sets of fans were goading each other like never before. It was obvious this had the potential to go horribly wrong; in fact it was a bit like standing inside a pressure cooker. Mid way through the second half a hundred or so Millwall thugs got through the railings at the front of the cage and spilled out onto the pitch in an effort to get at the Pompey boys at the Fratton End. I watched from the back of the Milton End as the referee took the players off the pitch as Police officers and Police dogs ran onto the park to keep the two factions apart.

The Fratton End were baiting the Millwall fans with "You'll never take the Fratton End, you'll never take the Fratton End" as more and more Police officers were drafted onto the perimeter of the pitch. The trouble was quelled and the ref brought the players back on to continue the match, although in all honesty it was little more than a side show which Pompey won 2-1.

As soon as the final whistle went the players ran for their lives towards the tunnel and the ground erupted. A huge roar went up and in an instant it started. The previously breached cage was pulled down at the front as hundreds of them spilled back out onto the pitch to be confronted by snarling dogs, eager for a bite or two. As they got beaten back into the cage so those immediately in front of us and to our right decided that they wanted to leave the ground right now in order to get at the Pompey fans leaving from the Frogmore Road exit. I found myself with Inspector Dave Watson and PC 1312 Dave Randell. We were being crushed and moved towards the turn stiles with the crowd. Dave Watson asked if we had our sticks with us. Obviously we had. He ordered us to draw our sticks and beat our way out of the ground. It was easier said than done, there was so little room to manoeuvre that it was easier to jab our opponents than swing out with a stick. We literally fought our way to the steps which were now a seething mass of bodies. Some of them were standing on the roof of the turn stile booths beckoning others to join them and directing operations from above. The three of us were the last coppers out of the Milton End and the large solid wood gates were heaved shut behind us. I was absolutely knackered, covered in brick dust and shaking like a leaf. The noise was incredible and now we were being pelted with lumps of concrete rubble, broken off from the terracing and other structures. I saw two officers take direct hits in the face and blood poured from their wounds.

The gates started to bow outwards. We were ordered to keep them shut and several of us put our shoulders against them in an effort to push them back. But it was no good, there were about a dozen of us versus a couple of hundred of them at least and within seconds there was an almighty crack as the wood splintered away from the hinges and the whole lot toppled on top of us. I managed to scramble out of the way just in time but Dave Randell was trapped under both doors. The Millwall fans sort of stopped for about two seconds, just long enough for me to grab Dave's arm and pull him out from underneath. We managed to hold them there for about two minutes, which was just long enough for one PC to grab the feet of one of those standing on the roof and heave him off and lead him away. We all retreated to the edge of Carisbrooke Road some 30 feet behind us and formed a cordon. The brick rubble now resembled rain as it was hurled high into the air from the terraces towards us. To my left I caught a glimpse of the Pompey yobs at the other end of Carisbrooke Road being held back by another cordon. Why don't we just let them beat the shit out of each other I thought? The Millwall fans were now exiting the ground in their hundreds as one of the metal turn stiles flew through the air. How much brute force did it take to rip that out of its concrete footings? And then they broke through the cordon and ran on mass along Apsley Road towards Goldsmith Avenue. The Pompey fans saw this and ran along the parallel Frogmore Road to head them off. With truncheons drawn we raced after them. Goldsmith Avenue resembled a scene from a medieval battle ground with bodies laying all over the road, with desperate looking policemen trying to keep the two warring tribes apart. The hatred on some of the faces on both sides of the divide was incredible. Some how most of them were kept apart and as the Pompey fans were pushed along Goldsmith Avenue towards Fratton Bridge so the Millwall thugs charged down Haslemere Road. There must have been over 1000 of them and they filled the entire street. They jumped on cars, demolished garden walls and used the masonry as missiles to throw at us or smash residential windows. Tricia's parents lived here and as I ran past their house I could see that my prospective father-in-laws Morris Minor had a huge dent in the roof and another on the bonnet. The mob turned right into

Devonshire Avenue and there were several skirmishes along the way. Slowly but surely we split them up into smaller groups and escorted them back to Fratton railway station to herd them onto trains back to London.

Although I had quite a bit of experience in dealing with violence now I hadn't been prepared for the sheer scale and the absolute determination to do as much damage as possible, whether that be human or material. It was truly frightening. As I rode my motorcycle from Albert Road back towards Haslemere Road there were residents out on every street, looking at a damaged wall or car. Some were sweeping up the debris whilst others just shook their heads in disbelief. As I turned into Haslemere Road I was shocked at the amount of rubble strewn along the road still. As I entered the house everybody was clearly very upset and frightened, none more so than Tricia's cousin Sue, a 16 year old Canadian on her first visit to England. She'd never seen anything like this in Canada! Apparently as the mob came running past the house Sue was so intrigued that she pulled back the net curtain in the front room for a better look. At that moment a Millwall thug had a steel manhole cover in his hands and threw it towards the window. Tricia's sister Sheelagh pulled Sue back but by some miracle the metal disc smashed through next doors lounge window instead. It had been a very long day.

I hadn't watched much TV in the last three years or so because I couldn't afford one in the flat. But I was spending more and more time with Tricia's family and by a happy coincidence caught the very first series of Hill Street Blues. I was hooked from the very first episode because even though it was set in the USA I could identify with every aspect of it. The story lines were based on true Police incidents and it showed, being both funny and sad. The characters were fantastically cast with my favourite being Andy Renko, who I have to confess I could relate to in a big way. It was a timeless and very human series showing the seedier side of life in a big city and those empowered with policing it.

I'm not sure whether I was relieved or disappointed that in my first few weeks of service, despite being warned that I would be targeted,

I never became the subject of a welcoming initiation ceremony, although I was still not entirely convinced that the testing of the air raid siren wasn't mine! But I'd seen plenty more since then, many of them repeated as new proby's came in.

Some of Southsea's involved utilising the local landscape in conjunction with an official looking telex message. One involved the annual swan count down at the canoe lake. Said proby would be dispatched to the lake, usually at 5am to count the number of swans, because as we all know swans are a royally protected species and Her Majesty was particularly interested in how her flock were doing. Once the count was complete the proby had to phone the control room Inspector at HQ Winchester to report his findings! The canoe lake was also the venue for another favourite where the proby would be handed a glass phial and some of those urine testing strips, the task at hand being the annual canoe lake water test. Having collected a sample of the water and inserted the strip the proby would return to the station and again report his findings to the control room. The annual deck chair count was one of my favourites though. The proby would be dropped off at the far end of Eastney seafront and made to walk the entire 5 miles along the seafront to Clarence Pier to count the number of deck chairs. They had to pay particular attention to those marked with BBC stencils as these belonged to Brighton Borough Council and needed to be returned. One of the funniest though was when Mick Keating volunteered to be hanged underneath South Parade Pier just as dawn was breaking. We had a new WPC on the Relief who had let it slip that she wasn't looking forward to seeing her first dead body. Mick placed a civvy jacket on and a Tesco carrier bag over his head as we 'hung' him so that his feet just touched the beach. He looked very convincing. Cathy Knight and her tutor PC 683 Dick Hanna, who was in on the whole thing were then sent by the control room to this suspicious incident beneath the pier. Dick went one side and deliberately sent Cathy to the other. She shone her torch across the body from outside the pier several times before she plucked up the courage to walk in and examine things further. She got right up close with her torch transfixed on the body, when Mick jumped at her and let out a blood curdling scream. Cathy actually left the ground and fell backwards onto the beach as we childishly leapt out from behind our hiding place laughing like naughty schoolboys. Welcome to Southsea!

One of the things that would really upset me in court was being challenged by a defence solicitor over the wording I had used in my pocket book in order to convict his client. Granted there are times when a play on words can mean one thing or another but generally speaking the over whelming majority of officers play by the rules and are as truthful as they can possibly be. But sometimes the offender can say things that nobody, especially his brief, is ever going to believe were actually said.

At midnight on night shift, most of us would pop back to the station for a quick ten minute cuppa. We would congregate in the front office and gossip whilst we slurped our tea and smoked a fag. There was a screech of brakes right outside the nick, followed by a big bang. We ran outside to see that a MK2 Ford Cortina had lost control and collided with a traffic island and a 'keep left' bollard which the car was now sitting on top of. As we ran outside the passenger was out of the car and trying to push it as the driver tried restarting it. Upon seeing half a dozen coppers emerge from the nearby building the passenger legged it, hotly pursued by some of Southsea's finest. I ran straight to the drivers door, opened it and the driver fell out onto his back into the road. I looked at him and said.

"Are you alright?"

"No I'm pissed"

"That's a fine way to treat your car"

"It's not mine I nicked it"

Thankfully he pleaded guilty and I was never challenged in court on that one!

Tricia and I got married at St. James's Church in Milton and held our reception at the Wedgewood Rooms on Albert Road. Graham was my best man. Tricia and I had a weeks honeymoon in France because that was all we could afford having recently mortgaged ourselves to the hilt buying our first house for £18,000. For me it was straight back to where I had started because the house was in Alverstone Road, thankfully right down the far end away from Eve and her daughter! It had a great view though. If you stood on the toilet seat, leant sideways about 45 degrees and then turned your neck another 20 degrees and looked out the top of the bathroom window you could see inside Fratton Park! Mind you it was probably the only house in the street where you couldn't see either goal mouth because the concrete base for the floodlights was in the way. And if you got carried away by the excitement on football days and clapped, you invariably fell off the toilet.

Buying a house and getting married also meant leaving Campbell Road which was rather sad, but I didn't lose touch with Steve and Mike as I would quite often use them as a tea stop. This also became a bit of a problem at our own house. On match days I found my house was becoming a very popular place to come and hide for more than ten minutes by a number of my colleagues who were either sheltering from the weather or hiding from the Sgt. It wasn't unusual to have more than a dozen in there at any one time as our kettle went into over drive!

After returning from our honeymoon I popped into the station to find out what my duties were for the following week and was strongly advised by Sgt Jock Campbell to "piss off home quick" because they were looking for RSG officers to go to Liverpool to help police the rioting in Toxteth.

I did manage to avoid going to Liverpool and commenced another set of nights upon my return from honeymoon. It was about half three in the morning on the Friday night shift as Craig and I drove slowly south along Clarendon Road towards the seafront. As we were about to pass the Calross Club so we saw Aubrey leap out into the road in front of us, frantically waving his arms. He was sweating profusely and panicking that something terrible had happened, but was in such a state we couldn't make out what the problem was. He grabbed my arm as I climbed out of the patrol car and ushered me across the car park towards the club. He was flapping about like a chicken worried by a fox and as we reached the steps to the club I could see a man laying on his back. His feet were on the bottom step and his head was close to the door. He was laying in a pool of blood and was unconscious. I checked that there was an ambulance en route and then got down the steps to join Craig who was trying to ascertain how serious the head injury was. In the darkness the man looked strangely familiar and there were two other men hovering about the edge of the steps. Aubrey said that the three men had been together all evening and had left at the same time and that all three were very much under the influence. Although he didn't know the other two he said the unconscious male was a local man by the name of Terence Keith Ross. He was a very well known business man who owned a string of second hand shops and antique stores and drove the only Rolls Royce in the city complete with personalised registration plate. Apparently as Mr Ross got to the top of the steps so he fell backwards, cracking his skull open as he landed. He died later that night in hospital. Four months later, Craig and I were interviewed by murder squad detectives from the Met Police, which came as a complete surprise to us. It transpired that on the night of the accident the two friends travelled to the hospital in the back of the ambulance with Mr Ross. As he lay dying one of these 'friends' carefully removed the solid gold bracelet from Ross's wrist and slipped it into his own pocket. The pair of them later sold the bracelet on in London but then argued about the split in the money. A fight ensued and one of them beat the other to death. Which just goes to prove that there really is no honour amongst thieves.

For several weeks now we had been plagued by a new group of youths who congregated by the bus shelter at Bransbury Park. Some times they would number 20 or more and they would harass passers-by, rip up the flower beds, throw stones at the Green Leaf Chinese Takeaway across the road, or passing cars and generally be a real nuisance. Every night we would go down there and they would run away across the park as soon as we arrived and ten minutes after we'd left they would be back and the whole cycle would start all over again. It was both tedious for us and became increasingly frustrating for the locals who saw the police as being powerless to stop it from happening. The youths were all aged 15 to 17 years old and were growing in confidence as the weeks went by.

During a particularly bad week with them Green Relief decided that a slightly more proactive course of action was required. As per usual they were performing one evening and so five of us entered Bransbury Park from the rear and sat in the bushes just a few feet behind them. They stoned the Chinese Takeaway and when the owner came out to remonstrate with them they threw stones and hurled racial abuse at him. A short while later a double decker bus stopped at the bus stop and the youths steamed on board, whilst some of the others started stoning it. That was enough for us, we had seen enough and could identify those who had committed the more serious offences. We raced out of the bushes and ran towards our respective targets. Mine was completely unaware we were approaching and was standing in front of the bus about to throw another stone at it. I grabbed him and arrested him, forcing him to drop the stone. The 16 year old youth I had detained was of swarthy complexion with dark swept back hair and was wearing a decent brown leather jacket. He was of Maltese extraction and came from a large family with four brothers and a sister. His name was George Scaberras. He was quite lippy of course but then so were the other five that had been detained. They were all taken to Central nick because Southsea was full up. Being juveniles of course we had to get their parents out before they could be interviewed and charged. Mr Scaberras arrived. He was Maltese and a very small, quiet man. He was polite and very apologetic over his son's behaviour. Both of them cooperated during the short interview and George confessed to his part in the proceedings. He was then charged and bailed to appear before Portsmouth Juvenile Court in a few weeks time. After completing the paperwork I escorted both of them from the cell block to the front door of the station where they were released. Mr Scaberras shook my hand and we said our good byes. I then went back into the front office and together with the SDO and a PC from Central we watched with glee as dad beat his son around the head several times, kicked him hard up the back side and generally knocked him about a bit, whilst verbally giving him a hard time as they crossed the road to the car park. If only a few more fathers would dish out such punishment we said as one, then maybe, just maybe things around here might improve a little. At the very least it might have curbed the problem at Bransbury Park.

I came into work the next afternoon and was immediately summoned into Inspector Danny Daniels office. He was a very tall, slim man, with impeccable manners who absolutely insisted that everything was done by the book. There was nothing officious about him you understand, he was a real gent but you knew that things had to be done correctly. When he told me to shut the door and sit down I knew I was in the shit. Straight away he cautioned me and then served a notice of complaint on me stating that I had assaulted one George Scaberras causing him actual bodily harm! He went on to inform me that Mrs Scaberras who had made the complaint also had a doctor's report and photographs of her son's injuries. What? This is a joke right? Is this my long overdue initiation ceremony? But no, it wasn't. The complaint was investigated by the Complaints and Discipline Department at HQ. Statements were obtained from young George who was now alleging that I beat him up in the back of the Police van, which I would have found difficult to do because I was driving it at the time! There was also a statement from Mrs Scaberras telling of her son's traumatic time at the hands of the brutal and fascist Southsea police. Strangely there was no statement from Mr Scaberras at all. I was interviewed under caution at great length by an Inspector from C&D and it was an experience I certainly didn't fancy repeating any time soon. My saving grace was the statements obtained from the officers at Central who watched with me through the window. The investigation took seven months before I finally got a single page note from C&D stating the complaint had not been substantiated. Well thank you very much for that.

Dave Martin took me into his office to ask me what I wanted to do in the future. I told him that ultimately I was looking at joining the Traffic Division but in the meantime I'd really like to get myself onto a Standard Car Course in order that I could become an Area

Car driver. I was delighted when he offered me the opportunity to do just that based on the fact that he was more than pleased with my progress since joining the Relief and that becoming an Area Car driver would be the right move for me and the Relief.

So in October it was back to Hulse Road for a four week Standard Car Course, which was without doubt the hardest but most enjoyable course I'd ever been on. We got to drive a variety of performance cars from BMW 520's, Rover SD1's, Volvo 240 GLT's and a MK5 Ford Cortina 2.3 V6. We drove all over the country learning the skills laid down by Road Craft and I loved every minute of it. Over the period of the course so the speeds increased as did the levels of concentration required. Some days I'd get out of the drivers seat absolutely knackered and dripping in sweat.

Then one lunchtime we stopped at Chichester nick in Sussex. My instructor was Ron Anderson again and he insisted that I and the two others in my crew ate the curry which was really good. Then he insisted we all ate two portions of the even nicer cheese cake that was on offer. We left Chichester feeling really stuffed and Ron insisted that all three of us sit in the back of the car. He drove down a country lane for a couple of miles and then entered a gateway that had an old sign on it saying RAF Tangmere. Within seconds the car was spinning around and around, sliding sideways and then doing complete 360 degree turns. We were on a skid pan and feeling incredibly sick! Once Ron had stopped pratting about we got out to regain some composure before our sessions of skid training commenced. Oh what fun we had. But it obviously had its serious side to and I learned more about car control in my hours driving on that skid pan that I had ever hoped to have learned in my previous three years driving experience. The following week we went back for a longer session which was thankfully before lunch this time. I passed the course and got my area car ticket. As far as I was concerned, at that very moment, I had arrived.

At last I got to drive Kilo Sierra Five One

It was back to Southsea with a bump because Millwall were back in town. It wasn't just the Pompey fans who were looking forward to it, so were Hampshire Police. We owed them something after the hammering we took just a few months before. More importantly we owed it to the residents of Portsmouth to ensure that this time the experience wasn't repeated. A huge Police operation was put into action with more than 400 officers greeting every train and coach that made the brief journey south. A zero tolerance attitude was adopted for both factions in order to keep them apart. Little or no trouble occurred before the match but inside the ground the cauldron of hatred was brewing again. Coins and bottles were being thrown across the corners of the north stand and the Milton End where the Millwall fans were penned in. Where officers spotted offenders so they were hooked out and removed from the ground. By half time there had already been minor skirmishes in the ground where rival fans had somehow found each other.

As I came out the St. John's Ambulance room having had my cup of tea I came across two of Pompey's finest. Both were in their late 20s, both were of very big build, with shaven heads, tattoos and a lot of anger. One of them in particular walked with what is locally referred to as 'the Pompey strut' that meaning that his legs are abnormally bowed, almost Chimpanzee like, his arms are placed out at 20 degrees and slightly bent at the elbows with fists clenched and upper torso barrelled outwards whilst swinging from left to right. It is a self assured, very cocky, look at me, I'm gonna ave ya, type stance. And this boy was definitely looking for somebody to ave. He was carrying his shirt and bare chested he was shouting in his mates face. Ray Harbour and I approached them both because it was clear that these two needed speaking to. Our bare chested boy had been stabbed in the chest, the blade piercing his sternum. There wasn't much blood coming from the one inch slit in his flesh and the last thing on his mind was going to hospital.

He wanted the "Millwall cunt wot done this to pay".

To be fair his mate was as concerned as we were that he get treatment first. We all stood there arguing with him as two ambulance men arrived. We weren't getting anywhere and neither was his mate. They were starting to fall out as bare chested boy kept trying to push past him. Then his mate suddenly pointed past him and shouted out.

"There they are".

With that our victim turned around to look and as he did so his mate punched him so hard in the face that he had rendered him unconscious before he even hit the ground. He turned to the ambulance men and said.

"You can take him away now boys".

I thought that was a touch of genius myself.

Towards the end of the game the Milton End was seething once again. My knees were shaking as we lined up across the end of Specks Lane looking at the same gates that had come crashing down on us last time. Lumps of concrete and stones were now raining down on us again as the gates were opened and out they swarmed, snarling at us like rabid Rottweilers. We had formed a massive cordon, some six officers deep across the exit. Those of us in the front row had truncheons drawn and swung them in an effort to keep the animals at bay. It started to work and they retreated a few yards back to the gates. I was then amazed to see Chief Inspector Don Emery standing in no-man's land with his back to the crowd barking his orders at us. As the bricks, stones and bottles fell from the sky, he not only seemed oblivious to it all but not one of them hit him! He pointed at the centre of the cordon and ordered it to break. As it did so, a line of officers armed with long shields and batons charged through the cordon and formed a front line cordon close enough to continue with a bit more summary justice. The Chief Inspector then produced a mega phone and politely explained to our London visitors that we could continue like this all night or they could bloody well behave like human beings and then we would escort them back to their trains! It worked and within five minutes a box had been formed and we walked the whole lot down Goldsmith Avenue to Fratton Station. The road had been cleared of Pompey fans by an equally determined group of officers who had pushed them over Fratton Bridge and up Fratton Road. Frustrated by their lack of interaction with their opposite number the Pompey thugs decided to vent their anger on the shop windows along Fratton Road, smashing dozens of them in the process. Two hours or so after the last train left we were still chasing our own youths all over the city. With every match now their numbers seemed to grow.

Driving and crewing the area car ensured that the level of my work increased significantly and so did the responsibility that came with it. The area car should generally be the first unit on the scene at most emergencies and the crew would be expected to have the capability to cope with just about anything they are presented with. It wasn't just a question of being able to drive fast, the actual policing was the important bit and you had to be capable of making quick decisions using your own initiative, sometimes in life and death situations.

Kilo to Kilo Sierra 51

Kilo Sierra 51 go ahead

Make Clarence Parade by the double bends, RTA, car into a wall, believed serious.

Kilo Sierra 51, 10/4

It was half three in the morning and we were sat outside the night clubs on the seafront when we got the call so we were there in less than a minute. A crappy old MK1 Ford Escort with five youngsters in it had been travelling west along Clarence Parade at high speed on a wet road when the driver braked hard on the approach to the first right hand bend, locked up and carried straight on, colliding head-on with the kerb. On hitting the kerb the car took off across the narrow pavement and was stopped dead as the bottom of the car hit the top of the two foot high stone wall that skirts Southsea Common. The Escort was balanced on top of the wall, with the front end about four feet above the ground and the rear touching the pavement. It was a scene of utter carnage. The driver and three rear seat passengers were scattered around the car having been thrown out on impact with the wall. They all had very serious injuries. Ken started doing a quick scan of the passengers whilst I went straight to the car because a girl inside was screaming. I had never heard anyone screaming like this, it was frantic and she was crying for help. I was horrified at what I found. On impact with the wall she had submarined from the front passenger seat and gone straight through the weakened rusty floor of the car and was now trapped by her thighs amongst a tangled mass of twisted, broken metal. I took a quick look under the car from the front and could see her legs hanging out from underneath. I'd never seen such injuries. Her legs were an absolute mess, with huge gaping wounds exposing broken bones and muscle tissue. They had been ripped to shreds. I immediately called for the fire service to attend in order to cut her free. She started screaming that her leg was on fire and that it was burning. I got back under the car and saw that her right leg was pressed up against the hot exhaust pipe and was being cooked. I could hear her flesh sizzling and cracking and there was a putrid smell that accompanied it. I couldn't pull it away because of the wreckage around her so ran back to the patrol car and grabbed the crow bar and a blanket from the boot. I managed to prise the exhaust away far enough to get the blanket in between it and her leg that was now badly blistered. She was in immense pain and I felt completely and utterly useless. No words of comfort from me were going to ease it for her and she was conscious enough to know that she was probably going to lose her legs before the end of the night. Where's that bloody ambulance I kept asking myself. Ken came over and told me the driver had just blown a positive breath test and was now under arrest. I held the girls hand as she sobbed because she thought she was going to die. I tried convincing her that wasn't going to happen and that we would get her out just as quickly as we could. The ambulance arrived and even they were shocked by what they were confronted with. I helped them as best as I could, holding up the saline drip they set up and trying to comfort the girl as she became slightly calmer once the oxygen mask they had placed over her face started working its magic. A doctor was called for and two more ambulances turned up. I knew that there was only one reason why a doctor had been called and I really didn't want to be around if they were going to amputate this young girls legs at the scene. The fire brigade arrived with two tenders and I was obviously now in the way. I had to get in the back of the car, still holding the drip and trying to keep her calm whilst all around her firemen and ambulance men did their utmost to get her out. They started to dismantle the car. First the roof came off, out came the windscreen, off came the doors and then slowly but surely they started to cut into the floor pan. By now the doctor had arrived and he was clearly concerned for her. It was going to be a delicate balancing act between saving her legs and saving her life. It very much depended on how quickly the fire brigade could extract her. He had rendered her unconscious through a number of injections so at least she was now unable to see or feel what was going on around her. It took another hour or so to cut the metal away from her legs. Her wounds were full of rusty particles and flakes of metal as very slowly she was lifted out and placed onto a spinal board and transferred to the QA Hospital. It had been an exhausting couple of hours and her screams will probably haunt me forever, but not as much as the feeling of being completely and utterly useless in such circumstances. Thank goodness for the skills of the Fire Service and the Ambulance crews at such incidents.

We learned a few days later that they had managed to save her legs and that although her recovery time would be months, maybe years, she would walk again. It's a pity her drunken boyfriend hadn't suffered in the same way.

I was about to work my fourth Christmas in a row. There isn't a good duty to work during the festive period but at least it's compensated by being paid at double time. Except Christmas Eve on late turn though. Christmas Eve was always my favourite time as a child, I think it had something to do with the build up to the big day which invariably ended in disappointment, but at least the tension and the excitement for what might lay ahead was always guaranteed. So far I'd only done early turn on Christmas Eve and this was my first late turn. Craig and Ken got the area car and I was designated to drive the van, a MK2 Ford Transit. It had been an exceptionally busy build up to the Christmas period and I'd been snowed under with work, so much so that my pocket book was more than a week out of date! I had pieces of paper with scribbled notes on, copies of charge sheets and numerous other bits of reference material to copy it all down from, it was just a question of time to get it done. And I simply hadn't had the time. But today I'd have to find it from somewhere because at 1600 hours I am due to see Chief Superintendent Ron West at Kingston Crescent for my annual appraisal. He was a stickler for going through every page to ensure you had crossed all the T's and dotted all the i's. Whose bloody stupid idea was it to have my appraisal on Christmas Eve anyway? It certainly wasn't mine.

We got turned out from parade to Commercial Road for a massive fight. Every unit in the city went. There were running fights all over the place. My van got filled with half a dozen prisoners that I took to Central and off loaded. I needed to get back to Southsea to get all those bits of paper. Half way back I got diverted to the Tricorn, more fighting. And in ten minutes time the pubs will close and then all hell will break lose. I ended up on the top floor of the Tricorn car park where there were several officers struggling to restrain about 20 drunken youths. As I got out of the van I saw one of them smack a PC in the face. I grabbed him and in the struggle we fell against the wall at the edge of the car park. At one point I was on my back, having been pushed backwards with this toe-rag on top of me with his forearm pressed hard against my throat as he tried to throw me over the wall to the ground three storeys below. He very nearly succeeded to. I eventually managed to get the better of him and wrestled him into the van. Several more prisoners were thrown in and the van was rocking from side to side as I drove back to Central to disgorge my next cargo. I was covered in crap and dust and I was knackered. It seemed like the whole city was fighting with calls for assistance coming from North End, Palmerston Road, Arundel Street, Fratton Road and everywhere else in between. It was now 1545 hours. I was starting to panic and I hadn't even touched my pocket book. I was starting to think up plausible excuses that Mr West might believe. I got called back to Commercial Road to collect another prisoner. I got to Central and there was a queue of prisoners waiting to get in. It was now 1605 hours.

Kilo to 2113

2113 go ahead

Mr West is waiting for you, what's your eta?

Er................about ten minutes, just dropping a prisoner at KC

Panic had now definitely set in. I managed to jump the queue and set off back to Southsea to get an old pocket book that I was going to present to Mr West in error! It sounded like a plausible excuse to me. I arrived at Southsea in a cloud of dust and slammed the van into reverse to back it onto the pad, an area of tarmac adjacent to the side wall, big enough to get three vehicles onto. I stopped the van and leant down to pull up the handbrake. In the rush my foot slipped off the clutch and the van shot backwards and crashed into the station wall. Oh fuck no, not now please. I leapt out of the van praying there was no damage. I didn't pray hard enough. The rear lights were smashed and there was a paint chip the size of a 10p piece next to it. As I looked at the damage so a couple of the Relief came running out having heard the smash.

Kilo to 2113

2113 go ahead

Mr West is still waiting. Do you have an eta?

Can you inform him that I might be delayed for some considerable time please

I kept my fingers crossed that he hadn't got his wife her present yet and was in a hurry to get to the shops before they closed. It worked.

Kilo to 2113

2113 go ahead

Mr West will see you in the New Year

Yes I bet he will, I thought. Craig was Acting Sgt today. He gave me two options. Either report the damage to him officially right now and get grounded from driving for a month, which is what happened to him the last time he bent the van or "ye can fuck off and get it sorted".

See you then. I drove straight to Hendy Ford's in Grove Road South. It was now fast approaching five o'clock. Hopefully they'll still be open I thought as I pulled up onto the forecourt of the all white, art-deco styled building. As I entered the show room I could hear lots of laughter coming from an area out the back. I rang the bell on the counter. Eventually a bloke in his 30s came out from behind a closed door. He looked and smelt pissed. And he was.

"Have you got a rear off-side light lens for a 79 Transit please?" I enquired as if it was just any old day.

"Why, have you smashed it then?" he laughed, as he opened the door to the rear of the office again.

"Ere lads, I've got a copper out here trying to cover up some damage to the meat wagon".

Oh God, how embarrassing is this. With that three more pissed comedians came out to join in. I took it all with a knowing grin. It got even worse when I asked for a can of Diamond White spray paint.

"That totals £27.50 mate"

"How much?" I winced.

"Take it mate, have it on us, you've given us the biggest laugh we've had all year. Merry Christmas to ya"

"And to you" I said as I ran for the door.

"Oi mate, one last thing" I stopped at the door "Make sure you don't use the shiny new screws in the packet, always use the old rusty ones, otherwise everyone will notice".

Sound advice indeed. After meal break myself and a couple of the Relief took the van to a deserted car park where we changed the lens, complete with rusty screws and performed a minor miracle on the paintwork.

CHAPTER 6

1982. We are at war

You rarely get to see your Chief Constable and when you do it's either because he is commending you for some brave deed or because he's about to rip your head off for bringing the force into disrepute. There is seldom any middle ground. John Duke was one of those Chief Constables with a presence. He could enter a room with 200 officers in it and without saying a word the room would fall completely silent. I think it's a mixture of stature and respect for the man himself. Every now and then he was prone to issuing force wide memo's to press home a particular beef of his at that moment in time. On parade this particular morning came news that Mr Duke was, from this day forth, banning the use and carrying of clip boards by officers. If they wished to make notes they were to use their official pocket books. And by the way, any officer not wearing his helmet or flat hat would be reported for being incorrectly dressed. There were plenty of mutterings from those of us gathered around the table. How petty, clip boards are so much more convenient, doesn't he have more important things to worry about, how's he going to know whether or not we use a clip board anyway some of us quipped? We were still griping about it as we came down stairs to get ready to go out on patrol and by mid morning we'd all forgotten about it anyway.

Kilo to Kilo Sierra 51

Kilo Sierra 51 go ahead

Non injury RTA Goldsmith Avenue by the roadwork's

Kilo Sierra 51, 10/4

Goldsmith Avenue was subject to major road works at this time which meant that only half the road was open, with temporary traffic lights in operation. The weather was awful with high winds and lots of rain and it was because of the weather that the accident had occurred. As a car was passing the temporary traffic lights, so a big gust of wind blew the lights over onto the bonnet of the car causing considerable damage. After sorting it out and sending the driver on his way I went over to the workmen's hut to have a further chat with them. They offered me a cup of tea, which I gladly accepted and whilst waiting for it I chatted away with half a dozen workmen who were sat inside the hut. There wasn't room inside for me so I stood outside. In fact I was leaning against the hut, with no hat on, both hands in my pockets and with my trusty clip board tucked under my arm, when a green Jaguar drove slowly passed. I caught sight of the rear seat passenger. It was the Chief Constable. He glared at me and I withered and died on the spot. No hat, hands in pockets and a clip board. At the very least I'll get sent to the Russian front or worse, Shanklin! I expected to receive a call any minute to return to the station to face the Superintendent who had probably just had his head ripped off by Mr Duke and now it was my turn. But it didn't happen. And I never stopped using a clip board either.

Green Relief lost Dave Martin on promotion and his place was taken by Sgt Dick Turpin who had spent his entire career to date out in the sticks at New Milton and other far flung outposts of the county. He was in his late 40s and of quite big build with silver grey hair and a full beard. He wore glasses and was generally speaking somewhat untidy in appearance. This was his first encounter at city policing and he made it known straight away that he was very left wing in his views and wasn't afraid to voice them either. He had already made up his mind that he didn't want to be here and that *we* would have to change the way we did things. This was going to be interesting.

An old idea was resurrected by the powers-that-be to reintroduce the crime car on a temporary basis. It meant that the area car would have an experienced Detective Constable as the observer instead of a uniformed PC because the DC might know the local villains better. We had been suffering from a lot of burglaries and car crime recently and the move made sense and was one of those ideas that actually worked if you had the right combination on board the car.

I had been working with DC Mick Hiscock for a week when we found ourselves driving along the Airport Service Road following a tractor of all things. You don't get many tractors in the city! This particular tractor was towing a large trailer loaded with scrap metal and on the top of the pile was a large metal water tank and the whole lot was tied down with a single length of string. It wouldn't have been so bad but the wheels on the trailer were two completely different sizes which meant that the trailer and the load were leaning over at a rather precarious angle. I thought I'd pull it over just to a have a quiet word in the driver's ear and advise him to either tie the load down more securely or preferably get the wheels changed. Well I couldn't have picked on a bigger arsehole if I'd tried. He started shouting at me straight away that I was wasting his time, he paid our wages, haven't we got anything better to do and why don't we go and fight some crime. Well we will be just as soon as we have finished with you. I have to confess that when challenged in such circumstances most cops will be equally as awkward as their customer, if not more so. I started examining the tyres on the trailer and on the tractor because they were full of splits, some of them big enough to get your thumb nail into. One of the tyres had no tread on it at all. I pointed out the offences to him but still had the intention, even after all the abuse he had given us, to merely offer him some sound advice.

"Are you gonna do me for this then?" he shouted.

"I'm considering it, yes" I replied.

"In that case if you're gonna do me you'd better do yourself, take a look at that" and with that he pointed at the front near side tyre on the area car, which was pointing slightly inwards towards the kerb.

It was completely bald, as smooth as a baby's bum. I did a double take on it because I couldn't believe what I was looking at. He stood there with his arms folded, looking all smug. He was the type of bloke who if I'd said, look mate, you go your way and I'll go mine and we'll say no more about it, he would have gone straight to the nearest

Police station to complain. I had no choice but to call for a Traffic Sgt and let him deal with both of us. I was in serious trouble. I hadn't checked the car before I started duty and I could hardly bullshit my way out of this one! A few minutes later a Traffic BMW arrived and a Sgt got out to be greeted by my tale of woe. He examined the Volvo tyre and shook his head in disbelief. Then he looked at the front offside tyre and found that was in the same state. And when he checked the tyre pressures he found one of the rears was 14 pounds under pressure. Could it get any worse? He cautioned me and then stuck me on for all three offences. He followed that up by reporting the tractor driver for a number of similar offences before he called the Police workshops recovery truck to the scene to collect the area car and transport it to workshops for further examination and repair. It was the lowest point of my career to date and even if I served another hundred years I'd never live it down. But worse was to follow, because all eight area car drivers at Southsea also got reported as did the Chief Constable for permitting the car to be used in that state. I hope he doesn't remember my name I thought. A file would now be prepared and sent to the Director of Public Prosecutions (DPP) for their consideration. I would have to sweat on the result for several weeks yet, but in the meantime and forever after, I checked every inch of every patrol car I ever drove!

It was one of those Friday nights, tense and electric. We'd had numerous skirmishes at pubs throughout the city and after closing time so they came down to the seafront in their hundreds. Taxis would arrive in convoys to off load their fares whilst others walked in large groups along Clarendon Road and Clarence Parade towards Nero's, Joanna's and the two bars on the pier. Big queues would form outside all of them and trouble would flare up when some were refused entry or others were ejected for being drunk or for fighting inside. Two or three foot patrol officers would keep watch over proceedings whilst those of us who were on mobile patrol would always return to the seafront in between other calls, like birds returning to the nest. It was partly our comfort zone but more to do with a show of numbers and to enable an immediate response should things really get out of hand. We were always joined by one or two Naval Provost vans, whose main responsibility was to police the huge numbers of sailors that would come ashore at the weekends. They carried Police radios so that we could contact them direct if we needed them to come and collect an errant sailor rather than us detain them for merely being drunk and incapable or for some other minor offence. Most Naval Provost personnel were built like brick shit houses and were always a very welcome sight when things went wrong. Their vans were usually doubled up for Police use when we ran out.

Just after one o'clock Craig and I came in for our meal break, together with a couple of others, leaving the seafront to the foot patrol officers. Only half an hour later came a frantic call for assistance. The canteen emptied and we headed back to the seafront and as we made our way there so there were further calls for help. As we turned onto the front it seemed like there were separate fights going on all over the place. The main focus seemed to be the Gaiety Show Bar on the pier, which is where it had all started and where our colleagues were. It was like something from a Wild West saloon, with tables and chairs flying through the air, glass smashing all around us, women screaming and the sickening thud of fist against face. I think all of us called for further assistance over the next hour or so, as the fighting spilled out onto the promenade and even the beach. We ran out of vans and desperately needed more having used all three city units plus the two Naval Provost vans. We eventually got vans and further reinforcements from as far away as Aldershot and the New Forest. The seafront was jammed solid with Police vehicles and eventually we managed to restore some order. Many of those arrested were Naval personnel, which made a change from dealing with our usual crowd of trouble makers.

Early turn is the favourite time to get calls to a sudden death as relatives or neighbours discover that someone close to them has passed away.

Kilo to Kilo Sierra 51

Kilo Sierra 51 go ahead

157 Francis Avenue please, possible sudden death

Kilo Sierra 51, 10/4

I was single crewed this morning because Craig was busy doing some paperwork. I arrived at the house to be greeted by an elderly lady whose sister wasn't answering from behind her locked bedroom door. The two spinsters had lived in the same house for years, one on the ground floor and the other upstairs. I knocked gently on the door but got no reply. I tried several times but got no response. The sister gave me permission to put the door in. There wasn't a great deal of room to get any sort of run up to shoulder barge it so I decided to give it a good kick. It popped first time and swung violently to the right. There was a sickening thud, followed by a sort of groaning noise. I went in and found the elderly sister had suffered an apparent stroke during the night and her head was partly slumped out of the bed towards the door. When I kicked the door it scored a direct hit on her forehead causing a nasty gash. I felt terrible.

I had to pick Tricia up from St. Mary's Hospital where she worked and was horrified to hear the news on the car radio. I was still listening to the details when she got into the car.

"What's up?" she asked

"Apparently we're at war with Argentina" I replied.

A few days later I stood on Southsea seafront with thousands of others as the Naval Task force, headed by the aircraft carriers HMS Invincible and HMS Hermes left Portsmouth to head towards the South Atlantic. There was no cheering; we all stood there in virtual silence. The mood in the city was sombre but business like as we saw convoys of army trucks entering the dockyard and helicopters buzzing about above us. The Police were tasked with escorting various convoys through the city and into the dock yard or to escort at high speed some high ranking Naval officer or politician in the rear of a darkened limo. Most people had never heard of the Falkland Islands let alone knew where they were and in truth most of us believed that a last minute diplomatic solution would be found. Nevertheless Portsmouth became the epicentre of the war machine that was gaining momentum with every passing day. My brother was an aircraft technician in the RAF and was sent out to Ascension Island so I now had a personal interest in events.

Meanwhile it was business as usual. It was a warm and reasonably sunny spring afternoon.

Kilo to Kilo Sierra 51

Kilo Sierra 51 go ahead

Make South Parade pier, serious assault

Kilo Sierra 51, 10/4

I was driving and had Dave Brown as my observer. We arrived at the pier to discover a young man laying on the ground. He had a very nasty head wound and was bleeding heavily. He said he had got into an argument with an old adversary by the name of Gary Northolt and that Northolt had hit him whilst wearing a solid brass knuckle duster and had made good his escape on a heavily modified racing scooter. While we were talking to a couple of witnesses we saw a noisy scooter ride past. The witnesses pointed it out as being the one but it was too late, all we could do was note the registration number as it rode away. A few minutes later it came back towards us along Alhambra Road and it rode straight over the pavement towards the pier. Dave ran out into the road to stop it but the scooter roared off and out of sight again. We got into the Volvo and started looking for it. Half an hour went by before Mick Smith piped up on the radio that it had just passed him on Eastney Road towards Milton and so I headed towards the area. A few minutes later as we were driving north along Winter Road we saw the scooter come across Goldsmith Avenue towards us, overtaking a line of cars as it did so. There was smoke pouring out the exhaust which was incredibly loud. The scooter passed us going the other way and I turned the Volvo around as quickly as I could. The scooter accelerated away flat out overtaking another line of cars as it did so and then disappeared out of sight. As I passed Evans Road on my left I could see that the bike had turned off left. I had no choice but to go down to the next junction and turn left to try and head it off. I made good progress and took the next two left turns and there it was coming straight towards us in a narrow side street. He hit the brakes hard and slid sideways to a halt, almost falling off. He did a U turn and accelerated away from us, colliding with the front off side of a Citroen. There was barely enough room for it to squeeze through but it managed to do so. With that the door of the Citroen flew open and a Royal Marine in full combat gear leapt out of the drivers seat and grabbed Northolt's jacket in an effort to stop him from fleeing. The scooter accelerated away hard. The front wheel came off the ground about 18 inches as he dragged the Royal Marine along the road for about 50 yards before he had to let go. As I drove past his car so the insecure drivers door swung open and scraped all down the side of the area car. The scooter turned left back into Winter Road and as I arrived at the junction it had gone. However there were dozens of shoppers around and all of them were frantically pointing down Heyshott Road but as I drove down there it had disappeared.

I went back to the Royal Marine to ensure he was all right. He was more angry that the polish had been scraped off the toe caps of his bulled boots! He had just left his parents house after saying his goodbyes because he was quite literally on his way to Southampton to board the QE2 en route to the Falkland Islands. I took his details, thanked him for his efforts and wished him luck on his journey. The irony wasn't lost on me. There was a young soldier about to go into battle to rescue fellow countrymen and here we were chasing a scumbag like Northolt. An hour or so later we got directed back to the seafront because Northolt had phoned the control room and wanted to give himself up.

Danny Daniels called me into his office. He had the result from the DPP. No further action, not in the public interest. You could have knocked me down with a feather because I was convinced I'd be looking at a court date. Mr Daniels looked at me over his reading glasses and said "Lesson learned?"

"Absolutely" I replied, breathing a huge sigh of relief.

I was now senior enough in service with almost four years in to be taking proby's out on their area car attachments and teach them how to do the job! How scary is that? We had a new boy on the relief, PC 1205 Chris Robinson, a very shy, polite lad and he was currently doing his two week area car attachment with me. We were on late turn, it was dark and it was raining quite heavily.

Kilo to Kilo Sierra 51

Kilo Sierra 51 go ahead

Injury RTA, Milton Road junction with Locksway Road, ambulance en route

Kilo Sierra 51, 10/4

On went the blue light and two-tone horns as we headed north along Victoria Road North. Around the roundabout at Bradford Junction and along the link road towards Fratton Bridge, which was basically a big one-way system with a Nat-West Bank and the London and Edinburgh Building Society building stuck right in the middle of it. We entered the one-way system, drove past the exit to Fratton Road and BANG we stopped dead. Chris and I were thrown violently forward before falling back into our seats. I looked forward again and saw that our bonnet was folded in half and there was steam or smoke coming out from underneath. I looked closer and saw that we had collided head on with another car. The two-tones were still blaring and I slowly reached forward to press the purple rocker switch to off to cut out the noise. We were in a daze but our natural instincts were to get out fast. Neither of us was injured and we just opened the doors of the Volvo and stepped out. I looked at the Chrysler Alpine that had collided with us. It was in a bad way and the female driver was crying out. I couldn't open the driver's door because of the damage but eventually managed to prise the passenger door open. Her feet were trapped underneath the pedals and were quite badly cut. I called up the control room to tell them what had happened requesting an ambulance and the fire service to our location plus another unit get dispatched to the original RTA. The poor woman couldn't understand what had happened and neither could I to start with until she told me that she had come down Goldsmith Avenue and had then turned right onto the one-way system, against the flow of traffic! The fire service arrived and it took them half an hour to cut her free, although she wasn't too badly injured considering. I stood there looking at both cars and thanked my lucky stars that we had been in the Volvo. Although the frontal damage was extensive at least the passenger cell had remained intact.

The TV news was essential viewing as things in the South Atlantic seemed to be hotting up. We were all surprised a couple of days previously when we learned that one of our submarines had sunk an Argentine cruiser called the Belgrano. All of a sudden this conflict as the media called it seemed real.

I was back on nights and was at home getting ready to come into work. It was about 9.20 pm as I gathered all my bits and pieces together. There was a news flash. An MOD spokesman by the name of Ian McDonald, a sort of grey man who spoke like a subdued Dalek delivered a bomb shell to the nation. There had been an attack on HMS Sheffield.

He said: "In the course of its duties within the Total Exclusion Zone around the Falkland Islands, HMS Sheffield, a type 42 destroyer, was attacked and hit late this afternoon by an Argentine missile. The ship caught fire, which spread out of control. When there was no longer any hope of saving the ship, the ship's company abandoned ship. All who abandoned her were picked up."

Tricia and I sat there in a stunned silence for a couple of minutes. HMS Sheffield was a Portsmouth based ship. I left for work a few minutes later and of course as Green Relief met in the canteen for our pre-shift cuppa the only talk was of HMS Sheffield. At 9.45 we walked down the corridor to the parade room. Only five minutes into parade the phone rang. It was the control room turning out the area car to the Ferry Road Naval estate at Eastney because there were TV camera crews knocking on the Naval houses asking the wives if their husbands were on the Sheffield! As Craig and I made our way to the estate we were still asking ourselves how it was that the media had got there so quickly and what on earth possesses them to ask such questions?

Kilo to Kilo Sierra 51

Kilo Sierra 51 go ahead

We've had another call, this time from the BBC, apparently one of their camera's has been damaged.

Kilo Sierra 51, 10/4 we'll be there shortly.

As we arrived there was pandemonium in the street. There were women hugging each other and crying, some of them were screaming and sobbing and you could hear others in nearby streets doing the same. Small kids in their pyjamas stood in doorways to several of the houses. At the entrance to one house was a group of a dozen women who had surrounded two men, one of whom I could see was holding a large TV camera. The women were all shouting at them and the atmosphere was extremely tense. It transpired that at this house the ladies husband was indeed on board HMS Sheffield and at this time nobody knew who was dead or alive. Understandably she had become extremely upset at the media intrusion, so much so that she had grabbed the camera and smashed it on the ground. We took the camera crew to one side to speak to them. Craig and I were almost speechless when they insisted we arrest the woman for causing criminal damage to their property. They really couldn't see that they had done anything wrong and they were still insisting we nick the lady. I could see Craig bubbling up beneath the surface.

"Er..........gents, that's nae gonna happen, but allow me to tell yea both what is. You've got thirty seconds to pack your stuff in your car and get the fuck out of this city, before I call the Naval Provost down here and I'll let them deal with yea. Understood?"

Craig had a way with words and to huge cheers from the Naval wives the two BBC men heeded his advice and headed out of town. We sat in the patrol car for a few minutes watching these poor women drifting from house to house, hugging each other and trying to give each other support. We wondered how many of them were about to have their lives turned upside down by unfolding events several thousand miles from here.

During that same week of nights we heard that Ado Watts, who I had been on White Relief with, had been seriously injured whilst attending a burglary. He had recently transferred to Havant and had been dispatched to a break-in on Hayling Island. As he walked around the rear of the premises in the dark he took a crow bar in the chest which broke two of his ribs and punctured one of his lungs. He was in serious but stable condition in hospital. Of course the next evening as we congregated in the canteen before parade it was the only topic of conversation. We were agreed that Ado always seemed to be the target for being assaulted and yet was one of the nicest people you could ever wish to meet, it didn't seem fair somehow. As we all nodded in agreement up piped our new Sgt who had already raised some concerns amongst us by declaring that he sympathised with the cause of the IRA and the PLO, was an active member of the Labour party and heralded Arthur Scargill as the saviour of the British worker.

"Of course the only policemen who get injured on duty are those that ask for it" he declared.

"What?" we all replied as one as we spluttered out mouth fulls of tea.

"It's obvious isn't it" he continued "some coppers just go looking for trouble and get what they deserve".

We all looked at each other in disbelief. I looked at Craig. His eyes were bulging and his face was bright red. He looked like Mount Etna.

"Yea listen to me" he exploded "I spent almost a year in Glasgow Infirmary with a smashed pelvis and two broken legs. I really don't think I deserved the injuries I got just for doing my job, Jesus Christ, what kind of a cop are yea coming out with crap like that" and with that Craig turned and stormed off.

"It's just my opinion" Dick Turpin said as he shrugged his shoulders, seemingly as surprised by Craig's outburst as we were about his.

The Falklands conflict was now in full swing and we were taking casualties every day both at sea and now on land. The troop supply ship RMS Sir Galahad was bombed and there were extensive casualties. The control room took a call from a lady up north whose son in law was on board. She had been trying to get through to her daughter for several hours but her phone was constantly engaged and she needed to talk to her, so she wondered whether the police might pop around to her daughter's house and ask her to phone her mum. Inspector Daniels tasked me with the job. I refused stating that the lady was likely to freak as soon as she saw a police officer at the door. Surely her mum could be a little more patient I asked? Mr Daniels more or less ordered me to go and do it immediately. Still muttering under my breath I drove to the house and reluctantly tapped on the door. It was opened by a little girl of about 6 years of age. I could see her mum through an opaque glass partition and could hear her talking.

"Can I speak to your mummy please?" I said.

With that the little girl turned and ran indoors saying "mummy, mummy there's a policeman at the door"

I heard the phone being launched across the room as the woman let out an horrific scream "nooooo"

"It's not what you think, it's not what you think" I shouted "phone your mother, phone your mother".

She collapsed onto her knees at the door, as the little girl burst into tears.

"I'm just here to tell you to phone your mother, she's been trying to get through to you for ages" I blurted out.

"I thought................I thought........." she whimpered

"Yes I know what you thought but that's not the case, really it isn't, please just phone your mother" I pleaded.

They didn't cover that one at Ashford.

As more and more casualties were reported there was a definite change within the city. For years the local yobs in and around the Queen Street area of Portsea had taken part in a traditional sport known as 'skate bashing'. Groups of youths would ambush an unsuspecting, lone sailor en route back to the dockyard and beat the crap out of him. This appeared to be a perfectly acceptable local custom, a right of passage for many an up and coming hooligan to partake in. However, Portsmouth seemed to be bearing the brunt of the casualties in the South Atlantic and the locals were proud to be as involved as they were and suddenly became very protective of those same young men who only a few weeks before had been considered as fair game.

If I had a pound for every hour I had wasted at court so far then I could have taken a very nice holiday with it. The whole court system, whether it be magistrates or crown court is geared towards those who work in such establishments and the system employed there couldn't give two hoots about inconveniencing members of the public, especially prosecution witnesses and victims and in particular police officers. If you are a defendant the system will bend over backwards to accommodate your every whim, it will believe the most unbelievable excuses as to why you can't attend and will only pay lip service towards keeping any real discipline in court if intimidated by enough of the defendants mates sat in the public gallery. If you are a witness or even the victim then it really doesn't matter that you had to take time off work for the fifth time in this case and it doesn't matter that you had a 250 mile round trip to be here to give evidence only to have it adjourned yet again because poor little Johnny had a headache this morning and couldn't possibly attend. If that isn't bad enough, it's the attitude from the court itself that causes the most upset in that no explanation is given, certainly no apology and you are forced to accept that "that's just the way things are I'm afraid".

But try being a police officer and attending court. I am firmly of the opinion that as far as the courts are concerned the police officer is right at the bottom of the food chain. His rights, his concerns, his feelings, his rest days, his annual leave, his sickness, the fact that he only finished a night shift at 6am this morning actually count for nothing. I've known officers threatened with jail time if they don't cancel or return from a foreign holiday immediately merely to give evidence in a traffic related matter. I've known officers physically lifted from their sick beds and transported to court to answer questions. I've known officers having had their rest day cancelled in order to attend court and on arrival are glibly told we don't actually need you. I've known officers turn up on rest days or in the middle of annual leave to be told that the defendant has changed his plea to guilty and "oh didn't anyone tell you?" and on one memorable occasion I actually got locked inside the witness waiting room at Juvenile Court because they all went home, having forgotten all about me!

But perhaps the most annoyed I ever got was at Portsmouth Crown Court. Despite my protestations I ended up having to attend court on all three of my rest days, meaning that by linking them to two full shifts I would end up working 17 days on the trot. To cap it all it wasn't even my job and was a joint CID and Southern Electricity Board investigation into the mass abstraction of electricity by one man at his three houses and several business premises. I spent two and a half days pacing up and down the carpeted hallways bored to tears, watching the traffic from the third floor window and doing my best to people watch on the tiny figures below. Just after lunch on the third day, finally, I got called into court. I bowed to the judge, climbed into the witness box, took the oath and gave the court my full details. The QC then got to his feet and rather laboriously commenced his questions.

QC "Officer, on the 28th October last year did you attend 47 Albert Road, Southsea and there did you liaise with two SEB officials?"

2113 "Yes your Honour I did"

QC "And did they hand to you this electricity meter?" which he picked up from the table beside him.

2113 "They did"

QC "And what did you do with it?"

2113 "I immediately returned it to Southsea Police Station where I booked it into the Crime Property Store"

QC "Thank you officer. I have no further questions your Honour"

The judge then looked at the Defending Council and asked if he wished to cross examine the witness. The bloke barely moved as he uttered "No your Honour".

The judge then turned towards me and said "Thank you officer, you are released".

Released? Released! I've spent three bloody days stuck outside and just given less than two minutes worth of meaningless evidence and you say I'm released as if I should be truly grateful. And they wonder why there are no policeman out on the streets!

Every police area in every town, city and neighbourhood has its regulars, whether that be certain drunks, specific problem areas, regular domestic disputes or constant problems at one business premises. Whilst some of these can be a real pain in the arse, especially the domestic disturbance cases, others often yield a more positive response because you are almost guaranteed a prisoner. In Southsea's case it was the Prom Café on the seafront. This secluded, out of the way little cafeteria was located on the promenade next to the Rock Gardens. It had been broken into so often that a silent Home Office alarm had been placed inside and we would get dispatched there at least once a month and nine times out of ten we would find the burglars still on the premises. These alarms consisted of a pressure mat placed under a rug or door mat or sometimes an infra red beam laid across a doorway might be used. The alarm would be triggered and would send a signal to the control room. A silent approach from the police was always used and it nearly always paid off.

Kilo to Kilo Sierra 51
Kilo Sierra 51 go ahead

Make the Prom Café, intruders on premises, Kilo Delta 53 is en route to assist

Kilo Sierra 51, 10/4

It was just after midnight as we made our way along the seafront towards the café. The Kilo Delta unit was a dog unit and from the voice on the other end of the radio it was PC Rowdy Yates and his dog Ajax. I'm not quite sure who was the fiercer of the two of them, but they were always a very welcome sight. Rowdy was a loud, hard faced man with a deep Lancashire accent. His hat had a slashed peek and the football yobs were terrified of him. Ajax was the biggest, hairiest German Shepherd dog I've ever seen and the football yobs were even more terrified of him! As Craig and I arrived from one direction, so Roger Hogben arrived in a panda from the other. We quietly shut the car doors and crept towards predetermined points around the perimeter whilst we awaited the key holder. I went straight to the north west corner by the toilet window because it was a favourite entry point and sure enough I found that the louvre windows had been removed. I heard the dog van arrive and could hear Ajax barking in the back together with Rowdy's muffled barks of "shut up" which are the two words a police dog handler uses the most!

As I stood there beneath the window I could hear a rustling noise coming from the bushes behind me. It grew louder and then to my horror out from the undergrowth came Ajax, on his own without Rowdy. He stopped and stared at me. His top lip curled up to reveal his shiny whites and then he started to growl. Oh shit. Now several years ago, as a spotty young cadet, myself and several others had been 'specially selected' to take part in the Regional Police Dog Trials to be used as dog fodder. Being cadets meant that we were expendable and that should any of Britain's finest Police dogs actually eat any of us, well that was fine, just so long as the dog didn't choke. The one thing I learned from that experience was that you stand absolutely still and as I stood there all statuesque like, so Rowdy appeared swinging his lead.

"Ya fuckin stupid mutt, can't you tell the difference yet" Rowdy growled as he slipped the choke chain over Ajax's head.

"Evening Steve, where's the point of entry?"

I showed him and Ajax suddenly got very excited. Rowdy was convinced that somebody was still in there; however the window was too high and too small to get a dog through so we would have to wait until the key holder got here. A couple of minutes later he arrived and opened the front door. Ajax could hardly contain himself and in he went. Within seconds he was barking out loud and in between times you could hear an anguished scream, followed by Rowdy shouting at the intruder to lay on the floor. With that we all piled in and there on the floor was one of our regular oikes, Peter Croucher. He was a burglar and shop lifter and not a very good one at that. He did it all to fund his glue sniffing habit, which really was quite revolting to watch. He would take a plastic bag and fill it with any solvent he could get his hands on, whether that be Copydex or the stronger carpet laying and industrial strength glues and then place the bag over his nose and mouth and inhale. He would keep it there for ages until his eyes and nose were streaming with water and snot. The toxic fumes caused large sores to form on his face and some of them had burst open. Somehow he got pleasure from it but like all addictions of course every fix needed to be better, stronger and more often. But there was something missing tonight or rather someone missing, because wherever Peter was his twin brother Andrew would be right beside him. Both of them were hardened glue sniffers and they did everything together, including all of their crime. We searched the building twice but couldn't find him. He has to be here somewhere. Rowdy dispatched Ajax again and he paid particular attention to the kitchen area but we had searched everywhere, even the cupboards. And then Rowdy opened the oven. There he was, on his knees with his head tucked in between them, looking just like a roast chicken. Quite how he got in there is beyond me and he very nearly got away with it and from then on every time we got called back there it was the first place we checked!

It had been a quiet night so far thanks to the rather damp weather and Dave Brown and I were just slowly cruising around looking for something or someone as we chatted away. The streets were almost empty and yet it was only half midnight.

Kilo to Kilo Sierra 51

Kilo Sierra 51 go ahead

Make Goldsmith Avenue junction with Priory Crescent asap, Traffic have a fail to stop Triumph motorcycle from the Havant area, believed doing a drugs run to Southsea. Can you assist them by blocking off Priory Crescent please

Kilo Sierra 51, 10/4

Block off Priory Crescent? But that's about four cars wide that road, how are we supposed to do that we asked each other as I raced towards the location. As we neared the junction so we heard a brief item of pursuit commentary coming over the radio. It was very brief but I'm sure they said they had just turned into Priory Crescent. Sure enough just as I was about to turn left into the junction so I saw a Triumph Trident bike at 70 mph plus, with a rider and passenger on board travel straight over the crossroads and into Winter Road without even slowing down. It was a Jeeessuus Chriiiist moment! The bike was immediately followed by a Traffic Division Volvo 240 GLT being driven by PC Keith Annals. The GLT Volvo's were a treasured toy on Traffic because Hampshire had the first ones in the country and they loved them.

I turned right and raced off after them. We travelled down Winter Road at 80 mph and I could just see Keith ahead of us as the bike went straight across the Devonshire Avenue crossroads at a similar speed. I saw the brake lights come on on the Volvo, followed by a huge spray of sparks as the rear nearside of the car seemed to slide sideways slightly towards the kerb. Keith flew across the junction as I started to brake hard; I didn't fancy doing the same. The car slid sideways ninety degrees and I skidded across the crossroads fighting to regain control on the damp road surface. We slid to a halt in the middle of the junction. Sod this; I'm way out of my league on this one I thought. We continued to monitor the commentary and were amused to hear that the passenger had leapt off the bike at 60 mph and now needed an ambulance. The pursuit ended in Telephone Road close to a shop that specialised in the sale of old British motorcycles. The rider had run off leaving the Triumph laying on its side in the middle of the road. The seat had come off and taped to the under side of it were four large cannabis soap bars, which were the first large quantities of drugs I had ever seen. Despite the interest in the drugs and the pursuit in general, most of our attention was focused on Keith's shiny Volvo and the rear nearside wheel. That shower of sparks I had seen was Keith colliding with the kerb and the reason we were all looking at the wheel was because prior to hitting the kerb the Volvo had five spokes on its alloy wheel and now it only had one! Keith was quite impressed because even after losing 4/5ths of his wheel, he was travelling at over 100 mph at times with no adverse effects.

Just like actors who traditionally steer clear of working with children and animals so Police officers are just as wary when dealing with certain types and in my case its shoplifters or kids, doubly so when they are juvenile shoplifters. My observer was PC 1435 Steve Moore and we spent most of our days laughing at just about everything we dealt with. He had an infectious laugh and a permanent smile on his face and we were great mates.

Kilo to Kilo Sierra 51

Kilo Sierra 51 go ahead

Can you attend 'The Shop' at Fort Cumberland Road, Eastney report of two juvenile shop lifters

Kilo Sierra 51, 10/4

Marvellous, my favourite, I thought as I slowly drove half way across the patch towards our latest deployment praying we'd get diverted before we got there to something slightly more serious. But today wasn't our lucky day because before I knew it we were pulling up outside. 'The Shop' was the only store on the Naval estate and provided a lot of goods. We entered and found the manager and she led us into a back room where she told us that these two juveniles had attempted to steal a large bottle of lemonade and were currently being kept in another room by a member of staff.

We entered the room and both Steve and I were rendered completely speechless, which was a first for Steve. Why? Because our arch criminals were aged five and three. They sat there all angelic and innocent looking, swinging their legs from the chairs because their feet didn't reach the floor. It transpired that young Margaret and Tommy Dollar were from the Gypsy camp about quarter of a mile away and were obviously below the age of criminal consent although it was quite obvious they knew they had done wrong. We put them in the patrol car still shaking our heads in disbelief and drove to the Glory Hole. After dodging several dogs we found their caravan and we were immediately surrounded by several travellers and lots more kids. We located Mr Dollar, a huge man wearing a grubby white vest and three days stubble. We took his off spring inside the caravan as dozens of the other kids kept throwing questions at us and our two lemonade thieves. Mr Dollar was clearly not pleased with his children but we got the distinct impression that it wasn't because they had been trying to steal but more because they had got caught!

On July 21st HMS Hermes was due to return to Portsmouth following the end of hostilities in the South Atlantic. Portsmouth was expecting thousands to turn up and cheer the aircraft carrier home and an operation was put in place to help police it, which in part meant closing the High Street and Broad Street to vehicular traffic. Although Craig and I had nothing to do with the operation we fully intended to see Hermes come in if we could. I think the city council and other authorities miscalculated the number of people who might turn up because by mid morning the seafront area was packed and it wasn't due in until 1pm. By 1230 Craig and I were starting to panic because there was just nowhere to stop and look, so we decided to try the High Street. We drove through the barriers and were amazed to see that the road was completely blocked by pedestrians all rushing towards the harbour entrance. There was nothing else for it but to abandon the area car and walk. We were now caught up in the fervour and excitement as people with union flags, wearing red, white and blue, some with painted faces, others with multi coloured hair all surged forward towards any vantage point they could find. The atmosphere was electric and it seemed like the whole country had descended upon Portsmouth.

Craig and I got to within 50 yards of the harbour entrance when we were approached by a man who had his hands on a young boys shoulder. The eight year old lad was crying because he had become separated from his parents and despite the efforts of this stranger they couldn't find them. Oh bloody great. Craig and I gave each other knowing looks. We ascertained that young Peter was from London but he couldn't remember where they had parked, what his parents were wearing, in fact nothing useful at all. It was getting close to 1pm. There was nothing else for it but to push our way through the heaving crowds in an effort to find this boys parents. We were just passing the door to the Still and West pub which is located right at the end of Broad Street and directly over looks the entrance to the harbour. The pub was full to capacity; in fact I doubt you could have squeezed another human being into the building. I could tell Craig was getting more and more annoyed, he hated things like this. Stood in the doorway was a man in his 50s who asked if the boy was lost. He leant forward and asked him if he had come to see the ships come in to which young Peter, still crying said yes he had.

"In that case" said the man "you'd better follow me" and with that he turned and beckoned us into a hallway and up some stairs, which led to a flat roof on top of the pub.

He was the landlord of the Still and West and the roof overlooked the harbour entrance, in fact it was the best seat in the house, you really couldn't get any closer. His family and close friends were there and they had a trestle table decked out with tons of food and within seconds young Peter had a glass of coke and Craig and I were being offered all sorts of alcoholic refreshment. I settled for a glass of coke as I was driving whilst it didn't take too much arm twisting to see Craig with a scotch in his hand and a big grin on his face. Plates of food were generously thrust our way as we heard the crowds below and to our left becoming ever more excited. And there she was, the rusting relic that was HMS Hermes complete with a Sea Harrier sat on top of her ski ramp deck and escorted by tugs spraying huge arcs of water, majestically entering Portsmouth harbour. The crowds cheered and waved their flags, the band of HM Royal Marines played *A Life on the Ocean Wave* as young sailors lined the decks of the carrier to wave back towards us. Helicopters circled above us and there were hundreds of small boats and pleasure craft jostling for position along side her. I couldn't help it but tears welled up in my eyes. I felt a bit embarrassed but then I caught sight of Craig and the tears were streaming down his face. It was quite simply one of those 'proud to be British' moments, a once in a lifetime experience, unrehearsed, genuine affection and gratitude from the people towards those brave young men who had suffered such terrible loses so far from home.

After filling our faces it was time to find Peters parents, although Craig suggested it might be easier if we stay up here and allow the crowds to disperse a bit first. Nice thinking Craig, I'll have another plate of food then. To be fair he was right because within half and hour after leaving we had located mum and dad almost half a mile away by the funfair. It transpired Peter had the better of it because his parents never got to see a thing. And he didn't need any lunch either!

It was one of those balmy summer mornings where the air is almost completely still, the sky a radiant blue with a few wisps of thin white cloud interspersed with the ice trails from passing passenger jets. I'd already spent an interesting few minutes talking to an elderly couple outside the nick whose job it was to clean out and then paint the red phone boxes. They were a retired couple and they did a brilliant job and by the time they had finished each one it not only looked shiny and bright but smelt better too, because the lady scrubbed the floors with disinfectant to rid the box of the smell of urine! Surely nothing could spoil such a lovely morning?

Kilo to Kilo Sierra 51

Kilo Sierra 51 go ahead

You're gonna like this one, apparently we have an out of control hot air balloon heading towards Eastney from the city centre. It's already caused some damage to roof tops along the way, if you spot it can you let us know please

Kilo Sierra 51, 10/4

A hot air balloon in Pompey? No sooner had I stopped smirking than another unit piped up to say he'd just seen it flying very low over the houses in Devonshire Avenue and it was heading south east. I was in Highland Road at the time and so I should see it any second. And sure enough there it was literally bouncing off a house roof and bringing roof slates crashing to the ground. It flew over Henderson Road roundabout and hit another house, this time demolishing the chimney. I turned right into St. Georges Road and watched in horror as it descended straight into the Royal Marines Barracks. What if this was an IRA assault? It's just the sort of publicity seeking stunt they would pull. Although the Royal Marines Barracks was no longer in full military use there were still a fair number of troops based there, certainly enough to warrant a strike by terrorists. I informed Kilo and raced towards the main gate. The two civilian gate guards were completely oblivious and their faces were a picture of abject horror when I told them what had floated down behind them only seconds earlier. I demanded they raise the barrier so that I could drive in and locate the balloon whilst they sounded the alarm. I turned right through an archway and towards the seafront side of the barracks and spotted the balloon straight away. Sure enough it was on the ground and the basket was laying on its side. As I pulled up beside it I could see a man trying to pull down the lines whilst at the same time assist a lady from the basket. They clearly weren't IRA terrorists.

"I say, that was jolly exciting" he said with what must have been the largest plum in mouth accent I have ever heard in my life.

"I don't think the people whose houses you have damaged will see it quite the way you do" I said somewhat sarcastically.

It was only then that I noticed what he had landed on. Of all the open spaces he could have picked both inside or outside the barracks he chose to put his balloon down on the Royal Marines prized bowling green, gouging a furrow some two feet wide across its entire length.

This really was jolly exciting now because through the archway came the RSM, complete with slashed peak and tip stave slung beneath his arm. He looked for all the world just like Windsor Davies from *'It Ain't Half Hot Mum'* and as our intrepid pilot was about to find out, he sounded like him to.

"Oi, just what the fuck do you think you're doing laddy" he bellowed. Before laddy had a chance to answer, the RSM saw the damage to the bowling green, which I think he took very personally.

"What's this? What........what.......what have you done to our bowling green you fucking imbecile?"

"I'm terribly sorry old bean" said our pilot in his Sunday best accent.

"Don't you old bean me you fucking idiot, who's going to pay for this lot then and just what do you think you are doing landing inside a military establishment anyway" he continued, still obviously trying to comprehend the enormity of it all.

"I do have some jolly old insurance you know, I'm not completely stupid" said Biggles.

"You're doing a pretty good impression of somebody who is" retorted the RSM.

I felt that things were getting a little bit emotional so took the RSM to one side whilst I took the balloonists full details to pass to all those who might need to make a claim against his jolly old insurance company.

Public disorder on our streets was now a weekly, almost daily occurrence it seemed. I don't just mean one on one assaults but the mass violence that we normally associate with football hooliganism was now being waged every weekend in pubs and clubs throughout the city. It became the norm for a large group of lads to go out openly looking for confrontation with another large group for the most ridiculous of reasons like "are you looking at my bird" or "what you looking at" which was usually followed by "do you want some then, ay?" And then both groups would do their utmost to inflict as much damage on each other as possible. Sometimes when investigating such incidents it wasn't possible to determine who started it or why, because none of those involved actually knew why. This wasn't just a Portsmouth problem, although I did hear once that some of Pompey's youth would fight the nearest lamp post if there was no-one else to scrap with! This was now a national issue that was so common place it barely got a mention on page seven of your local paper. But occasionally it was so big it made the front page.

We were on nights, it was a Friday and the atmosphere was thick with anticipation. As the hoards of revellers came down onto the seafront it just seemed like there were a lot more down here than usual. The queues for the clubs seemed endless and at midnight they were still trying to get in. Although the age of disco music was dead there was another fashion coming in, the New Romantics, with big hair, loads of make-up for the girls as well as the boys and some outrageous, almost theatrical clothing. The bouncers at Nero's in particular seemed to be having a busy night, ejecting more than the usual number of customers who were ready and willing to have a right go back but were ushered away from the premises by the foot patrol officers. In turn they were becoming increasingly concerned by everybody's attitude this evening, it seemed like everyone wanted to have a go. They asked for the mobile units to stay around if possible or to return as soon as their last deployment had been dealt with.

Just after 1am Craig and I were sat in the area car on the other side of the road together with the van and a couple of pandas. Something was going on just inside the door to Nero's, we could see the bouncers struggling with a man who they were trying to eject. Two of the foot patrol officers were already standing by the door and within seconds of being ejected the man was in handcuffs on the ground. But it was clear looking through the windows that further trouble was brewing. The gold statue of the Emperor Nero almost took a tumble as the bouncers and customers fought it out in the entrance foyer. We all ran across the road and were told by one of the staff that they desperately needed our help because there were loads of them fighting upstairs. We called for further back-up from other city units as seven of us went in and climbed the wide red carpeted stairs to the night club itself. As we turned left at the top and stood at the entrance way it seemed like everyone in there was either throwing punches, being punched, running away, screaming, crying, or had blood coming from a wound and was being treated by a tearful friend. I was amazed by the huge number of people in there. I'd been to Nero's loads of times socially and had never seen it so busy; they must have been way over their limit. There were glasses flying through the air and the sound of breaking glass could be heard above the music, which was still blaring out. To my amusement there were half a dozen girls still dancing to *'Eye of the Tiger'* as if nothing were happening! There was just so much going on that it was impossible to know where to start. Four officers from Central arrived and joined us at the top of the stairs. Within seconds PC Jim Dignam got hit just above the eye by a flying pint glass. He hit the floor as blood poured from his wound.

Enough's enough, time for us to wade in and sort this out. At that very moment a big fight broke out by the bar to our right, so a few of us headed over to break it up. There was one man in particular who was throwing punches and Craig grabbed him from behind and shouted at me to grab his legs. I bent down and grabbed what I thought were this man's legs. Indeed one of them was but the other belonged to Craig and as I put both of them together and folded them under my arm pit to start marching them out so I heard Craig screaming out to let go of his leg. I turned around to see him hopping. He didn't look too pleased with me! Inspector Daniels then let out a large scream and I saw a woman had sunk her teeth into his right arm. She clung onto him like a hamster does when it bites a child and it took two officers to drag her off. She bit straight through his jacket, a jumper and his shirt and still drew blood!

It wasn't just the girls dancing who were carrying on doing their thing, so was the DJ. I suggested to Inspector Daniels that we get him to turn the music off and switch the lights on so that we could clear the place and close it down. He agreed and we both set off across the dance floor whilst the glasses whizzed over our heads. To my surprise and annoyance the DJ arrogantly refused to cooperate and carried on as if we weren't there. Mr Daniels then let him know that if he didn't do as we had asked then he was quite sure that the licensing magistrates would be very interested to learn of tonight's events and that he would probably end up having to join the three million unemployed! He reluctantly switched it all off and turned the lights on. He then handed me the microphone and said "You tell em".

In fairness they took it quite well and seemed resigned to the fact that it was inevitable that it was going to end that way. By putting the lights on it proved that the club was massively over its limit and even though we were physically pushing many of them out of the club it still took us nearly an hour to clear it. I shudder to think how it might have ended had there been a major fire. In the end there were over 20 arrests and three injuries to police officers.

I'd been on early turn and I was knackered. I still hated getting up at sparrow fart and it made me a grumpy bugger for the rest of the day. About 6pm I got a phone call from Sgt Jock Campbell.

"Be at Kingston Crescent for 7pm with your full RSG kit" he said.

"What for?" was the obvious question from me.

"Buggered if I know" he said "I'm just passing the message".

Two van loads of the usual suspects met at Kingston Crescent and nobody had the slightest idea where we were going or what the job was. We just had to be at HQ by 8pm. It was already dark and bitterly cold with clear skies and a severe frost forecast. I took my usual seat in the rear off side corner of the Transit minibus as we headed north. There were lots of rumours flying about and even more when we arrived at Winchester and met up with another five PSU's. Whatever this was it was pretty big. We took the lift to the fifth floor canteen where we filled our faces with chicken curry after which our Sgts were called to a briefing. They returned half an hour later none the wiser, other than we had been tasked with patrolling the north of the county and were to await further instructions. By now it was gone 10pm as we drove further north to what K Division officers thought were the northern wastelands of Hampshire. It wasn't long before I fell asleep. An hour or so later I was woken by the others. We were stopping at Whitchurch nick for a comfort break and a fag. It was absolutely freezing up here. It was incredibly dark, with hills and trees and things us city boys never got to see. We met up with a couple of the other vans who were still none the wiser about our deployment and as we sipped on our Maxpax hot chocolate drinks we were convinced that within the next couple of hours we would all get sent home again. We got back into the carriers where I assumed my previous position and went out like a light.

I was woken up by the sounds of our Sgt screaming "everybody out, out, out" and with that I went straight into automatic pilot. On went the helmet as I swivelled on my backside, turned to my left and opened the rear doors. I leapt out of the carrier and the first thing that hit me was the cold, it must have been -5 degrees. As I opened my eyes I saw a few feet ahead of me a chain link fence with roles of barbed wire along the top. Behind the fencing were several lines of armed soldiers and behind them was an American Police car with its red and blue lights flashing away. Above us and hovering very low was a helicopter with its search lights on and chained to the fence were hundreds of wailing women.

"Where the fuck am I?" I said to myself "What planet is this, who are these women, why are they all screaming?"

There were TV cameras and press photographers everywhere and we were being barked at by RSG Commanders to form a cordon in front of these women and then arrest teams were deployed to remove them from the fence. But no sooner had one been removed then another female took her place. They were shaking the fence back and forth in an effort to pull it down. Just to the right of the main gate it looked like they were starting to succeed. I started to notice officers from other forces like the Met, Thames Valley and Surrey were also with us, but where the hell are we? These women all seemed to have braided or plaited hair, they wore those hippy type dresses with beads around their necks and sandals on their feet. Others were slightly more butch looking with shaven heads and Doc Martin boots. The noise was incredible, a good number of them were constantly blowing whistles, there was a deafening chorus of screaming and a red Indian type whooping noise and that bloody helicopter isn't helping at all. We were picking them off one by one to lead them away. They seemed passive enough when detained, although sometimes a completely passive prisoner is more difficult to deal with than a scrapping one, because they just become dead weight and you end up using all your energy trying to drag them away. Do a couple of those in an hour and you are exhausted. I had reached the front of the line and saw a female in her mid 20s I suppose cutting the wire fence with a pair of snips. I took hold of her arm and it was all slippery. She turned to face me and I was somewhat taken aback because she was completely silver! Her face, her arms, her legs, every part of her exposed skin was painted in silver gloss paint. And it was still wet. I know this because my hand was already covered in the stuff and as I went to take the snips from her so I got covered in a bit more. Then as I took her left arm to lead her away so I got covered in a load more of it. I got her to the mobile custody unit where we had our photo taken for ID purposes and she was duly booked in for causing criminal damage. She was pleasant enough and she was highly amused when I asked one of the Thames Valley custody officers where we were!

"This is Greenham Common" she said "Don't you lot know anything?"

All I know is I'm covered in silver paint. I had heard of Greenham Common because over the last few weeks it had become quite news worthy on the Southern TV news because a growing number of women had set up a Peace Camp at the entrance to the American Airforce base in protest at the possible deployment of Cruise missiles there. But tonight some 30,000 women had descended to 'Embrace the Base' and Thames Valley Police had called in Mutual Aid from adjoining forces. As the base was little more than 500 yards over the Hampshire border we were the obvious first choice. This was a big escalation in the women's tactics and this protest now catapulted their cause onto the international stage. By the time I got back to my unit much of the original demonstration had calmed down, although there were still thousands of them milling about. Tents had been set up on a grassed area by the entrance and these now stretched into nearby woodland.

The next night we were back up there again. No magical mystery tour across the Hampshire countryside first though, this time we went straight there after having a proper briefing at the nearby Newbury Police Station. My unit got deployed to the east of the main gate just behind the tents. Our objective was to patrol in pairs along a section of the perimeter fence, which stretched for over five miles to ensure that the women did not cut the fence and gain access to the base. If they did, then the military inside would deal with them. The perimeter pathway was nothing more than a trodden path through woodland and bog. In places it was almost impassable because it was so wet. We had to make our way to certain points to relieve those officers who had been there since mid afternoon. It was gone 11pm when Roger Hogben and I found our two colleagues huddled next to a small open fire they had lit in order to keep themselves warm. It was bitterly cold with temperatures plunging below -7 tonight. In the distance we could hear what sounded like a couple of chain saws being used but couldn't work out why. Roger and I collected some more wood and made ourselves a lot more comfortable. Every now and then a couple of the women would walk past and so we would follow them onto where the next two officers were to ensure they didn't do any damage. It was a bit cat-and-mouse like but mostly the tactics worked. We could still hear the chain saws though, which considering it was now 2am did seem a little strange. Roger and I got relieved by another crew and we inched our way back towards the van. As we reached one of the boggier parts of our route so we heard;

"psst, oi lads, over here".

It was coming from inside the fence. We peered through and in the darkness were two squaddies, in full combat gear, complete with blackened faces. They pushed a length of cable through the lower part of the fence and asked us to tie it to the base of a big tree the other side of the pathway. When it was stretched out it lay right across the bog. We'd only walked another 50 yards or so when we saw two women coming towards us.

"Good evening ladies" Roger and I said politely.

"Piss off" they said as one.

Like naughty school boys we hid behind the nearest tree to see if the squaddies might spring their trap. It was quite difficult to see but the scream and the splash said it all. As we came out from behind our tree we were just in time to see that one of them was on all fours in the swampy mud and in her effort to rescue her friend so the other one fell over to.

The next night it was just as cold and somebody had hit on the great idea that to relieve a bit of the boredom during the early hours, that we bake potatoes in our little fires. So quite a few of us had come ready prepared with spuds wrapped up in foil, ready to bake. At the briefing the Thames Valley Chief Inspector said that he wasn't going to ban us lighting fires; however he had received complaints from several locals that the Met had cut down a load of trees and somebody's garden fence the previous night using a chain saw! This practice was to stop immediately. If you needed fire wood there was plenty of it on the ground already.

It was appraisal time and after formal interviews with your Sgt, then the Inspector, then the Superintendent it was up to Kingston Crescent nick to see the Chief Superintendent, who of course I had kept waiting last Christmas eve! Thankfully he had since retired and this year I was to see his replacement, Chief Superintendent Eddy Day, known to everybody as Happy Day. I hadn't yet had the pleasure but I understood him to be a bit of a character and a lot more moderate than his predecessor. At least my pocket book was up to date this year. I knocked on the door and heard him say "Enter".

I opened the door and stood in front of his desk, saluted and gave him my name. He looked up from behind his glasses and beckoned me to sit down.

"Woodward, Woodward, why does that name ring a bell with me?" he asked, which is rarely a good sign. Then he snapped his fingers, took off his specs and said.

"I know, bald tyres on the area car"

"Er.........yes sir" I sheepishly replied.

"Biggest fucking laugh I've had all year, especially when I found out the Chief had been stuck on as well" he roared as he slumped back into his chair.

We then spent the next half an hour talking it all through, with him chuckling about the whole thing and about two minutes spent looking over my appraisal. He thanked me most sincerely for a good years work but I left wondering whether I would ever live down the tyres saga or would it haunt me for the rest of my career?

Christmas morning on early turn is generally a quiet affair. If you get called out, well, it's unfortunate but it's not likely to be anything too serious and just as soon as you've finished its back to the nick to resume the consumption of food and the playing of cards, which is the only day of the year that such relaxed behaviour is ever tolerated. After parade we trooped down stairs, where we rearranged a couple of tables, got the cards out, opened some tins of mince pies and cake and commenced our own little festivities. Being a bank holiday of course meant that we were down to minimum strength, which in reality meant that we had more manpower than normal. It was 6.45 am.

Kilo to Kilo Sierra units, can you turn out to 109 Francis Avenue please, someone has just thrown a house brick through the front room window.
Kilo Sierra 51 and Panda 9 attending.

Charming, Merry Christmas. Who does that on Christmas morning for goodness sake? The front room was a mess. There was a big hole in the front bay window and the brick had scored a direct hit on the family Christmas tree which was now laying on its side. The presents were strewn everywhere and the two young pyjama clad kids looked somewhat bewildered. We helped them clear things up the best we could and I helped dad secure the window with a piece of board. They didn't appear to have any enemies and we put it down to a random attack. We then resumed and headed back to the mince pies.

Kilo to Kilo Sierra 51

Kilo Sierra 51 go ahead

Can you assist ambulance please, Victoria Road South for a suspected cot death

Kilo Sierra 51, 10/4

Oh please don't let this be true, not just because its Christmas morning but just because. Craig and I spent the rest of the short journey in silence. We met one of the ambulance men at the door. It was a confirmed death of a five month old baby boy. They were just waiting for a GP to arrive to confirm death. There were no suspicious circumstances but even so we had to inform the duty CID officer to attend.

Craig and I entered the meagre flat on the first floor. The young mother was sobbing uncontrollably on the settee whilst her boyfriend did his best to comfort her. Craig and I had a legal obligation to view the body in order to report to the Coroner. It was a truly pitiful sight. We entered the tiny but immaculate bedroom and as the ambulance man pulled back a small blue blanket that covered the body, I felt my stomach tie itself up in knots. He looked so small, so vulnerable, laying on his back, wearing just a nappy with his arms and legs spread out. We all stood there in complete silence. The peace was shattered by a woman's voice downstairs.

She was screaming "where's my baby, where's my grandson".

We rushed to the stairs to see the grand mother running upstairs towards us. As she did, her daughter came out of the lounge screaming for her mum. They collapsed together on the floor hugging each other, crying out that it was so unfair. The boyfriend looked completely lost and unable to help them or himself. I took him back into the lounge. He grabbed me and threw his arms around my neck and burst into tears. I hugged him back. I felt it was the least I could do. His own parents had died a few years before and his brother was banged up in Camphill Prison, so his girlfriend and his only son were his life.

The GP arrived to confirm what we already knew and then did what he could for the poor parents and the grand mother. The duty DC arrived, followed by the DS then the DI and eventually the Co-op undertakers in their black van. I stayed with the young father as he clearly needed someone to talk to and I have to confess it helped me to deal with the situation myself. The worst bit for me was looking around their flat and seeing the tree and all the little presents lined up for their baby's first ever Christmas. Life for both of them would never be the same again. I'd never been to an infant death before and I certainly don't want to go to another one, not on any day.

As we were finishing off I had become aware via radio transmissions that a unit on Central's patch had found a car registration plate laying in the road and upon checking the details found that it belonged to a stolen Cortina. Over the next half hour or so I heard that said Cortina had been found in nearby Dean Street, Portsea outside the home of two well known brothers. As Craig and I left the house in Victoria Road South so there was a 10/10 shout from Dean Street. We made our way across town to Portsea. The 10/10 shouts kept coming and in the background you could hear all manner of shouting and screaming. We arrived with several other units and it was chaos. There were about 30 people out in the street, all wanting to fight with the police at 1030 on Christmas morning! Like rats from the sewer they had emerged from the nearby flats, not having a clue what the original concern was, but were accusing the police of heavy handed tactics on Christmas Day. This did not sit well with Craig and I. In hindsight perhaps we shouldn't have gone. In hindsight we were definitely a little bit emotional. And it has to be said that one or two of them bore the full brunt of that emotion. In total 17 people were arrested for assaulting police officers, ABH on two police officers, affray, theft of a motor vehicle and drunk and disorderly. Portsmouth Central custody centre was like a war zone. It took us over two hours just to get them all booked in and no sooner had we resumed we were deployed to our next job.

Kilo to Kilo Sierra 51

Kilo Sierra 51 go ahead

114 Essex Road please for a vulnerable misper

Kilo Sierra 51, 10/4

Christmas is traditionally a time of great emotion for many people. A time when they reflect on friends and family no longer with them. Now mix that emotion with alcohol and it can become a recipe for disaster. The lady was reporting her husband Barry missing and as suspected he was in a depressed state following the death of his father a couple of months before. He'd had a lot to drink and had taken a rope with him and she feared he might hang himself. The obvious place was the pier which is where we started our search. Thankfully there was no trace of him there or anywhere else. After an hour we were on the point of running out of places to look when we got a second call from the control room sending us back to the address because our misper had returned. We went back and found him sobbing in the arm chair. We did our best to console him but in the end we left it to his wife.

"Can we go and have something to eat now?" said Craig. It was half twelve and all we'd had so far today was a mince pie at 6.30.

Kilo to Kilo Foxtrot 51

Kilo Foxtrot 51 go ahead

Make Copnor Bridge please, serious RTA, ambulance attending

Kilo Foxtrot 51, 10/4

Kilo, do I have other units to back up please, further reports coming in that this could be a fatal

Kilo Sierra 51 we are free

Kilo Sierra 51, yes please, make towards

Kilo Sierra 51, 10/4

Just north of Copnor Bridge a car had collided with a pedestrian who was running across the road towards his own car, having just bought some cigars from a nearby shop. He died in front of his young daughter who was sitting in the car. Two Traffic units attended to deal with the RTA itself whilst the rest of us busied ourselves with witness statements, road closures and general running about.

In the end I felt a bit numb, sort of shell shocked by the days events and as Craig and I drove slowly back to Southsea, more than two hours late getting off duty, we wondered if there had ever been a worse Christmas morning? Peace and goodwill to all men didn't seem to fit somehow. I knew Craig would go home and down several shots of malt whisky; well he is Scottish and that was his way of dealing with things. As I walked through my front door Tricia could tell straight away that it had been a particularly difficult day. She was getting rather good at letting me off load my thoughts and feelings and it certainly helps having somebody that not only listens but can offer you some moral support or a good kick up the arse, whichever she felt was more appropriate! But this was Christmas Day and there were still all the traditional things to do and it's incredibly difficult to put on a smile and some festive cheer when all you can think about are two families mourning their loss whilst all around them are having a good old knees-up. In the end our own Christmas was rather subdued; I just couldn't do the celebration thing.

CHAPTER 7

1983. Kilo Sierra is dead

It was all change on the 1st January and none of us were very happy about it. The force made a number of boundary changes and in the process also changed the names of the Divisions and their respective call signs. K Division was changed to Eastern Division and within our area the old Kilo call signs mostly disappeared to. Out went Kilo Sierra to be replaced with Victor Sierra. Out went Kilo Foxtrot to be replaced with Romeo Foxtrot. The only station to retain its status was Portsmouth Central which remained as Kilo Charlie. It felt like the powers that be at HQ had finally swept aside the old Portsmouth City force and K Division was dead. We were very much in mourning. The only consolation was that F Division at Southampton had also been ripped to shreds and was now Western Division.

It was all change on the domestic front for me to as Tricia and I moved from Alverstone Road up to Jenkins Grove at Baffins, which by a quirk of fate was only ten doors away from Andy and Sues house! It was an incredibly cold January day when we moved and the house had no heating in it except for a two bar electric fire in the front room. Nobody had lived in the house for over six months and when we came downstairs on the first morning there was a thin sheet of ice on the kitchen wall.

The cold spell continued throughout January and into February and on nights, as always seemed to be the case we got lots of snow. Whilst huddled in the front office at midnight drinking much needed hot tea we were joined by two lads from the Oscar Mike unit, or the street offences squad as it was known. These guys wore casual street clothing and would either patrol in an unmarked car or out on foot to detect more serious street offences that wouldn't occur in front of a uniformed presence. Whilst we all chatted they told us that they had just stopped and spoken to two student types in Clarendon Road who were pushing a huge double wardrobe along the snowy pavement. Upon questioning the pair they stated that they intended to dump the wardrobe on a nearby building site because it took up too much room in their bed-sit just around the corner in Kenilworth Road. After taking their details the two Oscar Mike lads suggested that they take the wardrobe back home and dispose of it in the proper manner during day light hours.

As we came back into the station at 0400 for yet another cuppa one of the Relief mentioned that he had just seen this wardrobe dumped on said building site. Cheeky sods. This was a gauntlet that Green Relief just had to pick up. So after downing some tea we all got into the van and drove down to the building site on Clarendon Road, where we picked up the very heavy oak wardrobe and placed it into the rear of the van. We then drove to number 6 Kenilworth Road where you could clearly see the marks left in the snow where they had been pushing it. You know what it's like when it's been snowing. It's incredibly quiet, in fact at that time of night you could hear a pin drop. We were desperately trying not to laugh as we heaved the wardrobe from the van and out onto the pavement. Then, ever so carefully we lifted it over the low front wall, opened both the wardrobe doors and placed it hard up against the front door to the house so that when they came out in the morning they walked straight into the wardrobe! The best bit of all was that they must have known it was the Police but there was bugger all they could do about it.

Dick Turpin was still upsetting us all with his views and it was clearly designed to be provocative. Even his fellow sergeants were starting to distance themselves from him and it was clear that one or two inspectors were now keeping a close eye on what was going on. He had decimated Green Relief as one by one officers looked to get away from his politics and strange decision making by getting transfers onto various squads and departments. We were down to the bare bones and were virtually working alone as a shift with little or no input from him at all. What do naughty school children do when they want to get their own back on a teacher? It usually means surreptitiously attacking the teacher in a covert manner and then hiding behind the bike sheds giggling about it. Whilst one of the Relief kept him talking in the office, those of us who were left went outside into the snow and placed a 'no-waiting' cone onto the roof of his car. We then covered the cone in snow and sculptured it into a huge penis with two testicles attached to it. It was a real work of art and sadly we were laughing too much to really appreciate our efforts. At 0600 as Dick Turpin left by the front door we all ran out the back door and peered around the corner of the station wall. He walked across the road and stood there looking at our handy work.

"The fucking little wankers" he protested.

With that he raised his arm and took a huge back handed swipe at the phallic sculpture. The trouble was the cone beneath it was now frozen solid and the impact almost broke his arm. That seemed to make it all the funnier.

Catching burglars is every coppers top priority. It makes no difference whether you are a CID officer, Traffic or Section cop, bagging a dwelling burglar produces bucket loads of self satisfaction. Breaking into people's houses is one of the lowest forms of crime in my book, especially if they have ransacked the place or worse defecated on the carpet or spread it over the lounge walls as some of them are inclined to do. Why would you do that anyway? I asked a burglar I had in custody once that had done just that and he emphatically denied having a dump in the middle of the lounge floor. He fully admitted that the blood found on the window was his, he admitted ransacking the house and stealing all the jewellery, cash and other valuables but it definitely wasn't him who squatted down and left his calling card behind. Even when I put it to him that he had done something similar on a number of previous occasions he still denied it. He blamed the owner's cat, even though they didn't have one!

Kilo to Victor Sierra 51

Victor Sierra 51 go ahead

Make 7 St. Bartholomew's Gardens, believed intruder on premises, informant is next door neighbour. Owners are away on holiday.

Victor Sierra 51, 10/4

It was nine in the evening and we had a huge thunderstorm over head. No rain, but plenty of noise. St. Bartholomew's Gardens was a small island of 1970s built houses that now occupied a plot where St. Bartholomew's Church once stood and as we arrived outside so we were met by the concerned neighbour. His two teenage sons' were standing guard by the side door that had had the glass smashed. They had a spare key and so in we went. I stood just inside the door to cover the exit as two of the Relief commenced the search. The thunder rumbled above us. After searching the ground floor they went upstairs and found jewellery stacked at the top of the stairs ready to be taken away. This was a good sign that our intruder was still in the house. But to my surprise they came back down stairs empty handed. That wasn't possible said the two lads, they had heard the glass being broken during a thunder clap and were here in seconds. It wasn't possible for anybody to have got in and out before they arrived. They sounded very convincing. OK said my two colleagues, we'll look again. I tried calling up for a dog unit but the only one available was conducting another search over in Gosport some 15 miles away. After another thorough search they returned empty handed. I was annoyed now because I too was convinced that nobody could have made good their escape so quickly, especially as the stash had been left at the top of the stairs. I decided to take a look for myself. After looking in every cupboard and the oven of course I went upstairs. An untidy search had been made in two of the three bedrooms with drawers pulled out and left upside down on the floor and property strewn all over the bedroom. After looking inside and behind the wardrobe, I moved over to the double bed. It was one of those divan types that rolled on castors with the base very close to the floor. I got down on my hands and knees and looked underneath. All clear. As I stood up something told me to look again. I bent down and took a closer look. There was something hanging down but I couldn't quite make out what it was. So I lifted up the side of the bed and out fell our burglar. He had managed to secrete himself up inside the bed frame by hooking his feet and hands onto the wooden framework. He wasn't happy either and he put up a big fight in an effort to get away from being arrested. It took four of us to pin him down and hand cuff him, but yet again it showed the desperate lengths that burglars will go to in order to avoid arrest and that a really thorough search is essential.

The beauty about being a Police officer is that you never know what's around the corner. It could be an RTA, a fire, a juvenile shop lifter, a domestic, an assault, a big street disturbance, a missing person; the possibilities when dealing with human beings are endless. The trouble is we generally only get to see the end result, after it's all gone horribly wrong.

Kilo to Victor Sierra 51

Victor 51 go ahead

Make 12 Sovereign Crescent report of an explosion, fire and ambulance service en route.

Victor Sierra 51, 10/4

It was mid afternoon and explosions on 1970s built housing estates aren't exactly common place. Craig and I weren't too far away and were the first to arrive. There were plenty of neighbours out in the street and we were beckoned through a side gate into the garden by one of them. It was certainly an unusual sight, for there was a man, in his 50s I'd say laying prostrate on the lawn. Most of his clothing had been blown off him and his skin, particularly his face, was blackened and badly blistered. He was in severe shock and was shaking all over. His wife was kneeling beside him trying to comfort him as she tried damping his face with a wet towel. Every touch made him scream. Thankfully the ambulance crew arrived shortly after we did. The garden was covered in debris, most of it glass.

As the ambulance crew tended to the man's injuries we took the wife to one side to try and ascertain what had happened. It transpired that the man was revamping the kitchen which had been extended slightly a few years previously to include a set of sliding patio doors. He was making up some new work tops using ply wood and Formica, which needed gluing into place. He was using a strong form of copydex adhesive whereby you paste both the work top surface and the wood, before bringing the two surfaces together. He'd done two and was working on the third one, when the build up of fumes from the adhesive had reached the ceiling and were now falling back down to ground level because there was no ventilation. As they passed beneath the work top he was standing at so the fumes were ignited by the gas boiler flame, causing the explosion which blew our DIY man straight out through the patio doors and into his garden. He survived but no doubt suffered a great deal over the next few months.

Entering people's houses and bed sits, no matter what the reason means that you are getting a pretty good glimpse into their lives the instant you walk through their door. I have always found this to be a fairly accurate yard stick and can help prepare me for what might lay ahead. And I'm constantly amazed at the manner in which some people live. I'm quite a neat and tidy person on the whole and whilst I would never judge a person by the way in which they choose to live I have to confess I quite often stand in someone's lounge and think 'yuk, how revolting'. I'm not talking about the décor or their choice of fabrics but the squalor that many end up creating themselves and seem happy to live in. There's no class divide here either, I've been into some truly immaculate council flats in the roughest parts of the city and conversely found myself retching at the smell emanating from a supposedly decent looking property in the posher parts of Southsea. And it's that smell that gets to me every time; it is as unique as the smell that lingers in cell blocks, only worse. It's a combination of cigarette smoke, damp dogs, body odour and chip fat. It's ingrained into what's left of the thread bare carpets, the never-been-washed-ever net curtains that droop in the middle of the window, that can't be opened to ventilate the room because it's been nailed shut. There's always a huge pile of damp washing that smells like a saucepan of over boiled sprouts, that has been left on the kitchen floor for several weeks now and the big 'John Smiths Bitter' ashtray they nicked from the pub that now sits on the arm of the settee is literally over flowing with fag ends. The chip pan and the grill pan sit in a lake of cold, solidified fat that is an inch deep and burned onto the cooker in several places. A number of fag butts are lined up along the edge of the kitchen worktop next to the cooker and have been left to burn out as the occupant prepares dinner, whilst the kitchen bin, if they actually have one, has no lid and should have been emptied a week ago last Tuesday. Meanwhile the blue bottle flies dive bomb the remains of the Chinese takeaway as I watch the mangy and rather elderly Alsation dog lick out the contents of a mug placed on the floor by the settee.

"Would you like a cup of tea officer?"

"Erm……no thanks" I invariably decline, but nonetheless they make me one anyway, picking up that same mug from the floor and making the excuse that Muttly does like his tea. When it arrives it's usually luke warm with far too much milk in it and with the tea bag and a few dog hairs floating on top.

You are invited to sit down but you can't until they've cleared away a large number of clothes and a filthy old quilt from the settee, which when you sit on it collapses under your weight and you sink to almost ground level. If you ever manage to get back up again you spend the rest of the day picking off a large number of dog hairs from your uniform trousers, which are now also engrained with *that smell*. The very worst houses are those that you can literally smell from outside as you raise your hand to knock on the door! I'm not joking either. On many occasions you have to wipe your feet on the way out of the property so as not to tread their filth back out onto the street.

Sometimes you just feel sick to the stomach with the brutality that senseless people are prepared to inflict on innocent victims. It's even worse when you know the victim and can't find the culprits.

Kilo to Victor Sierra 51

Victor Sierra 51 go ahead

Make Albert Road please body found in the road, not sure at this time whether it's a hit and run RTA or an assault

Victor Sierra 51, 10/4

It was 3am and had already been a busy night with a high number of assaults and fights in clubs and restaurants. As we arrived in Albert Road, just down from the traffic lights with Waverley Road, we could see a taxi with its hazard lights on with the driver crouched down beside a body. The driver said he had just found him like it and although he was conscious he couldn't get anything out of him. I was dreading this because as soon as I arrived I knew who it was. The little yellow hand cart was the give away. It was Alan, the road sweeper. I bent down next to him. He seemed to be sobbing as he lay face down in the gutter. Craig took the taxi driver to one side to get his details and check his car for damage, just in case. I called to Alan and told him it was me and that he was safe. I needed him to roll over if he could. I could see blood on the side of his face and could now hear him saying "Why?"

It took a while but eventually I got Alan to roll over onto his side. I was horrified by what I saw. Alan had been beaten and kicked so severely that his face was barely recognisable. Both his eyes were swollen shut, he could hardly see out of them. His bottom lip was split in half and blood was pouring from his nose. I was most concerned about his skull because there was so much blood coming out of his left ear that I couldn't tell whether it was because it had been badly cut or that maybe he had a fractured skull and that the blood was coming from inside his ear. But it was his pitiful sobbing that will haunt me forever.

"Why Steve, why did they do this to me?" he asked, desperately trying to look through his eyes. "What did I ever do to them Steve, why did they have to do this?"

I didn't have an answer for him and felt terrible because of it. To make him and me feel a little better about things I sat beside him in the gutter and got my fags out.

"You do know it's your turn to splash the fags Al?" I quipped.

"Can you let me off just this once" he smiled back.

"Just this once then you scrounging old git" and we sat on the kerb waiting for the ambulance as Alan tried his best to draw on a fag with a split lip, whilst it got soaked in his blood.

I tried getting a description of the mindless scum that had attacked him and all he could say was that he was sweeping the road when he heard someone running up behind him and the next thing he knew was that he was on the ground and could feel himself being repeatedly kicked. He went on to say that he thought there were two of them because he could hear them laughing. We called in as many units as we could and got them to stop and turn over every male they came across and to pay particular attention to any with bloodied shoes. Despite everyone's best efforts they were never found.

I travelled up to the QA Hospital in the back of the ambulance to keep Alan company. His closest relative, an elderly sister lived in Cosham and we sent a unit to go and collect her to bring her up to the QA. As we headed towards the hospital I kept looking at Alan and it was plain to see that his world had been torn apart by this meaningless assault. And as he kept saying at the roadside, why? Why him, what had he done? He hadn't looked at some blokes bird or knocked over some geezers pint, which were the usual pathetic excuses we would be handed in many cases. All Alan was doing was his job, keeping the streets clean for us all, unseen by most and from now on, unseen by any of us ever again. We visited him in hospital the next evening where he tearfully told us that he had decided to retire. You could tell he didn't want to but he knew it was for the best. I'll miss having a sneaky fag with him.

On the 9th June the country went to the polls and I ended up doing the late shift at the same polling station I'd been at in 1979. It was just as mind numbing as it had been the last time and Maggie Thatcher swept to power for a second term.

Sometimes you get sent to incidents that just make you laugh, even if the victim involved is hurt, the circumstances surrounding it just make you smile. You can't help it.

Kilo to Victor Sierra 51

Victor Sierra 51 go ahead

RTA, believed injury, Eastney Esplanade

Victor Sierra 51, 10/4

Now I've seen some messy RTA's but this was truly awful. There was chicken curry mixed in with chowmein, egg fried rice and bean sprouts spread all over the road surface and a large quantity of spring rolls covered in sweet and sour sauce. Somewhere amongst that lot was a moped rider covered in most of the aforementioned food and quite a lot of blood, looking at the state of his face. But how had he come to such a sticky position? It transpired that he had popped down to his local Chinese takeaway on his moped to buy dinner for him and his mates. He had four plastic bags to carry and had slipped two on the end of each handlebar and started to ride home with these things swinging in the breeze. On the nearside of the esplanade the carriageway is lined with large ornamental rocks, each one about the size of an arm chair. He had somehow lost control of the moped, the front wheel slipped away and down he went, face first into the rocks. He only had an open faced crash helmet on which afforded him very little protection. We all winced when we realised just where the impact was. His face was covered in blood, very swollen and he couldn't speak. The ambulance scooped him up and carried him off to the QA. We then swept the Chinese into the gutter and left, mocking the poor lad for being quite so daft. About an hour later we got called back.

Kilo to Victor Sierra 51

Victor Sierra 51 go ahead

We've had a request from the staff at QA. Can you return to the scene of the RTA. Apparently your boy has lost seven teeth and the doctor says that if we can retrieve them there is every chance they could save them

Er............yes 10/4, we'll try

Craig and I argued all the way there about who was going to sift through this concoction of cold and gloopy takeaway to look for seven teeth. It really wasn't very nice flicking bits of rice from your fingers, whilst lengths of cold chowmein were like slippery eels to the touch. Found one, just by the rock he'd kissed. Found two more. Because we had swept the remains into the dusty gutter complete with quite a lot of blood it had turned the whole lot into a sort of kid's mud pie. As we pulled it apart and examined each portion like concerned archaeologists so we found numbers four and five. As people drove slowly passed us they stared in disbelief.

"What's up" shouted Craig "have ya never seen cops scavenging for food before? If you lot paid us more we would nae have to do this" he laughed.

Just as we were starting to lose hope of retrieving all of them so I found the last two under the nearby shrubs. We placed them all in a small brown envelope and hot footed it up to the A and E department. We proudly presented our findings to the doctor who seemed quite hopeful that the surgeon might just be able to put them back in. Mind you it might be a while before our boy could do anything except maybe suck through a straw.

Sometimes it just goes horribly wrong. No matter how well prepared you think you are, no matter how well briefed, the unexpected just leaps up and bites you in the arse. We were in the station when Kilo asked us to phone them. Craig did the honours and I watched him scribble down some notes. We had a death message to deliver and it was an unexpected one for the family concerned. So off we went to the house to do what all coppers hate doing the most. As Craig had taken the details down he decided that he would do the dirty deed. We knocked on the door and were greeted by a young man in his late 20s. His wife was sat in the kitchen and we all sat around the table. Craig told the young man that his father had died. He sat there in stunned silence whilst his wife just flipped and ran upstairs crying. We all sat there for another three or four minutes in total silence, letting him absorb the dreadful news. Then slowly but surely he started to ask us questions like how, where, when and why? Craig couldn't really answer him so handed him a piece of paper with contact details for an officer at Havant who could help him further.

"Havant Police?" he enquired "Why Havant, my dad lives in London, I don't understand".

Neither did we but the alarm bells started to ring as Craig looked at me with a frown.

"My father-in-law lives in Havant though" he went on.

Craig reached for the phone to ring the control room and confirmed our worst fears. It wasn't his father who had died it was hers. The three of us sat there in complete silence. Craig and I had dealt with some tough things over the last couple of years but this was, without doubt the worst. How are we going to tell her that it's actually her father that has died? The husband put us out of our misery by volunteering to do it himself, he felt it would probably be kinder that way, in fact the more he thought about it the more he insisted upon it. In fact it might be better if we leave right now. We sat in the patrol car for a few minutes in an embarrassed silence. Who got it wrong, us or the control room? Craig showed me the notes he had made from the initial phone call which tended to suggest that we had done nothing wrong, but it didn't make us feel any better.

I love my cars and bikes. I am a self confessed petrol head, always have been and doubtless always will be. I've spent and lost a small fortune over the years on various means of motorised transport and I doubt I will ever change. If my numbers ever come up I wouldn't know which show room to start at but would probably visit them all. And I'm not the only one.

Kilo to Victor Sierra 51

Victor Sierra 51 go ahead

RTA, Eastern Road junction Tangiers Road please, no injury but road partially blocked

Victor Sierra 51, 10/4

Eastern Road is one of the main arterial routes into and out of the city. In fact Portsmouth must be unique in that it only has three routes for motorists to use so if one of them gets blocked it can cause chaos for hours. This particular junction was a notorious black spot especially if cars were trying to turn right out of Tangiers Road onto the four lanes of the Eastern Road.

Upon my arrival I found that only one southbound lane was blocked with a damaged vehicle and the other vehicle involved was on the grass verge. The two vehicles were at opposite ends of the spectrum. On the grass verge was a 1920s Rolls Royce with gleaming open back coach work, wooden wheels on hard rubber tyres, beautiful brass work lights and bright red leather seats. The rear offside wheel was completely smashed and laying underneath the car whilst the hand made mudguard was twisted and broken and a large hole had been punctured through the body work causing some damage inside. The Rolls Royce was one of only three left in the world and the very proud owner who was driving it home from auction for the first time was on his knees crying his eyes out! This car was a childhood dream. He had a picture of one on his bedroom wall and in his adult years had scoured the planet looking for one. He was less than a mile from home when he got wiped out by the tattiest, rustiest, crappiest old red Simca van you are ever likely to see on the road. It was a huge insult to the Roller to be hit by something quite so vulgar. Its owner was equally as tatty and hadn't washed or shaved for some days and to really rub salt into the wound, he couldn't give a shit. Life can be so unfair sometimes.

I'd been on nights and was sleeping like a baby when the phone rang. Normally I'd ignore it but it just kept on ringing and ringing. In the end I had no option but to pick it up. It was Jock Campbell and I was required at Portsmouth Crown Court right now, "the Judge is waiting for you" said Jock.

It was just gone half ten in the morning. As I hurriedly got dressed into my uniform I kept asking myself, what job is it then, I wasn't warned to attend court, why does the judge want to see me, what have I done? Crown Court Judges don't summon you for nothing. From the time I leapt out of bed to the time I had got into my car was about ten minutes. Except this wasn't my car, I'd borrowed it from one of the guys on the Relief whilst he repaired mine. It was a MK1 Ford Granada which was a bit of a wreck and every panel on it was a different colour and it was full of rust! I was still wondering what on earth it was I was required for as I turned left onto Baffins Road and hit the accelerator. Baffins Road was the first main road I had come to and I wasn't hanging about, I was under a lot of pressure. As I approached the bottom of the road I saw a Police officer step out from the pavement with his arm raised and pulling me over to the kerb. Oh shit, I don't believe this, not now. It got worse; it was Bob Scorey the same officer that had stuck me on the last time. I'd obviously just gone through a radar trap, which if I'd thought about it was a regular haunt of theirs on Baffins Road. He peered through the window and saw I was in full uniform. I blurted out what had happened and that the judge was waiting. He took a step backwards and just waved me away, shaking his head in disbelief as he looked at the state of the car I was driving.

I got to Portsmouth Crown Court and ran upstairs to Court 6. I let the Court Usher know I was here and then took a look at my watch, less than 25 minutes since I got the phone call, not bad I thought, he can't complain at that. Half an hour went by and the Prosecutor came out, thanked me very much for coming down at such short notice but they had managed to sort out the query now and I wasn't required.

"I hope we didn't inconvenience you too much" he said and disappeared back into court.

"You have no idea" I mumbled.

Being a Police officer you expect to be called names, it comes with the territory. But that doesn't mean you like it or find it acceptable. Mostly you just take it on the chin but sometimes an opportunity arises whereby you can turn the tables. Steve Moore and I were crewed up together on a busy Friday night. It was really humming at pub kick out time as hundreds of people spilled out of the pubs and started heading down to the clubs. It was quite warm and so we had the windows on the patrol car open. As we drove slowly round the

Strand roundabout there were dozens of revellers about. Standing on the corner of Clarendon Road was a group of about six or seven young women. They looked pleasant enough, all dressed up in their rah-rah skirts and big Dynasty styled hair but as we drove past so they bellowed out as one "PIIIIGGGGGSSSSS" and they shrieked with laughter. Steve and I were rather offended by this and so I did a quick U turn and we returned to the roundabout. The girls were still standing on the same corner and had stopped laughing and now looked somewhat apprehensive as we returned. We didn't stop but as we drove past them we bellowed out "SLLLAAAAGGGGSSSS". Priceless.

It was a Sunday night and Green Relief was down to the bare bones for some reason. Apart from me and Craig the only other PC on duty was Roger Hogben and as we sat down to parade with Dick Turpin we discussed which vehicles would be the priority. Craig and I would crew the area car obviously and Roger would take the van out. Dick Turpin disagreed and said Roger should take a panda out instead. But what if we need a van we collectively asked? But it's a Sunday said Sgt Turpin, we shouldn't need one.

"What do you mean it's a Sunday and we won't need one?" protested Craig who had recently passed the promotion board to Sgt and was awaiting his posting.

But Sgt Turpin stood his ground for no other reason than to piss us off. His parting shot was that if we really needed one then we could always call Centrals or Frattons to attend. With that he got up and left the room, leaving us all shaking our heads in disbelief yet again.

Less than an hour later Craig and I picked up a disqualified motorcyclist on the seafront. After a brief chase he gave up and stopped in Clarendon Road. As we got out of the area car so he jumped from his Suzuki GS1000 and at the same time pulled out a huge length of chain from under his jacket. The chain had a heavy padlock on one end and he started to swing it around his head. He came straight at us shouting out.

"Come on then you fuckers, do you want a piece of me" and within seconds we were locked in a nasty brawl with him.

He punched, kicked and scratched us and did his absolute best to inflict some damage. It took us three or four minutes to restrain him enough to put in an urgent call for a van, any van. Roger arrived first in his panda and with his help we eventually managed to get some handcuffs on the bloke. We then lay on top of him absolutely exhausted, whilst he continued to struggle. A Kilo Papa Naval Provost van arrived and between us we lifted him to his feet and threw him in the back and shut the doors. I stood there, bent forward with my hands on my knees trying to get my breath back as Craig leaned against the van doing much the same thing. Sgt Turpin arrived in a panda.

"You alright lads?" he enquired.

"You, you fucking idiot, get out of ma sight, I don't wanna see you again for the rest of the night" raged Craig as he lurched towards him pointing an accusing finger "No van on a Sunday night, what kinda crap decision was that?" he continued.

Dick Turpin did the first wise thing he'd done since arriving at Southsea just over a year ago and heeded Craig's advice and quickly drove off. In fact we didn't see him again until 0430 when he poked his head in through the front office door and asked.

"Is it safe to come back in yet?"

In October I got roped into doing a football duty for an evening game. Pompey were playing Aston Villa in the Milk Cup and a capacity crowd was expected. There's always something special about evening matches. I'm not quite sure what it is but the atmosphere is generally a lot more buoyant. I took my place at the top of the Fratton End and you could tell that tonight was going to be different almost as soon as you entered the ground. There was a real buzz about the place and the atmosphere was electric. The noise was incredible. I'd never heard Fratton Park in such fine voice or so loud. It was a constant wall of noise and was quite intoxicating. It was a terrific match that ended in a 2-2 draw and I had suddenly and inexplicably become a Pompey fan! Graham would be mortified if he knew.

November 1983 saw the first deliveries of Cruise missiles to Greenham Common airbase, flown in by the USAF in massive Galaxy transport planes. Quite how those things actually flew I've no idea and it was amazing to watch them fly in and lands, as the weight of their wings almost seem to make them flap like a bird. Roger and I started to get sent up to Greenham on a more regular basis than we had been in the past as the so called Peace Camp grew in size and changed tactics. Most of the time they spent sitting in or by their tents until the press turned up. Then all hell would break loose as the women performed for the assembled camera crews. It wasn't unusual to have more than a hundred of them suddenly run out onto the main road to start a peaceful sit down protest or block the main gate into the airbase using a similar tactic. They had also started a dirty campaign by stringing used tampons on string and hanging them around their necks or wrists. Some of them had covered their hands in shit so that when we took hold of them so we got covered in it to. They really were quite revolting people and it looked like they were here to stay.

By December the IRA had started another Christmas bombing campaign on mainland Britain and we were all horrified when they changed tactics and planted a huge car bomb outside the Harrods store in London, detonating it earlier than the time they had stipulated in their phoned warning, resulting in the deaths of six people, including three Police officers who were trying to clear the area. Every day seemed to result in us receiving more and more calls from the public about suspicious packages and cars and we were all on high alert, particularly around our shopping areas.

It being the Christmas period of course meant that it was annual appraisal time and it was with some trepidation that I sat down with Sgt Turpin to read his views on my years work because I knew he wasn't keen on me. I wasn't alone because he wasn't keen on anybody on the Relief. After all the various boxes had been ticked as mostly average it came to his written account. It consisted of a page and a half. Three lines on my years work and the rest of it on how many times I had been late for early turn!

"Do you expect me to sign this?" I enquired.

"I think it's an honest appraisal don't you?" he threw back.

"Sorry no I don't and I won't be signing it to say that I agree with its content because I don't" and with that I left the room.

I was livid. If JB or Dave Martin had written it I would have bowed to their opinion because I had immense respect for both of them and therein lay the problem, none of us respected the man. He was petty and spiteful.

Two days later I had to pop upstairs to see Inspector Daniels. He read through my appraisal, sat back, took off his glasses and said.

"I can't see you liking this very much Stephen".

That was a bit of an under statement and I let him know exactly what I thought of it. Now Danny was a very straight laced man. He did everything by the book, there were no grey areas with him and you knew exactly where you stood with him. Except on this occasion. I fully expected him to say 'just grin and bear it' and that as far as he was concerned I was a good egg and that he was quite satisfied with my performance. He sat there and pondered for a few moments and then tore my appraisal into two pieces and dropped it into the bin!

"I'll ask him to reconsider what he has said and get him to write a more balanced one" he said.

Another two days passed and he called me into his office again to inform me that Sgt Turpin had refused to write another appraisal. He had therefore written a brief one for me explaining that there had been a clash in personalities and praising me for my years good work. There was no mention of early turn either. We then had a long discussion about me taking the promotion exam as he said I was now ideal sergeant material. I declined and stated I really wasn't that interested. He was astounded at my reaction and couldn't quite comprehend why I wasn't interested. I told him that I wanted to continue being a street policeman and that driving a desk just wasn't me. But Mr Daniels persisted.

"Can you see yourself still driving the area car in ten years time then?" he asked.

"If I'm as happy in ten years time as I am now then yes, why not" I replied.

He sat back in his chair with a smile and then admitted that actually he quite admired me for saying that because there were times when he would watch us from his office window, as we rushed out of the station and off to our next job whilst he was left stuck indoors and that he felt quite envious. That was my point, sir.

CHAPTER 8

1984. Arthur Scargill pays my mortgage

The start of the year was one of personal sadness for me because I lost my partner as Craig got promoted to Sgt and transferred to Kingston Crescent. I'd been his official interpreter for two and a half years and enjoyed every minute of it. More importantly I had learned so much from him. He was very street wise, which I have to confess prior to teaming up with him I certainly wasn't. He got me into lots of trouble but I loved him for it, although his driving scared the crap out of me. A few weeks prior to Craig's departure another area car driver from a different Relief had transferred across to Green Relief. PC 1171 Rod Briggs was a big lad with a bit of a 'jack the lad' type reputation. He was certainly a good laugh, hated the yobs and was handy to have around if things got a bit hairy. In other words he was very much like Craig except that he spoke with an English accent.

Another change centred on our radio system. Hampshire dumped the 10-code system it had been using for several years in favour of a more recognised national system which meant that we now used the term *'Roger'* to acknowledge transmissions instead of *'10/4'* and it felt totally alien to us all, in fact most of us hated it. But at least we had some first rate controllers at the recently renamed control room. Out went the term 'Kilo' and in came 'Charlie-One' which kind of sounded OK. With controllers like Stef King, Vernon Ellis, Bob Bradley and Paddy Draper to guide us and quite often take the piss out of us, it was a comfort to know that they were right there looking after the interests of those out on the ground. Their job was vital to the success of policing the streets effectively. Not only were they Police officers and knew how we operated and how we might think things through but they knew the city as well as the rest of us, which is of paramount importance.

Roger, Steve Moore, Dave Brown and I seemed to be doing more public order training or potty training as it was frequently referred to now, than anything else. It almost seemed like a weekly exercise, but was born out of necessity because of the growing unrest within the country. I even spent my evenings running around the field at Baffins Pond in order to keep my fitness levels up. And you know how much I hate cross country running! As a reward for being the super fit, go-anywhere types that they wanted on the RSG so we were given lovely blue and yellow holdall bags with 'Hampshire Constabulary' emblazoned along the sides to carry all our extra kit in. We were quite proud of them.

At the end of January Pompey were due to meet their arch rivals Southampton in the 4th round of the FA Cup. It was the first time they had met in a competitive match for a generation. There are many people in Portsmouth who simply won't even say the word Southampton and will instead refer to the area as 'that lot up the road' or as 'scum' or 'scummers'. It was years before I found out what scummers actually stood for and where it originated from. It stems from a 1930s dock yard strike when all the dockies at the Portsmouth yard walked out. The management were desperate to keep the dock yard working and brought in labour from nearby Southampton. Legend has it that not only did they cross the picket lines but that they called themselves the 'Southampton Community Union Men' and in so doing handed the Portsmouth workers the perfect label and its stuck ever since.

The two communities are geographically just 15 miles apart but there is a world of difference between them. In footballing terms Southampton was in the top tier of English football whilst Pompey was still languishing in the lower divisions and that really hurt. In hooligan terms though Pompey were easily in the top four of the premier league. They had a truly terrible reputation at both home and away with the 6.57 Crew growing in both stature and notoriety. Although Southampton had a sizeable following they didn't possess a hooligan 'firm' like Pompey, Millwall, Chelsea, Cardiff or several others. In the days leading up to the match you could tell the Pompey boys were starting to get rather excited at the prospect of meeting the scummers. Freshly painted slogans appeared on various walls around Fratton Park all in an effort to welcome their guests. Every incident we attended was met with a barrage of anti Southampton songs and chants.

The good news was that I wouldn't be attending the match as part of the support group because Rod and I were 2-10 area car that day. I was both relieved and disappointed all at the same time.

We managed to stay away from the ground before and during most of the match, occasionally receiving updates on the score from Charlie-One. With less than 10 minutes to go it was still 0-0 as Rod and I stopped in Goldsmith Avenue close to Priory Crescent to chat to a Traffic motorcyclist we knew. He said that although it had been noisy before and during the game, so far it had past off peacefully. With less than two minutes to go before the final whistle it was heading for an honourable draw. Then some idiot Pompey 'fan' up in the north east terrace threw a coin at the head of a Southampton player. It scored a direct hit. After the player had received medical attention the Southampton team took their free kick and as a result scored. The ground erupted and within minutes it had spilled out onto the streets of Portsmouth.

Rod and I decided it was time for us to leave the area and let those who were on football duties deal with whatever was about to hit them. I started the Volvo, put it into first gear and moved off, turning right into Priory Crescent. I had driven less than 50 yards when several hundred Pompey yobs appeared from Carisbrooke Road and out into Priory Crescent where they filled the entire street. I stopped the car. About the same time I looked in my mirror and saw a couple of hundred Southampton fans behind us in Goldsmith Avenue. Rod and I were trapped in no-man's land.

"Lock the doors" said Rod "If they charge us, just drive, don't stop, just drive".

They all seemed to look at each other for a few moments before a huge roar went up from the Pompey side and they charged forward. Stones, rocks and bottles rained down in both directions. I hit the throttle as Rod hit the blue light and two-tones. I think I shut my eyes as we steamed through the mob. I could hear the car taking a beating and then the rear window caved in. There was glass everywhere. And in an instant we were out the other side. I stopped a hundred yards later and we looked back to see a full scale pitched battle being waged behind us. The assistance calls from various units in and around Fratton Park started at the same time. Specks Lane seemed to be the main focus of where the trouble was and at one point we heard that personnel carriers were being overturned and set on fire. Rod and I got out and inspected the damage. Both front wings were dented, one rear wing dented, one of the two aerials was missing, a rear light cluster smashed and the rear window had a big hole in it. I was livid. Over the next three hours we chased and split up various groups who were hell bent on getting at anything in red and white.

In Goldsmith Avenue, Milton Road, Rodney Road, Fratton Road and various points in between we pushed and shoved the yobs away. They went on the rampage in Fratton Road smashing shop windows and damaging cars. Up by St. Mary's Church, which is more than a mile away from the ground so the Police fought running battles with the Pompey yobs. A half house brick hit the bonnet of the Volvo and caused yet more damage. We had no idea where it came from. Dozens were arrested and there were several nasty injuries on all sides. Major damage had been done to houses, shops, cars and other property, but the biggest casualty was the Hampshire Constabulary who lost 16 personnel carriers, several of which had been overturned and two set on fire. It was a gruesome afternoon.

As we traipsed back to the nick we were all in a state of shock. The front office was full of coppers with torn shirts, scuffed boots and filthy dirty trousers all sat on the floor or on tables just swapping stories, not in a jocular manner but more in disbelief at the pure hatred that we had witnessed. Most of us were nursing minor cuts and abrasions with a couple of the lads needing hospital treatment.

In the middle of it all walked Superintendent West who stood in the middle of the front office and surveyed his rather battered troops. He slapped his brown gloves across his palm and said.

"Well I think we got away with that rather lightly don't you?" he enquired.

"What fucking match were you at then sir?" came the reply from PC Derek Russell, a beat officer, somewhat senior in years, who was slumped on the floor with a big hole in his trousers.

With that Mr West entered his office and shut the door.

Long weekend was always something to look forward to. Having only one off a month meant that they were treasured days of rest, a time to relax and catch up on much needed sleep. I don't tend to dream much but when I do they can be quite vivid, albeit slightly weird in places. I had slept in on the Monday morning because I was due to start nights that night and Tricia always left me in bed. I'd had a really strange dream that night that involved a big car chase and that it ended with the target car crashing and ending up broadside across the road. The driver then got out, leant over the open door and pointed a handgun at us. My instinctive reaction was to drive straight at the door but as it slammed shut so it chopped the gunman's head clean off. As in many dreams one part of it kept repeating itself and it was the sight of his head coming off and rolling across the bonnet. It was such a vivid dream that I rather ghoulishly told Tricia all about it when I eventually got up.

Rod and I were crewed up in the area car and after policing the 10 pm Monday night under 18s kiddie disco turnout from Nero's, which for once didn't end up in a big fight, we moved on.

Charlie-One to Victor Sierra 51

Victor Sierra 51 go ahead

Can you look around the Milton area please for a white car that has been driving on the pavement at pedestrians? No other details other than it's a white vehicle

Victor Sierra 51, Roger

We drove around the area for about 20 minutes or so and found nothing. We gave up and decided to head back towards the seafront. As we were passing Milton Park I happened to look to my right, through the park towards Goldsmith Avenue and saw a set of red tail lights going sideways.

"Erm........that doesn't look right" I said

At the same time I saw the van coming into Goldsmith Avenue from Eastney Road. All three vehicles met at the junction. The tail lights belonged to a white Renault 18 Turbo which was currently broad side across the road facing the driver's door of the Police van. As Geoff got out the van to speak to the driver, so the Renault just drove straight into the side of the van, reversed and then drove off back down Goldsmith Avenue. I drove off after it as Rod put the blues and twos on.

Goldsmith Avenue is a fairly wide main thoroughfare but felt quite narrow at 80 mph. Rod was busy commencing a commentary for the control room and other units to follow when I saw a red Ford Capri at the junction with Priory Crescent. It stopped for about one second before pulling out straight in front of the Renault. The Renault braked hard, with smoke billowing from its rear tyres and it swerved to its right and somehow managed to drive behind the Capri and then continued westwards along Goldsmith Avenue. Its speed didn't dip below 70 mph as we raced passed the lorry park and continued towards Fratton Bridge. The car was all over the place as it braked hard and locked up its wheels. At the same time the driver tried turning left onto the one way system but completely lost control of the car and it spun three times. There was smoke coming out of the tyres and the whole city must have heard the noise it was making. Just as it came to rest, broadside across the entrance to Fawcett Road so we saw that it had collided with a young lady on a pedal cycle, knocking her off her bike and onto the pavement. It was a very minor collision but that wasn't the point. Rod called up for another unit to attend the location and ensure that she was alright as the Renault turned right into Fawcett Road and then immediately left into Orchard Road. It accelerated away flat out along the narrow side street with cars tightly parked on both sides of the road we hit 60 mph. At the end of the road was a minor crossroads and sat at the junction was a Hillman Avenger. Without slowing down the Renault hit it straight in the rear and I saw the Avenger literally take off across the junction and smash into a parked car. The Renault now had extensive front end damage and parts of the car were still falling off as it turned right into Talbot Road and then immediately right into Telephone Road. It accelerated away again at full pelt, hitting 60 mph as it sped back towards Fawcett Road.

It was never going to make it. The driver barely touched the brakes as it went straight out into Fawcett Road and smashed into the very same Capri it had missed earlier! Both cars came to an immediate halt, the Renault now a complete write off with both front wheels pointing in opposite directions and water, oil and smoke spewing out from the exposed engine. It was broad side across the exit from Telephone Road as we pulled up facing it. The driver's door opened and the driver started to get out. My instinct was to stop him from getting away and so I drove straight at the door to prevent him from getting out. As soon as I did so it all came flashing back.

"Oh fuck me his head" I screamed.

"What?" said Rod somewhat confused as he jumped out of the area car.

To my absolute relief I hadn't chopped his head off although he seemed mightily pissed off that I'd trapped his ankle in the door! After freeing him he was hand cuffed and arrested for failing to provide a breath test. His passenger, a work colleague in his early 30s was crying like a baby. He was being given a lift home from work and understandably he was absolutely terrified. Sadly we had to allow the driver to go to hospital for treatment to a minor leg injury and so whilst Rod went up to the QA in the ambulance with him I set about clearing up the mess we had caused. A decent sized crowd had now gathered and I kept calling out for the driver of the red Capri but no-one came forward. Eventually a little old man tugged on my sleeve and spoke to me.

"Are you looking for the driver of that red car?" he enquired.

"Yes I am do you know where he is?" I asked.

"Yes he ran away after the accident, flat out he was, ran straight down Fawcett Road and disappeared" said my elderly witness.

I did a check on PNC on the registration and it transpired that the Capri owner was in fact disqualified. I'll have to catch up with him later.

After receiving treatment at QA our mad driver was brought down to Central custody for interview. He blew a borderline breath test that put him just under the limit and during the subsequent interview he said he'd driven like that for a laugh. It was his car and he had a full time job as a milkman, although I doubt he delivered his milk as quickly as he drove his car. At Portsmouth Magistrates Court a few weeks later Stephen Bull pleaded guilty to reckless driving and various other offences and was disqualified from driving for just 12 months. It should have been a lot more.

Our Ford Capri driver was quite possibly one of the only disqualified drivers I've ever really felt sorry for. He voluntarily gave himself up to me at the nick the next evening. During a brief interview he said how he had actually laughed and thanked the other driver out loud after the near miss in Goldsmith Avenue. He said he couldn't believe his luck that the Old Bill was chasing somebody else and not him and that for the first time in ages he could have a nice relaxed drive home. He was as sick as a parrot when the same car hit him a couple of minutes later.

Feelings between Sgt Turpin and the remainder of the Relief were at an all time low, especially since Craig had departed. We were in the canteen having breakfast on earlies and whilst listening to the news on the radio we learned of the latest IRA attack in Northern Ireland where yet another British soldier had been shot dead. I'm quite certain that Dick Turpin did it purely to wind us up but he never knew when to stop and all too often he crossed the line. He started his usual diatribe about how we should pull out of Northern Ireland and that the Provisional IRA had a legitimate fight against the British and that any soldiers over there should lay down their arms and refuse to fight the politician's war and if they didn't and subsequently died, well, that was their hard luck. We'd heard a lot of it before but the line about soldiers deserving to die was a new one on us. Dick Hanna was a former squaddie who had served in Northern Ireland and seen friends and colleagues die. He flew across the canteen table on both his knees and as he landed the other side he grabbed Dick Turpin by the neck and pushed him hard up against the wall. He put his breakfast fork up to Turpins throat and told him in no uncertain terms that if he ever said anything like that again he would not be responsible for his actions. Dick then let go of him and Turpin slumped back into his chair as Dick stormed out of the canteen and along the corridor towards Chief Inspector Hipkiss's office. We could hear Dick from the canteen demanding that the Chief Inspector get rid of Sgt Turpin immediately or the whole Relief would put in transfer requests, which was news to us! We heard the office door shut and things went very quiet. Dick Turpin meanwhile reckoned he was the victim of a gross over reaction. We all made our excuses and left him on his own. It was the last shift we ever had with him because the Chief Inspector took a lot of notice of Dick Hanna's rant and Turpin got an overnight move to Fareham custody centre and we didn't have to put in for transfers elsewhere.

On 14th March we were on late turn and were busily attending to all the usual routine calls. We came in for grub about 6pm and I got called into the Station Sgts office. Roger was already in there and Jock Campbell told us to go home and pack a bag, we were going to Nottingham at 8 pm tonight.

"Nottingham? What for, what's going on up there?"

"No idea" he said "Just go and get ya kit and get yourselves to Fratton for 20 hundred hours" as he lit another fag "And can you pick up Steve Moore from his home address on the way up there?"

As ordered Roger, Steve and I arrived at Fratton for 8 pm where we met up with all the other RSG lads and we boarded a carrier and headed up to HQ at Winchester. We got fed the usual chicken curry and then assembled downstairs in the large hall for a briefing from Chief Constable John Duke. Nottinghamshire Police had called upon several other forces for assistance in policing the Nottinghamshire coal fields because flying pickets were being sent to Nottingham from neighbouring areas like Yorkshire and Derbyshire. The National Coal Board, backed up by Prime Minister Margaret Thatcher had recently announced the closure of Cortonwood Colliery in Yorkshire. This was to be the first of 20 pit closures with the loss of 20,000 jobs. The National Union of Mineworkers (NUM) led by Arthur Scargill had responded by calling for a national strike. The big problem was, the strike was declared unofficial as no secret ballots had been held, thus making the dispute technically illegal. Miners were split, especially in the more moderate county of Nottinghamshire and those who chose to work had the lawful right to do so and it was the role of the police to ensure that they enjoyed their legal right to work without fear of reprisal. That was the theory anyway. The reality was that Nottinghamshire Police were completely overwhelmed by the demands for policing the dispute and brought about the biggest mutual-aid programme that this country has ever seen with officers throughout England and Wales being drafted in to protect the moderate Nottinghamshire miners.

It was a big operation and they had no idea when we would be home. Mr Duke then made a huge mistake in telling us that uniform stores which were in the basement at headquarters would be open for us to go and help ourselves to any items of uniform or equipment we hadn't had time to pack or needed to replace. It was just like the first day of the New Year sales on Oxford Street, with coppers coming out with arm fulls of goodies; new jumpers, helmet badges, torches, hand cuffs, new truncheons, in fact anything they could carry. If it was shiny it got lifted.

Almost 200 officers, the whole of the Support Group then boarded four coaches to head north to Nottingham. Whilst en route we listened to the news on the radio and were horrified to learn that a miner had died during scuffles outside a Nottinghamshire pit. The mood changed from one of schoolboy-on-big-coach-trip to one of sombre anticipation. It was 2am by the time we arrived in Nottingham. Nobody seemed to know where we were supposed to go or what we were to do when we got there. Gaggles of senior officers could be seen making phone calls and attempting to ascertain where we were to go next. We drove around the countryside until it got light and then drove around a bit more. We were getting hungry and there's nothing worse than a large group of hungry coppers. I think I'd rather face a charging bull elephant. We got directed to Sherwood Lodge, Notts Police's headquarters for breakfast. There are four big car parks at Sherwood Lodge and it was utter chaos, with hundreds of Police vans from seemingly every Police force in the country all trying to either get in or get out of the car park. And no wonder it had all gone wrong, because there in the middle of the crossroads desperately waving his arms around like a windmill was a Superintendent! It was hilarious.

Anyway half an hour later our intrepid coach driver had found somewhere to park up and we formed up beside it and then marched towards the main building. There were coppers everywhere in the car park and they took the piss out of us mercilessly. We were a disciplined unit and marched everywhere we went in what was loosely termed as 'orderly movement' but to the others was a source of much amusement. It really didn't bother us because it did look smart and disciplined. We joined the end of the queue for breakfast. It must have been 400 officers long and snaked out the front doors, down the steps and across the grass. It was another hour before we got in and sat down to eat a polystyrene plate full of sausage, egg, bacon and beans.

After breakfast we went back out to the car park where we met up with a load of our own carriers that had been driven up overnight by Traffic officers and then we got deployed to our first pit. It was quite a long drive from Sherwood Lodge to Pye Hill No.1 Colliery which we eventually found at the bottom of a steep hill. It was quite a small place and evidently very old. The place looked deserted until we got ushered into the pit canteen by one of the ladies that worked there. It was just like a school dining room really, with a big long counter where the food was served and lots of old Formica topped tables and those hard plastic, stackable chairs that grated across the tiled floor. We were made very welcome by the canteen ladies and they offered us breakfast, which we gladly accepted because we hadn't eaten for over an hour. They served us up sausage, egg, bacon and beans but on decent china plates this time and each server greeted us with a smile and said.

"Are ya all roit me duck?"

We smiled sweetly back. I've been called lots of things over the years but never 'me duck' but it didn't sound threatening or insulting so we assumed it was OK. As we tucked into our breakfast the Pit Deputy came in and welcomed us to Pye Hill. He said the lads would be glad to see us here when they came up from their shift about 1330 hours. He went on to tell us that both Pye Hill No. 2 (which was across the road) and No. 1 were fast approaching the end of their natural time anyway because the coal was just about dried up, so these two pits would be closing regardless of what Arthur 'bloody' Scargill says! He clearly wasn't fond of the NUM leader.

After he had left we split up into pairs to patrol the area on foot whilst others got an hours kip. Steve and I toured the local village and the pit which must have taken us all of 15 minutes. There wasn't a great deal to see and do. Considering we had been on duty now for almost 22 hours I didn't feel too bad. At 1330 hours we saw our first group of miners exit the lift shaft and head towards the changing rooms. The whites of their eyes pierced through their blackened faces as they stared at us in silence. One by one they left as the afternoon shift clocked on. They all seemed rather bemused by our presence.

Once they were down the pit we kept ourselves awake by playing 5 a-side football on the roughest piece of grass I've ever played on. We were all completely knackered after half an hour. Then at 6 o'clock they fed us again and an hour later we got relieved by a van full of officers from Sussex. But where the hell were we going to sleep? Nobody seemed to have an answer for that one until we got directed to what I think was part of Nottinghamshire's training department, a sort of large manor house in the middle of nowhere. We got directed to a room upstairs which turned out to be the firearms storage facility and the only place to sleep was the floor. There was no bedding and we merely crashed out where we dropped. There just wasn't enough room for all of us and so some of the lads settled down outside on the stairs. We had now been on duty for more than 30 hours and I felt sick where I was so tired.

They woke us up at 0100 hours to start work again. There were no showers and just two toilets, so it wasn't very pleasant. We drove back to Pye Hill to relieve the Sussex crew from the previous night. We followed the same routine as the previous day and at 1700 hours we got stood down and ordered to return to Sherwood Lodge. Then it was back on the coach and the long drive back to Winchester where we arrived at 2300 hours, some 22 hours since we started duty. My own bed had never looked so inviting. I think I slept most of Saturday.

At 3pm on Saturday the phone rang. It was Jock Campbell. Be at Fratton for 1400 hours Sunday, you're going back to Nottingham for a week. At least this time we were a little more prepared I suppose. And by the time we got up there at least they had somewhere for us to stay. It was an old army camp at Grantham in Lincolnshire. What a desolate, grey and dull place the town of Grantham is. I think it must have been left behind in the 19th century. The army base wasn't much better either and had clearly been hurriedly recommissioned to house hundreds of coppers from Hampshire, Sussex, City of London, Hertfordshire, Bedfordshire, Essex, Dorset, Greater Manchester and the Mct. We had to put together army issue camp beds and were given green sleeping bags that must have been made for a midget; they only came up to just below my chest. There were no wardrobes or anything to put your personal kit away in, so it just stayed in your kit bag on the floor. We queued for everything from the toilets to the canteen. Breakfast was quite nice though. It was sausage, egg, bacon and beans.

We were up to start work at 3 in the morning, which really wasn't very pleasant and then it was into the carriers and out to our pit, which again was Pye Hill No. 1. It was bloody freezing cold to. There was a severe frost, the likes of which us southern city boys just weren't used to. We arrived at Pye Hill about 0430 and Steve and I took the first patrol out by the main gate. As we stood around in the cold we started to notice that our uniforms were turning white with frost. I couldn't feel my feet or my hands and I was quite convinced that my ears were going to break and just fall off. Our one hour out on foot couldn't end soon enough and we practically ran back to the glorious warmth of the pit canteen, where at 0600 those delightful ladies served us breakfast. It was very nice and consisted of sausage, egg, bacon and beans.

Later in the day we were invited to actually go down to the pit face and see what being a coal miner was all about. It was too good an invitation to turn down and so in pairs we took it in turns to get a lengthy safety briefing and then got kitted out in an orange boiler suit, safety helmet and lamp before stepping inside a rusty, rickety cage that was actually the lift that dropped like a stone several hundred feet below. My heart was pounding as we stepped out the cage and onto the pit floor. It was actually quite windy and the walls were lined with loads of electric lamps. There were pipes and cables everywhere and in the distance you could hear drilling. We then walked for about half a mile, maybe more through a number of black tunnels towards the coal face itself. The further down we went the warmer it got and the thicker the air. It really did feel claustrophobic and I was starting to question quite why I was doing this. The noise increased and then there we were right at the coal face itself. I was amazed to see that some of the miners were actually swinging a pick axe at the wall and digging by hand. Two others were using pneumatic drills but most of the work seemed to be the old fashioned way. Our guide explained that because Pye Hill was so old that this was the only way to get the coal out. Other more modern pits used big boring machines but here it was full on hard labour. The heat here was incredible, almost stifling and mixed in with the coal dust it made it particularly difficult to breath. We stayed for about 10 minutes and then made our way back up to the surface. The fresh air never tasted so good and my admiration for the hard graft that these men endure every day of their working lives was huge. Every single one of us who went down there said the same thing and we would never complain about our own jobs ever again.

Boredom was starting to set in, as there are only so many foot patrol laps you can do around the pit perimeter. The tiny village attached to it hadn't seen a single policeman in the last 50 years and suddenly found itself swamped by 20 foreign coppers and it wasn't long before the novelty wore off on both sides. Once the miners were beneath ground there was very little to do until they resurfaced. Pye Hill was unlikely to get hit by flying pickets and so we were scratching around for things to occupy our minds. Roger had brought along a sponge tennis ball and between us we invented hand tennis which we played using the dining room tables in a sort of cross between table tennis and grass tennis. We started a league and it helped us build up an appetite for our next breakfast. After a few days we got really good at it.

On the Wednesday morning we heard rumours that a mass picket was heading towards Nottingham from Yorkshire and that a large number of PSU's (Police Support Units) were being sent to intercept them. We climbed aboard our carriers and set off from Grantham at about 0300. There was a really severe fog outside and our progress was very slow. Convoy driving is hard enough when you can see the other vehicles, it's even harder when you can't. I was sat in my usual seat at the back and we were the very last van amongst a convoy of more than 50 vehicles. It wasn't long before I fell asleep. Sometime later I woke up, aware that we had stopped.

"Where are we?" I sleepily enquired.

"On the M1" somebody replied.

I looked out the window and could just see the central barrier right next to us, which meant that we were in the outside lane.

"But we've stopped" I squealed.

With that we started reversing back down lane 3 of the M1 in the fog. I suddenly realised that I was now right at the front of the convoy and would be the first to get wiped out if our carrier got hit. We all screamed at our driver and the Sgt who basically told us to shut up. We were supposed to have crossed the M1 through the last Emergency Crossover Point (ECP) in order to form a solid road block using the vans across the south bound M1 to prevent the pickets from continuing their journey.

"What? A solid road block? Haven't they heard of Reading and the M4? They can't be serious surely?" I protested.

With that I saw a Traffic motorcyclist pass us in lane 2 heading south on the north bound! We found the ECP shortly after and then reversed across the south bound lanes and stopped on the hard shoulder whilst all the other carriers did the same. Although there was very little traffic around at this time it was still the M1 in the dark in pea soup fog! We were far from happy. A number of senior officers then gathered together and thankfully a sane decision was reached that in fact we wouldn't form a solid road block but would cover every south bound exit from the motorway in order to turn them back north again. It worked and no-one got wiped out either.

By mid morning we got directed to Sherwood Lodge for breakfast and joined another massive queue for the dining room. Our unit had just reached the doors when they were shut in our face. They were full and it would be another half hour before we could get in. There were two pay phones right by the doors so it seemed like an opportune moment to phone home to check that all was well. Tricia answered the phone to tell me she had been to the doctors that morning to confirm her suspicions. She was pregnant. Good job I'm doing loads of overtime then which I don't think was the right reply! It was terrific news and helped lighten the mood after our motorway madness experience earlier in the day. I got lots of good advice of course from people like Steve, Roger and Dave who were already fathers. Steve welcomed me to the club because his wife

Carol had only recently given birth for the first time in January. Then the doors opened and in we went for breakfast. What have we got this morning then? Hmmnn, sausage, egg, bacon and beans. I think I'll have some of that then. We sat down and the entire breakfast conversation consisted of gruesome nappy changing stories and how my life would never be the same again.

After grub it was back in the vans and we got directed to Hucknall pit, just outside the town of Hucknall, a much industrialised area that was black with soot. No sooner had we arrived than we got directed to Hucknall Police Station for breakfast. You could have anything you like so long as it was sausage, egg, bacon and beans!

One of our number was PC Mick Donnellan who had recently transferred onto Green Relief at Southsea. He sat next to me in the carrier as we were driving towards Hucknall that morning and asked me if I missed the Isle of Wight at all? It was a curious question but one that bore a purpose. Mick can only be described as one of those characters who always lived life on the edge. He was always doing the most outrageous things, not to impress, but because he was close to being an out and out nutter. After he had done something mischievous he would grin in a manner that made him look like he had just escaped from a nearby institution.

It transpired he used to live on the island and had joined the RAF with my brother and during their basic training they had travelled together on their bikes up to RAF Conningsby in Lincolnshire. Half way through their training a number of them entered a local Chinese takeaway one Saturday night and Mick took it upon himself, in his drunken state, to take the piss out of the staff there as teenagers are inclined to do. In the corner was a much older man waiting for his order. After witnessing Mick doing the very worst Chinese impersonations imaginable the man decided to intervene and requested Mick to refrain from such behaviour. Mick fronted him up and they had a serious nose to nose verbal confrontation. After the man left with his order Mick grinned in his usual manner. Come Monday morning he was no longer grinning as the new camp commander carpeted Mick and they yet again had a nose to nose verbal confrontation, only this time Mick kept his mouth very firmly shut! Within a couple of weeks Mick had been drummed out of the RAF for being unsuitable and had then joined the Hampshire Constabulary!

Whilst I was mulling over the irony of that last statement he went on to confess to buzzing another motorcyclist on the island. He would lay in wait about 9.30 every evening for a man on a Honda 200, wearing old fashioned white gauntlets, to ride through Northwood. If Mick timed it right he would overtake him at about 80 mph just as the man was about to turn right into a side road. I was amazed by this story because my father would complain bitterly about this maniac on another bike who would deliberately shoot past him so close that he almost fell off as he rode home from work each night! Donnellan grinned again.

As we sat down to eat our second breakfast of the day Mick was now in very high spirits, which is a dangerous state for someone of his unstable mentality to be in. He finished his food in about 30 seconds flat and then stated he was still hungry! So he set about eating the polystyrene plate and then for desert he ate his plastic knife and fork. But he wasn't finished yet. He then stood up and lifted a dart board from the wall and bit two chunks from it clean off and swallowed the lot. After being told by some of us to put it back he left the dining room to go to the toilet. He left via the twin swing doors and out into the corridor. The doors were the old wooden type fire doors with opaque glass, reinforced with wire mesh. About five minutes later we became aware of an argument developing outside the doors between a PC in a blue shirt and a senior officer in a white shirt. The blue shirt was Mick Donnellan. The argument was getting more and more heated and they were nose to nose, RAF style. It got so loud that a canteen with over 100 officers in it fell completely silent as we all tried listening in on the dispute. But then it got physical and both of them ended up on the floor, wrestling each other. Somebody ran over and opened the door to reveal Mick sat on top of an Inspector, who was flat on his back. Mick had hold of the Inspectors collar with his left hand whilst his right fist was clenched and drawn back ready to punch him in the face! There was a tangible sharp in-take of breath from every one of us. Then in an instant both of them leapt to their feet and laughed out loud as they brushed each other down. The Inspector was Mick's brother Paul and they had conspired together to wind everybody up. Seems the balance of the mental well being was a family trait.

After policing the area for the rest of the day we drove the 50 miles back to Grantham arriving there about half ten at night. As we walked from the car park back towards our billet so we came across a naked officer who was hand cuffed to a small tree. He pleaded with us as we filed past him to unlock the cuffs.

"What force are you from mate?" was the general question.

"The Met" came his reply.

"Sorry mate, can't help ya" was the response.

I'm not sure what he had done to warrant such treatment but being from the Met didn't exactly endear us towards him. Not that we had anything in particular against our London colleagues, it was just that they called us County Mounties and thought we all ate carrots for breakfast and they just did everything on such a massive scale. They also had some rogues amongst them and we were constantly amused by the stories and rumours that filtered down about some of their antics. One of their number was so bored with being up in Nottingham that he stole one of the Mets green Bedford buses and drove back to London. Another 'borrowed' his Chief Inspectors staff car to travel into Mansfield for the evening, got pissed and then wrapped it around a tree on the way back, whilst two others were arrested in Nottingham city centre for being drunk and disorderly! And they covered anything that moved in little round stickers that said 'I've met the Met' on them. They were on every door, window, road sign, pit canteen counter, toilet cistern, toilet seat, drain pipe, miners cars, on foreign policeman's backs, in fact everywhere you looked there was a sticker. On one occasion they completely plastered a Dorset Police carrier with hundreds of them. It must have taken them hours. We had to admit that one was quite funny!

By Friday afternoon we'd all had enough really, we were dog tired and slept like babies on the coach back south. We were all looking forward to a full weekend off, having been promised that we would not be coming back up to Nottingham next week. On Saturday afternoon my phone rang. It was Jock Campbell again.

"Pack ya bags Steve you're all going to North Wales tomorrow, be at Fratton for 1400 hours".

"North Wales?" I asked

"This dispute is escalating by the day, now the Welsh are calling for mutual aid" said Jock "With all this overtime I keep giving you RSG boys I hope you remember to buy me some fags" he laughed, although I knew it was the biggest of hints.

Roger and I teamed up again and after another HQ briefing at Winchester so we boarded coaches for the long drive to North Wales. Our accommodation was the Derbyshire Miners Holiday Village, on the outskirts of Prestatyn. It was a sort of Butlins holiday camp for miners who would have been mightily pissed off if they knew it had been taken over by the Old Bill. It was luxury in comparison with Grantham. Two to a room, with en-suite bathrooms, a decent bar and two snooker tables. We could get to like this.

We still had to get up at stupid o'clock though to drive 20 miles to the Point of Ayr Colliery which was right on the coast. Apparently the actual coal face was under the sea. It was a strange set up because the picket line was in a lay-by on the main road opposite the lane that eventually led to the pit itself. We were quite pleased to actually meet some pickets at last. They were a jovial bunch who were amazed to hear that we were from Portsmouth. There were about 200 of them I suppose and we were all getting along famously until the press turned up about five minutes before the convoy of working miners arrived in fully caged coaches. Then the pushing and shoving started, screaming out the word "Scab" at the coaches and throwing the odd stone. No sooner had they gone in than they said.

"Right, see you boyos tomorrow mornin then" and they all buggered off.

And that's how it was every morning. Except on the days when the media obviously had far more important things to cover and the pickets couldn't really be bothered with all that pushing and shoving stuff so they just shouted instead!

On the Thursday evening Chief Inspector Bob Dawes, our unit commander gathered us altogether in the bar, not to buy us a drink but to inform us that North Wales Police had requested that we stay for a second week. However there was a catch. Hampshire and North Wales had failed to reach agreement over payments and costs and it meant that we would have to stay here the weekend, without pay and resume duties the following Monday. If there was even one dissenter amongst us who really wanted to go home then all of us would have to return home and not come back. No one dared raise their hand, although it was quite obvious there were one or two seriously thinking about it. So we stayed the weekend in the great metropolis of Prestatyn! After walking around the town on the Saturday morning we just went back to our accommodation and watched TV and played a lot of snooker. During the evening we were joined by a number of Welsh officers who had heard we were in town and came to join us for a drink. One of our number, an extremely brash Yorkshireman by the name of John Small met his opposite number, a Welsh DC. Both of them enjoyed being the centre of attention, doubly so when they were pissed. I'm not sure how it started or who suggested it but a contest between the two of them was called for. The contest was to drink a pint of unbeaten raw eggs, on top of several pints of beer. There was lots of cheering and clapping as the two pint mugs were placed on the bar. They stood face to face and both of them downed their pint in a matter of seconds. It was stomach churning just to watch. It was declared a draw. Time for a second pint of eggs then. Another couple of dozen were broken into the glasses and then on the count of three they lifted their glasses and started again. The Welsh DC got half way through his and then puked everywhere. You've never seen 30 odd people move so quickly in your life. John Small successfully finished his second pint and was hailed the winner. And he didn't let us forget about it for the rest of the week either.

At the end of the second week it was time to return home and for the second time we were guaranteed at least a week off because by now the force were having to send up non RSG officers because of the huge number of commitments. However it wasn't a 'week off' per se because of the number of abstractions from front line duties it meant that those of us who were left each week now had to work 12 hour shifts instead of 8 hours. Upon returning to Southsea we met up with our new Patrol Sgt, Mick Moorse. He had been transferred from Fareham Traffic Division after accidentally driving a Police Jaguar XJ6 into the bucket of a JCB which then smashed through the windscreen of the Jag almost taking his head off. His punishment was to become our Sgt. If I thought it was going to take years before I was allowed to forget the bald tyres on the area car episode then I had nothing on what he had to endure. But he took it all in good heart and he was a breath of fresh air to Green Relief and exactly what we needed to boost our morale after Red Dick had done his damage.

After just a week back at home it was time to head back up to Nottingham. By now most of us knew what to expect and went fully prepared with little extras from home to make life that much easier. The latest must have gadget was the mobile Walkman personal cassette player and it either became a thing to be treasured during the long boring drives or a source of immense irritation amongst those who weren't into music because of the constant faint sound of guitars or vocals that sounded like they were on the end of a long distance telephone call. Personally I loved mine and took it everywhere listening to Michael Jacksons *'Thriller'* album, Nick Kershaw's *'Wouldn't it be Good'* or anything by Level 42. But the one song that summed up the mood of the moment was Frankie Goes to Hollywood with *'Two Tribes'*. Although the song was essentially about the American and Russian Presidents fighting over their stockpile of nuclear weapons, it also had huge significance for us because of the miners strike. Here were two tribes of human beings, miners and police officers, battling it out on a daily basis and that air raid siren at the beginning had a rather more personal meaning for me of course!

Another essential item became the TV and the video recorder. I've no idea how it started but it very quickly became the routine that first thing on a Monday morning your van crew would travel into the nearest town to your allotted pit and find a Radio Rentalls or a Redifusion shop where they would very kindly donate, on a weeks loan one TV and one VCR. Then a selection of video cassettes would be hired, purchased or brought from home and these definitely prevented the boredom from becoming too much in between duties at the pit.

The food distribution in Nottinghamshire appeared to have become slightly better organised now that the initial panic had eased and everybody had settled into a routine. Breakfast still consisted of sausage, egg, bacon and beans of course no matter where you had it. But another food supply was taking on legendary status on a daily basis; the doggy bag. Everyday we would collect our rations like prisoners of war collecting their Red Cross parcels. Every day they packed the same items into those little brown paper bags; a round of corned beef sandwiches, a Pork Farms Cornish pastie, an apple, a Mars bar, a packet of custard creams or bourbon creams and a wax carton of orange squash. The Cornish pastie, which looked like a crushed Armadillo, was a constant source of amusement or suspicion, depending on your constitution because the meat inside was always tinged green and most of us just tossed them into the nearest bin. However there were those officers who actually collected their colleagues unwanted pasties during the week, took them home and chucked them in the freezer to be used some other time. One such person was PC Mick Murphy who was based at Southsea but who hailed from South Africa. He actually thought these pasties were a delicacy and couldn't understand why we wouldn't eat them. He dined out on them for months!

The other food of note was the Maxpax instant drink. I wish I'd taken shares out in the company at the beginning of 1984, because they must have made an absolute killing. The hot chocolate was everybody's favourite, made with luke warm water from the green water carriers we had on board each van, it kept us alive during the freezing cold dark nights and early mornings. You could also get Maxpax coffee, tea and a sort of vegetable soup that looked like puke once you poured the water onto it.

Phoning home was a nightmare because the camp at Grantham only had four pay phone booths with about 500 officers all wanting to use them at once. It took over an hour to get to the front of the queues most nights.

After phoning Tricia one evening I walked into the lounge at 10 o'clock just in time to catch the news of the fatal shooting of WPC Yvonne Fletcher outside the Libyan Embassy in London. There was total silence throughout the huge lounge as we looked at footage of her hat and those three Police helmets rolling around in the road with no-one able to retrieve them. One of the Met PC'S left the lounge in tears. He'd been at Hendon with WPC Fletcher and knew her well.

The journey home always seemed to take forever. Friday night on the M1 was quite often a stop-start affair and it would usually take over four hours to get back to Winchester. Most of the time we just slept, but on a couple of occasions high jinks came into play. Hampshire had taken four coaches to Nottingham and our coach driver seemed to be having a bit of a race with one of his colleagues, no real speed involved, but lots of jockeying for position on the motorway. Sat in front of Roger and I were Mick Keating and Mick Donnellan, both of whom you could say were bordering on the side of madness, especially Donnellan. Both of them had given colleagues in the coach we had overtaken several times lots of verbal and certain hand gestures. They were as high as kites and things were going down hill rapidly. I saw Donnellan whisper into Mick Keatings ear and you just knew that something even worse was about to unfold. Our coach was in lane two and appeared to be about to overtake the coach in front of it. As soon as it manoeuvred to do so up they jumped, down came their trousers and underpants as they planted their backsides against the coach window and mooned towards their colleagues.

Except it wasn't a coach full of coppers. The look on the mostly female pensioners faces, obviously on a day trip out somewhere was something to behold, as one by one they all pointed and laughed. I think it unlikely they ever knew that it was two police officers that had mooned to them but the two Mick's were somewhat subdued for the rest of the journey!

After spending another week up there it was back to Southsea with a bump because Chelsea were in town and that meant as many officers as they could muster for what was surely going to be as bad as any Millwall or Southampton match. The Chelsea 'Head Hunters' had a fearsome reputation that the 6.57 Crew would want to test to the limit and visa versa of course.

It wasn't just opposing fans or Portsmouth's own residents that the 6.57 Crew liked to upset. Believe it not they even targeted the Pompey players! Whilst sitting in the van in Frogmore Road with Ray Harbour watching the crowds gather, we became aware that the upper crust of the 6.57 Crew were gathering outside the side door to 'The Pompey' pub. It was quite obvious they were waiting for something or someone. It was about an hour or so before kick-off. Then one of Pompey's star players Mark Hateley arrived on foot, resplendent in his shiny suit. As he approached the main entrance to the ground so he was surrounded, not by the usual autograph hunting kids but by the 6.57 Crew. They patted him on the back, brushed his hair with their hands and appeared to be chatting to him like a brother. Hateley smiled but appeared uneasy. He gave one of them something by hand and as soon as he had done so then they all broke ranks and allowed him to continue and sign the scrapbooks being wielded about by the aforementioned school kids. A few minutes later another player arrived. This time it was Alan Biley who was surrounded by the same group. He didn't seem too pleased to see them either and in fact at one point appeared to be pressed against the wall. As Ray and I approached, the group quickly dispersed and Biley made his way into the ground. We followed him in and caught up with him outside the players lounge. It transpired that each player is assigned a certain number of complimentary tickets per game and it was these that the 6.57 Crew were after. What had started as a one-off gesture of kindness by one of the players towards a member of the Crew a few weeks earlier had quickly degenerated into what they perceived to be a 'right' to free tickets from the players. By using intimidation as their main weapon they would basically mug the very people whom they claimed to passionately support. From then on the Police kept a very close eye on the players arriving at the ground and I believe that the rules governing such tickets were also changed.

Chelsea brought about 3000 fans down and the atmosphere was very tense. By half time you just knew it was going to end in tears. There were obviously Chelsea fans in the Milton End but there were also several hundred of them up in D Section of the south stand. The match ended in a 2-2 draw but it didn't matter. The final whistle might just as well have been the starting pistol to ignite the trouble. Those up in D Section ripped the hard plastic seats from their frames and used them like Frisbee's, throwing them at Pompey supporters and then at the Police. My section was ordered onto the pitch to face this barrage of blue flying saucers and once they had seemingly removed every available seat they then started throwing coins at us. Seats were easy to dodge but you don't see the coins coming and if you get hit by one they can do a lot of damage. The dogs were having a field day and keeping the hooligan element at bay so we got dragged back outside the ground to clear the Pompey boys away before releasing the Chelsea fans. As we moved along Specks Lane clearing it of Pompey fans so the noise at the north east corner got louder. And then just as in the first Millwall match so the old wooden gates came crashing to the ground and out they poured like a swarm of angry wasps, lashing out at everything that moved. Yet again the residents around Fratton Park had to put up with running battles as the now familiar scenes were played out from street to street. And yet again as we frustrated the two warring parties so it was the 6.57 Crew who vented their anger against the shop windows of their own city. As Police shield units were deployed so the yobs were pushed down Fratton Road and eventually dispersed.

And before I knew it we were heading back to Nottingham but this time in an altogether different style. We were convinced it was a wind up to begin with when told to report for duty at Southampton airport, because we were going to fly up to the East Midlands and collect our carriers from there. The force chartered two Boeing 737s from Orion Airways and Brittania Airways and the flight north would take just 18 minutes. As we paraded in a nearby hangar so John Duke gave us a speech that Monty would have been proud of just before D-Day. By reducing the total number of travelling hours for each officer from twelve to two each week the force saved an absolute fortune in overtime payments. But more importantly for us it meant that from the time I left home to the time I arrived in Nottingham was little more than an hour. It was great fun to. Special tee shirts were made with 'Hampshire First Air Bourne' on them and it was a bit like a giant lads outing. Even the cabin crew got involved as we all mimicked their safety briefing, pointing out the emergency exits fore and aft together with all the other movements and directions they give. It was a truly inspirational decision to fly us up there and back every week and we even made the front page of the national newspapers. Officers from other forces took the piss of course humming the dam busters theme whenever we marched past them or would do reverse googles using their thumbs and fore fingers but they only did it because they were as jealous as hell, because by the time I got home and sat in my front room, most of them were still trundling down the M1 and had another four hours travel time left. Who's laughing now?

The other new thing we had was a better place to stay. It was another disused army camp just outside the Nottinghamshire village of Ollerton and it was called Proteous. It was more like a German prisoner of war camp than an army camp, just like the ones you see in the films, with a number of Nissan huts used for the accommodation and a large canteen and a separate bar area. It felt nicer than Grantham did and was actually quite homely. Each of the huts housed about 30 officers in bunk beds and at least we had our own metal lockers and half decent showers and wash rooms. These were accessed via a concrete corridor that linked several huts together. In the centre of each hut was a coal fed boiler that heated the room although as this was late spring we didn't really need them yet. And at least we didn't have that 50 mile drive from Grantham and back everyday just to reach Nottingham before we even started work which was a relief. The food was better to although breakfast still consisted of sausage, egg, bacon and beans it was of a much higher standard than our previous place.

At the entrance to the dining hall there was a table with souvenirs laid out on it. Yes, somebody in Nottingham hit on the idea that perhaps policemen just might like a souvenir or two to remind them of this great big adventure we were on. And they were right, we bought dozens and dozens of replica miner's lamps, which came in three different sizes, together with figurines of policemen and miners carved out of coal and set in resin. They even made one of a copper with wings for us Hampshire boys. I had to have one of those! Over the next few weeks they introduced more and more products and must have made an absolute killing. Some of us had already starting collecting 'motty' tags from the various pits we visited in our travels. These tags were round brass plates, a bit bigger than a 10p coin and they had the pit name cast into them. Each miner had his own particular reference number and his number would be stamped onto his tag and before he entered the mine he would leave his motty tag on a special board so that in the event of an accident beneath ground the authorities would know exactly who was still down there. It wasn't long before we started collecting the tags from our pits and having our own collar numbers stamped onto them and placing them on our key rings. I've still got all of mine.

So far we'd experienced very little in the way of confrontation with any flying pickets, but that was about to change. My unit was based at the very modern Bevacotes Colliery for a week and whilst going about our patrols one morning we got hastily redeployed to Bentinck a few miles away because a mass picket was en route. It was a warm summer's morning as a convoy of some 50 Police vans and carriers filed into the main car park at the pit. There were pickets everywhere, hundreds of them with more arriving. My heart beat increased significantly, this looked like it might be serious. They were massing alongside an area outside the pit entrance. I looked on as more Police units arrived, including the Mets Mounted Units, dogs and two mobile custody units. More and more cars and vans arrived disgorging pickets whilst others arrived on foot. It was like watching a re-enactment of some medieval battle where columns of foot soldiers were formed up in squares with their generals sat on horse back on a nearby hill, directing operations, before sending out the message to charge.

One by one the Police units were deployed as the picket grew bigger and stronger. By early afternoon it must have numbered some 500 strong as they waited for the shift changeover to commence. Police horses were next to be deployed and stood between the police lines and the main gate as a last line of defence. Then my section got deployed and as we marched out to the assembled throng so my heart was now pounding. We took up a front line position as the picket line increased sideways. I was now face to face with hundreds of snarling Yorkshireman, all seemingly dressed in donkey jackets. We stood there glaring at each other in a sort of prolonged stand-off, each of us waiting for the other to react. Then came the order to link arms, which meant that the buses containing the afternoon shift of working miners was on its way. As soon as we did that the pickets knew to and it started. The screaming of the words "Scab" filled the air as the surge forward towards the gate commenced. The picket line must have been at least ten deep and I think I had as many Police lines behind me. Linking arms with your colleague is fairly easy and a reasonably strong human locking device. However the weak point is the hands. The technique involves you hooking your fingers together and if you have slightly long nails you can do yourself some serious damage. The weakness comes as pressure is exerted upon your line and the linked arms become stretched. No matter how hard you try your fingers will give way first and once that happens the arms unfold and the chain breaks. The trouble is no-one wants to become that weak link and so you are desperate to keep the line intact. The pushing and heaving from both sides was intense and went on for some considerable time. The noise was incredible with pickets shouting and screaming in your face whilst senior police officers bellowed out their instructions to us via hand held mega phones. Police dogs barked, sirens could be heard in the back ground as we pushed back against the picket line with every ounce of strength we could muster. The crushing sensation was awful and bloody terrifying; I'd never been in such a situation before. Suddenly though I couldn't breath. There was no oxygen. I stood up on tip toes quite literally gasping for air, trying to suck it down from above. I looked around me and it's as if time had stopped for just a second or two because all of us, both coppers and pickets were doing the same thing. Then the lines broke and we all collapsed onto our knees, dozens of us on both sides of the divide, all coughing and choking. As soon as we broke so the oxygen was allowed back in and we could breathe once again. It was a horrible experience and not one they had taught us to expect during the hours of training we had done. By the time we all got back to our feet a few seconds later the buses had swept past us and into the pit.

But the trouble just escalated from here on in. As the lines broke up I saw a number of police officers and pickets to my right fall to the ground, quite possibly for the same reasons I had just experienced. There were about 20 people on the ground and as some of them started to get to their feet I saw a picket standing on a low wall about ten feet back into the picket line raise his hand and throw a one litre sized Cresta bottle onto the head of PC Mick Southcott, a Southsea officer who I knew really well. The bottle smashed as it made contact with his helmet and the force of the blow knocked him back to the ground again. The picket was really distinctive in that he had short cropped, but really ginger hair and he was wearing a bright red tee shirt with a blue jumper tied around his waste. He saw me looking at him and instantly vanished into the crowd. Within seconds the pickets were breaking up and running in all directions, as Police officers who had clearly witnessed other offences taking place set about detaining those responsible. I saw my target heading back towards the main road. I told Inspector Dave Watson what I'd seen and he joined me as we ran up the hill towards the road. There were stones and bricks being hurled in all directions now as running battles seemed to be raging all around us. After sprinting for some 200 yards we caught up with our man and found him slumped across the bonnet of a parked car, clearly out of breath. I arrested him, cuffed him and led him back down the hill towards the car park. I took him to one of the mobile custody units where we had our photo taken together, to prevent any identification issues later and he was locked up in a cell. Mick thankfully was none the worse for his encounter with a Cresta bottle and as he wiped the juice from his face he smirked and said "Hmmnn, its frothy man".

It was several hours before things had quietened down enough for us to return to Proteous but when we did we were all completely knackered.

The following week we watched on TV as the mass picket switched from Nottinghamshire back to Yorkshire as the tactics changed from demonstrating at the colliery gates to preventing the coal from reaching the coking plant at Orgreave. Maybe we would get a bit of respite from the constant cat and mouse games down here we thought. The following morning there were rumours circulating that we would be heading north towards Yorkshire. It didn't happen straight away and we were almost disappointed when we got allocated a Nottinghamshire pit for the day. No sooner had we arrived there than we were redeployed northwards towards Orgreave. Having seen the pitched battles on the TV the night before we were obviously going to need riot shields. However none of our units had any, they were being used by other Hampshire units who were still in bed back at Proteous. We actually had to drive past Proteous to head north towards Yorkshire and requested permission from a certain Hampshire Chief Inspector to stop off and grab our shields. He refused and said we had to go there without them. We were absolutely furious and somewhat embarrassed at the prospect of turning up to assist our colleagues in a full blown riot situation but without the proper kit.

As a dozen or so Hampshire vans raced through the countryside, escorted by a couple of Nottinghamshire Police motorcycles we crossed the border into south Yorkshire. It was like entering a different country. It just looked and felt different. People glared at us, some openly swore at us or stuck two fingers up. It wasn't like Nottingham at all, they were pleased to see us there but not here, they all seemed to hate us. We arrived in a small village which had a traffic light controlled crossroads in the middle of it. The village buildings met the pavements and the whole scene was very narrow and claustrophobic. As we stopped I saw that the carrier immediately in front of us had stopped outside the local green grocers shop. There were two elderly women stood by the door gossiping and these two had been taken straight from the pages of a Giles cartoon. They had dark over coats on, wrinkled old stockings and one wore a head scarf whilst the other had a pill box hat on. Without even pausing for breath they casually leant forward and picked up handfuls of tomatoes and other vegetables from the stall outside the shop and began hurling it at the van in front, whilst screaming out "fucking pigs" and "fucking Thatcher's boot boys". It really was hilarious and as the lights turned green and the vans moved off, so they turned to each other and continued their gossip as if nothing had happened.

We arrived at Orgreave half an hour later. It was absolute chaos; I've never seen so many Police units in my life. We were ushered into a car park and greeted by a Superintendent who asked us if we were a shield unit. Our embarrassment was now complete as we were placed on stand-by. In other words, we'll only use you if you are the last we have. And there we stayed for over four hours. Other shield units came and went and we could hear much of what was going on about half a mile from our location but we were never called in. It was good to see Arthur Scargill getting arrested later on, although we had to watch that on TV too.

After more than three months of travelling around the country, not getting enough sleep, getting up at ridiculous hours of the night to start work and living on a diet of sausage, egg, bacon and beans most of us needed a break from it all. The second weekend in June saw all of Green Relief at home together for the first time since mid March. It was also Tricia's 21st birthday and so what better excuse than a big party at our house. Everybody came, it was packed and as the alcohol flowed it was the first time we had really let off steam for ages and it did us all the world of good.

But it wasn't long before we were back up there again, only this time a new tactic had been introduced; intercept duty. This concept saw us commencing work at 0200 hours to take up positions not at pits but at various road junctions and roundabouts to literally intercept cars full of pickets, turn them around and throw them back over the border into Yorkshire. Most of the time it worked. At the very least it frustrated the pickets and a lot of them never made it to that day's designated meeting point which meant that policing the actual picket was a lot easier on the Police. But it was a gutty duty. For a start it was mid summer and that meant if you were to survive the entire week you needed to get to bed at a reasonable hour and that meant by about six in the evening. That isn't easy when you are sharing a room with 30 others and it's just too hot to sleep. There was a change in our food to. We now bombed down the M1 to Leicester Forest services and were allocated an allowance of £1.30 each towards our breakfast and no it wasn't the usual fare, we could have scrambled egg, black pudding and toast here. Maybe intercept duties weren't so bad after all.

After breakfast one morning we drove back to our designated roundabout at junction 28 of the M1. We had been there for about an hour when a Derbyshire Police Mini Metro panda car pulled up in front of us. A huge PC got out and put his helmet on. He looked really miserable as he approached the passenger door of our carrier, where Inspector Danny Daniels was sitting.

"Excuse me sir" said the PC "but can I ask what you are doing here?" he droned in a monotone sort of voice.

Mr Daniels explained that we were on intercept duty and this was our designated point. The PC listened intently.

"I'm going to have to ask you to leave sir, this is Derbyshire, not Nottinghamshire" he said with a dead pan expression.

"I beg your pardon" said Danny "you can't be serious surely?"

"I'm just passing you the information sir" continued the PC "my Chief Inspector has told me to move you on, you aren't on mutual aid to Derbyshire so you have to leave I'm afraid".

There was uproar from the back of our carrier as the PC made his way back to his car. Danny got on the radio to Notts control room to clarify things and after much consultation we had to move to the other side of the roundabout, back into Nottinghamshire. And I thought we were all on the same side!

We had a Traffic officer by the name of Reg Waring as our driver one week and he was a scouser. He was very senior in service and a wily old fox. Now I liked Reg, in particular his great sense of humour. However there were a couple of guys on my section who decided that Reg was to become the butt of all their jokes and jibes for the entire week. And Reg didn't bite once. He just took it all in his stride. Until Friday morning as we returned to our pit after breakfast somewhere. As we drove through the pit gate we usually turned left to park up. Not today. Reg turned right and drove to an area right at the back of the pit, miles from the gate. He then drove our Transit into a lake of thick black coal slurry about 12 inches deep. This stuff was slightly thicker than water, stuck to everything it touched and really didn't smell too good. The lake was about 200 yards across. Reg stopped in the middle, rolled his trousers up to reveal Wellington boots, took the keys out of the ignition, smiled and said.

"I'm having the last laugh this week boys and its down to you lot to decide which one of you piss takers has to wade through this lot to come and get the keys" and with that he walked off towards the pit canteen.

It was a baking hot evening, one of those sultry, sticky ones that everyone complains about because they can't sleep. We were at a distinct disadvantage because we needed to get to sleep early in order to start work at 0200. But we were all in very high spirits and stone cold sober to. We lay on our beds just laughing and joking around, telling stories and generally just being laddish I suppose. In the bed next to me was Andy Guy. Now I'd joined the cadets with Andy and knew him well enough to know that he was the heaviest sleeper in England. In fact if they ever make sleeping an Olympic sport he'd win gold every time. By about half eight we were no-where near getting tired, except for Andy who stripped off bollock naked, lay down on his bed and pulled a single sheet over himself. He muttered something like.

"Why don't you wankers get some sleep" or something similar which just got ignored.

We all carried on mucking about for another hour or so, by which time Andy was gone. He was fast asleep and snoring like an old steam wagon. In the bed opposite me was Benny Cruikshank, one of life's naturally funny people, he thoroughly enjoyed making us laugh. Without saying anything he jumped off his bed and opened up the remains of his doggy bag. In it was a corned beef sandwich. He peeled the bread away and threw it in the bin before rolling the corned beef into a sort of torpedo shape. He was giggling like a five year old as he walked across the room to Andy's bed. He whipped off the sheet to reveal Andy laying on his side in the recovery position. Benny then carefully placed the turd shaped corned beef in between the cheeks of Andy's backside. Andy didn't even flinch and we were crying with laughter. Then Benny grabbed his uniform tie and started to tickle Andy's cheeks with it and as they twitched so the corned beef turd completely disappeared up Andy's arse! I really thought I was going to wet myself, I don't think I or anybody else in that room has ever laughed so much in their lives. At one point I could hardly breathe. I don't know what the funniest part was really, the fact that Benny even thought about doing it, let alone actually carrying it out or Andy for not waking up. It took us an hour or so to calm down and only after we had got Benny to promise to behave himself did we start to drift off to sleep.

At 0200 hours all the lights came on and the alarms starting ringing. Time to get up and start work again. Surely we've only just shut our eyes? I looked at Andy and he had his head under his sheet. He came back up with a handful of corned beef.

"Cruikshank. It couldn't have been anybody else but Cruikshank" he muttered, climbing out of his pit.

I looked across at Benny and he was still fast asleep with his mouth wide open. In a second Andy was at his bedside and before any of us could shout "no" Andy had shoved the corned beef down Benny's throat! What a great way to start the day.

Flying back and forth was now becoming routine. En route home one Friday evening there was some kind of technical hitch that delayed us from getting on board the aircraft. We were lined up on the edge of the tarmac in our section groups and had been for over half an hour. Underneath the wing of the aircraft was a gaggle of senior officers no doubt discussing the week's campaign when a PC marched out from within the rank and file officers. When I say he marched, I do mean marched out, in full military style. We then noticed that he was holding one of those old Bakelite type telephone hand sets in the palm of his left hand whilst swinging his right arm, perfectly straight and parallel with the ground. He halted with a crunch of his boots, lifting his right knee and slamming his foot hard into the concrete as he threw up his right arm in salute. At the same time he thrust forward his left arm with the phone in it and shouted out.

"It's for you sir"

"Why thank you very much" said the Superintendent as he took the receiver and said "Hello"

200 coppers got the joke but I don't think he did.

By early September the strike didn't look like it was showing any sign of weakening its grip and in some places was actually getting worse. One of those areas was Kent where the strike had started off solidly but now some of the miners had decided it was time to go back to work. It provoked a furious reaction from their colleagues and before we knew it we were taking the 12 minute flight from Southampton airport to Manston airport in Kent. A 12 minute flight? It was hardly worth taking your seat belt off before we were being told to put it back on again in preparation for landing. Manston was a former Spitfire base during the war and has to be one of the most desolate places in England. We boarded our carriers, which had been driven there over night and drove to the disused hovercraft terminal at Ramsgate for a briefing. We were shown a video that showed some of the trouble Kent Police had been experiencing over the last few weeks, with demonstrators quite literally swinging on ropes out of the trees and onto the convoy of buses bringing miners into work. The Police had suffered numerous serious injuries including broken legs and arms. This was going to be quite a week then, we thought as we mingled with colleagues from Essex and Sussex.

After being shown the pit and the narrow approach road we then got taken to our accommodation for the week. It was yet another deserted army camp and looked just like Grantham. Except there was one big difference. There was no accommodation as such. Because Kent had had to organise things with such short notice they hadn't had the chance to equip the rooms we needed. So the good news was that 300 of us had to sleep on the gymnasium floor, head to toe and shoulder to shoulder on thin rubber mats. If that was the good news then, what was the bad news? Well the bad news is we only have two working toilets, two sinks, one shower and no hot water, although they do hope to have the water sorted by tomorrow. It has to be said that coppers are bloody good at moaning. I mean really good at it. But come on, 300 of us sharing two toilets and one cold shower! It was going to be a very long week.

I don't think many of us got much sleep that night and if you were dropping off some tosser would tread on you as he made his way to or from the toilet block. I felt really sorry for those close to the door; they can't have slept at all. If you thought we were grumpy about all this before you should have heard us the next morning. God help any pickets that piss us off this morning. Maybe that's why they did it?

At 0400 we drove back to Ramsgate and parked the carriers on the old hovercraft apron as we sipped on our Maxpax hot chocolate. It was an incredibly clear night, in fact I've never seen so many stars, there were millions of them for as far as the eye could see, and it really was quite amazing. But that paled when someone shouted to look directly above us. It was an awesome sight, for there was the

Space Shuttle Discovery gliding by, orbiting the Earth. It was as clear as day and rendered most of us utterly speechless.

The actual policing of the pickets was no-where near as bad as we had been led to believe, in fact we spent most of our time on stand by at Ramsgate, watching an assortment of videos and just eating to relieve the boredom. Then it was back to our one star hotel to join the queue for the cold shower. It didn't help at all that the food was crap and that it didn't matter how much we complained nothing got sorted. A couple of Police Federation representatives arrived to inspect the camp and promised us that we would each receive £50 in compensation. We're still waiting for it!

By the time we got back from Kent, Roger and I had decided we really didn't want to do this any more. Not only had we played so many games of hand tennis that we were actually in danger of turning semi professional but we were genuinely tired. I mean dog tired. So tired we felt sick. It was really starting to take its toll. Not just on us but on our wives and families too. Many of us had young kids or babies and our wives were spending weeks alone having to fend for themselves. We were promised a couple of weeks off, although that still meant working twelve hour shifts back here.

I had a new partner in PC 2376 Geoff Tarvin who had passed his area car course whilst I'd been away. That meant there were now three of us to share the responsibility, which felt great. It didn't always work out like that though and it wasn't long before I was back on nights and Geoff was on annual leave and Rodders was sick. So I got Sgt Mick Moorse as my observer for the night and we talked a great deal about my eventually wanting to get onto the Traffic Department. He obviously recommended it highly and as soon as his punishment for bending the Jag was over he would be straight back.

As we bimbled about the sea front area so we noticed a couple of cars apparently racing each other. By taking a short cut I caught up with the MK3 Cortina and MK1 Escort as they headed east along the seafront. They hit speeds in excess of 60 mph as they entered St. Helens Parade, where the Cortina hit the brakes and turned left into Granada Road. For some reason we decided to stick with the Escort as it accelerated away from us. I hit the blue lights, but it was clearly failing to stop. It then turned violently left into Craneswater Park, with smoke billowing from its tyres. It was all over the place, swerving from left to right as Mick Moorse gave out a superb commentary to the control room. It swung left into Festing Road and accelerated away again before sliding sideways out into Albert Road. No sooner had it gained control than it took the first right into Henly Road where it collided with a couple of parked cars, before speeding off again and into Bath Road. Here it hit 60 mph, more than double the speed limit in a very narrow side street with cars parked on both sides. As it approached a major crossroads with Devonshire Avenue it drove the wrong side of the 'Keep Left' bollards and then drove straight across the junction at 60 plus and into Fernhurst Road, another residential street. As it braked hard at the end of the road it slewed all over the road before turning left onto Goldsmith Avenue, where it hit the kerb on the opposite side of the road. It accelerated away up to 60 mph again and just stayed on the wrong side of the road for about 500 yards before it braked hard and turned left into Francis Avenue and then first right into Orchard Road. It accelerated away again up to 50 mph and then just drove straight across the crossroads with Talbot Road without braking at all. Up ahead I could see another blue light and it was coming towards us. It was the van and it broadsided across the narrow road completely blocking the Escorts path. The car skidded to a halt as the drivers door opened and the driver was off on his toes. He ran like a bloody grey hound along Orchard Road across Fawcett Road and into Rugby Road where I lost sight of him. I was just starting to panic when one of my old cadet colleagues Kevin Emblen, who worked at Fratton came walking around the corner with my driver by the scruff of the neck. We called for the van to attend our location and after placing him in the rear he promptly threw up everywhere. He was way over the drink drive limit, was already a disqualified driver and had stolen the Escort to get home with. After depositing the driver in the van I had to walk back to the area car in Orchard Road where I met up with a smiling Mick Moorse who was sat on the bonnet of the Volvo puffing away on a cigarette.

"Enjoy your run?" he quipped

"Not really, running has never been my thing" I replied.

"I'd have driven the area car down to you but you took the bloody keys" he laughed.

I'd forgotten what normal policing was like and after a busy weekend it felt great to be back in Southsea. I never thought I'd say that.

By early October I was back up in Nottingham for what was becoming a rather tiresome and tedious duty. Most of the mass picketing had ceased due to the intercept duties we were performing with great success plus there were signs that the strike was starting to crumble. Arthur Scargill would have none of it of course but the facts were that more and more of his colleagues were feeling the financial pinch and starting to drift back to work.

Our routine was disturbed by a special request from Nottinghamshire Police to Hampshire Police. Could our officer's help police tonight's Milk Cup match between Nottingham Forest and Pompey? Given the 6.57 Crews growing notoriety when away from home it made perfect sense for us to assist them at the game. With childish grins we lined up on the platform at Nottingham's main railway station. As the train pulled in you could clearly hear the Pompey chants and could see the train rocking from side to side. As the doors opened and several hundred Portsmouth youths spilled out onto the platform we greeted them like long lost friends, calling to them by name. I wish I'd had my camera with me; it was a sight to behold! Once it had dawned on them that tonight they weren't going to be anonymous faces in the crowd they were almost completely silent. It was a magic moment. We boxed them in and herded them up to the City Ground where they were strangely subdued. Some of them saw the funny side of it whilst others were genuinely pissed off about it all, especially when they got told that this was now going to happen at all the away games because they couldn't behave themselves. It was one of the few victories we ever really had.

Two days later and nobody was laughing. We woke to news that the IRA had bombed the Grand Hotel in Brighton during the Conservative Governments annual conference, killing six and injuring dozens of others. Within minutes all the Sussex Police units had been rounded up and were headed straight back towards their own force. We watched the TV during the morning and cheered as one when Maggie made her defiant appearance in front of the cameras. No matter what your political persuasion you cannot allow the terrorists to win or to even think they are winning and to see her there, immaculately turned out as if she was on a shopping trip to Marks and Spencers just made you feel that all of us were sticking two fingers up to the cowards that are the IRA.

Before I knew it I was back at Southsea and back on nights. It was about 3.30 am when Danny Daniels gave me a letter to deliver to the old Portsmouth Police HQ in Queens Crescent, which had been sold off to Social Services a couple of years before. I left Geoff at the nick doing some paperwork as I drove onto the forecourt of Byculla House. I popped the letter through the letter box and stood back admiring the building and reminiscing about Bob Allen and his gorilla when I smelt smoke. I turned to face the wind and it appeared to be coming from the sea front area. I called up the control room to ask if they had any knowledge of a fire in the area and after checking with the fire service the answer was no. I decided to go and check things myself. I headed down Palmerston Road and the smell was getting stronger. I turned left onto Clarence Parade and about 200 yards away I could see a large group of people standing in the road looking upwards. I pulled up and looked towards a large building that was actually four old Victorian houses knocked into one giant block of bed-sits, spread over four floors. As I got out of the car I looked up and saw four people standing on the roof screaming and with good reason because there were flames coming through the roof all around them. I asked for the fire service obviously and some back up. I then shouted at the crowd of about 50 people to tell me the best way into the building. Out of the crowd stepped a completely naked young woman who said "follow me" as she darted across the road and up the concrete steps to a door. I told her to go back as I entered the building into a hallway. I ran up a flight of stairs and opened the door at the top. It opened out onto a sort of round communal hallway with about five doors leading off it. I could hear a strange noise coming from behind one of them and opened it. I was met by a wall of fire that was being sucked upwards with a tremendous roar. It was surely the gates to hell? The noise and the heat literally blew me off my feet and as I picked myself up I knew I had to get out of there and quick. I kicked the door shut again and as I made my way back outside I saw the first two fire appliances arrive. They knew straight away that this was a big one. Two more police units arrived and after clearing the crowd to the safety of the other side of Clarence Parade I asked the Chief Fire Officer if there was anything we could do to assist. He grabbed two axes from a fire engine gave them to me and PC 1855 Dave Murray and said he wouldn't normally do this but he wanted every single room checked to ensure that everybody was out. We weren't to put ourselves at risk but the building needed checking room by room. We were joined by Mick Moorse and Danny Daniels and as the four of us went in we agreed from the outset that we would stick together and not separate.

We went back in via another door and ran straight to the top of the building. After banging on a bed sit door, if it wasn't unlocked and we didn't get a reply the axe went through it until it did open. Once we had checked the room we quickly moved onto the next one. We were surprised by the number of people who were still in there and had no idea that the place was on fire, but there was no fire alarm sounding for some reason. Water was now coming through the ceilings as the fire service started pumping water onto the fire. The heat was incredible and all you could hear outside was more and more fire engines arriving. Then a ceiling caved in on top of us and covered us in a sort of thick white plaster-like paste. We put a door in on the second floor and came across a drunken male who refused to leave and just wanted to give us lots of abuse. We didn't argue with him and instead threw him down the stairs and bundled him outside. We moved into the next block and found several more people inside who were still asleep. The place was full of smoke and it made breathing really difficult at times. We were getting really tired to and although wanton damage with an axe sounds like a lot of fun the novelty kind of wears off after you've swung it at more than 50 doors. The water continued to pour through the ceilings and we were absolutely soaked and covered in this white residue. By the time we had reached the ground floor again we were exhausted, in fact I really couldn't lift the axe let alone put it through a door. I decided to kick this one in. I took a running jump at it and slipped on the two inches of water on the floor and accidentally toe punted the door. I was convinced I had broken the big toe on my right foot and screamed in agony. The room was empty. With that we all got out and into the fresh air. The hydraulic platform had rescued those on the roof as the 12 appliances tackled the huge blaze that had now engulfed the whole building.

As I sat in the back of the ambulance having my foot looked at a young man came up to the door and asked if he could speak to me.

"I told the landlord about the fuse box sparking two days ago" he said.

"What fuse box?" I enquired.

"Under the stairs on the ground floor. I told him if he didn't do something about it then it might cause a fire" he continued.

"What did he do about it?" I asked.

"Nothing obviously" he retorted.

I took him to the Chief Fire Officer.

"I think this young man has something to tell you" I said.

By the time he had finished listening he looked like he was ready to explode and then went hunting for the land lord. I heard later that he was taken to court and heavily fined for numerous offences under the Fire Safety Act. It was nothing short of a miracle that nobody died in this one.

In all we rescued 12 residents from that inferno and the only casualty was my big toe. It wasn't broken but it felt like it. By 10am the blaze was under control and we were relieved by the early turn Relief and trudged off home to bed. I hate fires and I don't think that until you have experienced the ferocity of a major blaze that you fully understand just how deadly they can be. Just like the firearms incident a few years previously there was no official debrief, no counselling and no commendations either. It was generally accepted by those of us who worked in the city that the dangers we faced on an almost daily basis were very rarely acknowledged in any official capacity but that if you worked out in the sticks and you arrested a violent drunk (something we did everyday) then it was almost guaranteed that you received a commendation certificate! Or was that just us being cynical?

On the 18th November Tricia gave birth to our daughter Kelly. As I sat there cradling this tiny little ray of sunshine with a tear running down my cheek something inside of me went pop. I was now responsible for this latest addition to the human race which meant that I had to start acting in a mature manner. Oh the heavy burden of fatherhood. There were two bonus's to becoming a parent though, two weeks annual leave, which meant no Nottingham and an immediate cure for my being late on early turn. How? Because when you have a baby in the house and it's asleep, you really appreciate it staying asleep and so the second the alarm clock went off at 0515 I was out of bed like a scalded cat.

By the time I started to go back up there the weather had turned distinctly chilly. It was certainly colder up there than it is down here, by several degrees a lot of the time. This meant that the boilers in our rooms at Proteous were taken over by those who saw it as their divine duty to fill and stoke the boilers every five minutes. They became positively obsessed by them, constantly lifting the lid and prodding at the burning innards and adding yet more coke just to ensure that it didn't go out. There seemed to be some kind of competition to see who could get there's the hottest and I started to worry a bit when ours was glowing a faint shade of orange. It was so hot in our billet that we had to open the bloody windows to cool off. Now you tell me what the point in that is? On one occasion the boiler had been fully stocked with coal just prior to us going over to the bar for the evening and upon our return the room was like a furnace, you couldn't breathe. My bunk bed was next but one nearest to the boiler and you couldn't touch the metal frame and the blankets on the end had been baked and literally crumbled and flaked when you touched them. But best of all, inside my metal locker which was several feet away from the boiler, my tin of black shoe polish had turned to liquid! Our own Captain Pyromaniac, one PC 2399 Steve Saxton was certainly very proud of that one!

The bar at Proteous was a big nissan hut about twice the size of the accommodation units. Every now and then it would get packed to the rafters with over 200 officers from various forces and it was time for a lot of inter force banter, lots of alcohol and some of the most disgusting songs I've ever heard in my life. Political correctness hadn't been invented yet and on this particular evening it had been snowing quite heavily outside and all of us were in quite high spirits, even before we got to the bar. All the Hampshire officers sat at one end and there were loads of Met at the other. Somewhere in between us were Surrey officers. The singing started with songs like 'Father Abraham' and 'Bestiality is Best' bringing howls of laughter from everyone, although the biggest laughs were reserved for the Dance of the Flaming Arseholes. Don't ask.

And then it started. Donnellan threw an empty beer can from one end of the bar to the other. This was followed by a retaliatory can lobbed back in our direction. Then all hell broke lose as cans, some of them half full were hurled through the air spilling their contents over the Surrey boys in the middle. Up went the tables to be used as shields as others built walls from chairs to protect themselves. It was like a scene from a Wild West bar brawl but without the fisticuffs. Quite what the bar staff thought of it I've no idea but they must have been mightily relieved when it spilled outside and the cans were substituted for snow balls. It was the biggest snow ball fight I've ever seen and went on for over an hour. Of course the Met cheated by breaking out riot shields from one of their carriers but by now we had been joined by Surrey officers and we outnumbered the Met by two to one. I'm not sure how we progressed to the next stage but somebody had found out that a Met section were doing the early shift and that a whole hut full of them were asleep. Somebody got hold of one of those large, heavy door mats and climbed up onto the roof of their hut and carefully placed it over the chimney from their boiler as over a hundred of us surrounded the hut armed to the teeth with snow balls. We only had to wait a minute as the windows came flying open, followed by piles of smoke, followed by three dozen semi naked, half asleep Metpol officers who got absolutely pulverised with snow balls. They squealed like girls as they cowered in defensive mode trying to fend off an avalanche of snow. That'll teach them for plastering everything with Met stickers!

A couple of weeks later and Green Relief held its Christmas 'do' at the Hansom Cab restaurant in Albert Road. We had the private function room out the back and it's a good job we did. It was the first time we had all been together since Tricia's birthday in June and so it was time to let the hair down again. You should have seen the wives and girlfriends faces as we stood on the tables giving our best rendition of 'Bestiality is Best".

CHAPTER 9

1985. You should be dead

The miners strike was definitely starting to crumble with the Christmas period forcing many more back to work. The grim reality of not being able to provide for your family was starting to take its toll on even the most hardcore of Arthur Scargill's troops. The number and frequency of flying pickets descending on Nottingham got less and less and accordingly the Police operation was scaled back until Nottinghamshire Police no longer needed mutual aid from other forces and by the beginning of February Hampshire's involvement had come to an end.

In all I spent 27 weeks away from home during that first nine months of the strike. From a policing point of view it was a huge success, mounted on a scale never seen before and unlikely to ever be repeated. We made many friends both with the miners, their families and the locals whose lives were blighted in so many ways during those twelve months. As Police officers we were humbled by the pride of the Nottinghamshire people in standing up for themselves in the face of massive adversity aimed at them by the very people they once called their work colleagues and friends. The scars for many will never heal. The dispute turned father against son, brother against brother and neighbour against neighbour. For those who have never lived or worked in such a close environment it may be difficult to comprehend that the divisions could run so deep and would now be life long. The thought of disowning your brother for life because he dared to break the strike and return to work probably doesn't sit well with most people. But then the bond between such workers is seemingly thicker than blood in such places.

But was it worth it? In the end Arthur was right, the Government and the National Coal Board closed down dozens of pits, forcing thousands of men to look elsewhere for work. But I doubt that Scargill could ever really comprehend just how much damage he did to thousands of families all for the sake of his massive ego. The names of those collieries will be etched into the memories of those who worked down them and yes, by those Police officers who policed them, forever. Pits like Pye Hill, Bentinck, Bevercotes, Blidworth, Ollerton, Worksop, Ilkeston, Hucknall, Calverton, Cotgrave, Huthwaite, Sutton, Clipstone, Bilsthorpe, Calverton, Epperstone, Manton, Welbeck, Newstead, Thoresby, Creswell, Harworth and Shirebrook. For those of us who spent many weeks up there, the memories will live on forever, some of them funny, some of them not, but mostly we returned with nothing but admiration for the miners and their families who endured so much, no matter which side of the divide.

Settling back into a normal routine was great, especially as we only had to work eight hours a day and not 12 or 16 hours as had been the case for almost a year now. But it also meant going back to deal with everyday issues on Southsea's patch and for me personally, things were about to get rather difficult.

There had been a marked increase in the number of public order incidents in the Eastney area of the sub division over the last year or so. Those youths who had plagued Bransbury Park in recent months were now starting to branch out into other areas, intimidating people, starting fights with other groups, shop lifting, stealing bikes and then cars and becoming part of the massed swell of Portsmouth youths under the 6.57 banner at football matches. A nucleus of about a dozen males was seemingly at every incident we attended, many of them just on the threshold of adult hood but equally many of them were still juveniles.

Charlie-One to Victor Sierra 51

Victor Sierra 51 go ahead

Make St. Mary's Social Club fight in progress, believed 50 youths involved

Victor Sierra 51, Roger

It was early evening as Geoff and I raced towards the rear entrance to St. Mary's hospital, where it's Sports and Social Club was located. It was an unusual call to receive for this establishment because it was mainly used by nursing staff and wasn't open to the public. As we drove along the approach road so we saw about 30 youths come running out the back gate. Amongst them were many of the Eastney boys. We drove into the hospital and saw another smaller group outside the club. They scattered in all directions upon seeing the Police and disappeared into the shadows of the hospital grounds. We spoke to a member of staff at the club who stated that the two groups had merely clashed outside and it had nothing to do with the club itself. We got another couple of units to stop the Eastney boys at the far end of Rodney Road so that we could have a chat with them. As we drove back down the road so we could see that further fighting was taking place just as the other units arrived. The two groups had met up again and they were really going for it. But as soon as we arrived and nicked a couple of them so they seemed to join forces and turn their attentions towards us.

One of those arrested was Angelo Scaberras, brother of George who had made that spurious complaint against me 18 months previously and who I had had numerous dealings with since. The Scaberras family were many and as well as George and Angelo there was John, Colin, David (otherwise known as Dolly) and Rachael. As Angelo was being put into the van kicking and screaming so Dolly came running up to the doors in an attempt to get him released. I ushered him away and told him to calm down. He kept coming back again and again and every time I pushed him away.

"Fuck off Woodward you cunt, I fuckin hates you, you bastard, let my brother go, he ain't dun nuffin" he screamed.

I pushed him away again and kept pushing him further and further down the road. Just when I thought I had managed to resolve the situation so I saw Dolly running straight back at me screaming.

"I fuckin hates you Woodward" and at the same time I caught a glimpse of something shiny in his hand.

I moved back and sideways as he swung his arm towards my face. I grabbed his arm and took a pair of nail scissors from him. He started to struggle violently and I grabbed his hair. He had a large mop of almost permed curly locks. He was kicking and screaming, flailing his fists like a wind mill and my only option was to lift him off the ground by his hair, which I'd never done to an 11 year old before. Yes, at 11 years old this little shit was quite prepared to stab me in the face with a pair of scissors. Geoff came and joined me and before we put him in another van we searched him and found a Stanley knife in his back pocket.

At Central custody centre I met up with Mr Scaberras again and he point blank refused to believe a word we said against his sons.

From then on it seemed that almost everything I dealt with had a member of the Scaberras family involved. A simple routine stop of a car had three of the brothers inside, a disturbance at The Glitter Bay Amusement arcade on the seafront involving George, an RTA involving Angelo, another RTA the following week involving Rachael, a gate crashed party at Eastney involving all of them. I was even at an RTA in Waverley Road one evening and was just in the process of breathalysing one of the drivers when a familiar voice behind me told the driver to do a runner. It was Angelo Scaberras. The accident had absolutely nothing to do with him and he was merely walking by but decided to come and stick his oar in anyway. He kept interrupting the procedure and in the end I grabbed him by the scruff of the neck and told him his fortune! He just laughed in my face. As the Eastney boys grew physically so their anarchistic tendencies grew to and it seemed like their very existence was to annoy, antagonise, intimidate, disrupt and upset as many people as they could on a daily basis and that included targeting certain Police officers, mainly those of us who just weren't prepared to tolerate their behaviour in any way shape or form and so we did our level best to annoy, antagonise, intimidate, disrupt and upset their criminal activities.

Domestic disputes are one of the jobs that Police officers hate dealing with the most. There are rarely easy solutions to be found and invariably both parties end up joining forces and shouting at you instead. Some of the arguments are just so futile and pathetic you really wonder why some people get so worked up about things. Amongst the list of ridiculous domestics I've been sent to resolve include an argument over who ate the last Weetabix, another over a debt of 50p and a full scale war between two neighbours over a packet of fags! Another involved a drunken husband and wife who were complaining about the noise from next doors dog and so he went out to shout at it. When that failed he picked up a house brick to throw at it but in his drunken state ended up throwing the brick through his own window! His wife then beat the crap out of him. And at one truly amazing incident Chris Robinson and I got sent to a violent domestic in a flat that involved two lesbians armed with knives. As if that wasn't bad enough I needed to call for another couple of officers, including a WPC to come and assist but needed to nip out into the alleyway upon their arrival so I could open the gate to let them in. Imagine my despair when opening the gate to find the Sgt and the PC having their own face to face argument because the PC wasn't wearing his hat! But sometimes there's not a lot you can do for any of those concerned.

Charlie-One to Victor Sierra 51

Victor Sierra 51 go ahead

Longshore Way please, report of a domestic dispute, sounds of breaking glass, informants are neighbours

Victor Sierra 51, Roger

The address was highly unusual in that this little cul-de-sac was a rather exclusive road that only had half a dozen very nice houses that overlooked Langstone Harbour. In fact I don't recall being sent to anything in that area before, let alone a domestic. As we approached the front door I could see that the glass panel in it was broken. The door was ajar. We listened carefully and could hear a woman sobbing. We announced ourselves and two voices said they were upstairs. We walked into the spacious hallway and saw that everything was broken. A mirror on the wall, a small telephone table, the phone itself, there were ornamental plates smashed to pieces all over the floor. A quick look in the lounge and the settee was on its back, an armchair had been ripped to shreds, a coffee table smashed, photo frames on the floor and broken, in fact there wasn't anything that hadn't been destroyed. Geoff and I went up the stairs, walking over other broken objects and entered one of the bedrooms. It was as bad here as downstairs. There, sat on a wardrobe that was laying on its side were the husband and wife, arm in arm, crying their eyes out. Their dispute had gone on for several hours and between them they had destroyed everything they owned in what started off as some kind of tit-for-tat squabble. Their beautiful house and every item of furniture had been severely damaged. They didn't need our assistance as both of them had now come to their senses and realised what they had done. They didn't need any legal advice either because he was a barrister and she was a solicitor! Happens to the best of them.

Being on Area Car duties meant that I attended most of the RTAs on Southsea's patch. It was an area that I was becoming increasingly good at dealing with and I was always interested in the mechanics of how certain accidents occurred. More often than not the answer was obvious because alcohol was involved.

Charlie-One to Victor Sierra 51

Victor Sierra 51 go ahead

RTA Nettlecombe Avenue, car has hit several parked vehicles, driver has been detained by local residents

Victor Sierra 51, Roger

It was 1 am and Nettlecombe Avenue is in the more affluent part of Southsea with big houses and even bigger cars. As Geoff and I turned into the normally quiet street it looked like a bomb had gone off. Several parked cars had been badly damaged and at the far end was the crappy old Datsun that had caused it all, buried in the side of its last victim, a rather nice Mercedes. The driver was pinned against the wall by several residents whilst his wife just sat in the car shouting at everybody. The driver was placid enough and had offered no resistance at all, but then he did smell very strongly of alcohol. He blew a positive test and I arrested him and placed him in the rear of the van when it arrived.

His wife meanwhile just continued shouting and swearing at everyone. We had to get her out of the car in order to move it to the side of the road to get it recovered. She became very abusive towards the already angry and upset residents. She swore at them and said it was all their fault. In the end I had no choice but to arrest her for being drunk and disorderly. We put her in the back of the van and then followed it to Central custody centre. Half way there we got called by the van driver to state that these two were now having a full blown domestic dispute in the back. He wasn't kidding either. As the van reversed up to the custody centre doors you could hear the pair of them shouting and screaming at each other. When we opened the van doors I was horrified to see that she had physically attacked him, punching him in the face several times, cutting him above the eye, blacking the other and causing blood to pour from his nose! We rescued him from his 'trouble and strife' and took him indoors.

"Breathalyser Sarge" I said as I entered custody.

Sgt John Barber looked over his glasses and said.

"Really? How did he get the injuries?"

"His wife did that and she's next in" I said.

Our driver confirmed this and thanked us for getting him out the van before she killed him. John Barber then commenced the breath test procedure and the man gave two breath samples. We waited for the Lion Intoximeter to do its work before it flashed up on the screen, 197 and 192. John Barber and I both said at the same time.

"Bloody hell, you've blown 197"

"Is that good?" said the man, oblivious to our disbelief.

"You should be dead" replied Sgt Barber.

"I don't feel dead" he said.

197 was the highest reading I had ever seen and upon looking through the machines log it was the highest ever recorded at Central at that time. The legal limit is 35 microgrammes of alcohol per 100 millilitres of breath. Our driver was therefore almost six times the drink drive limit and yet he could still walk, stand and hold a reasonably intelligent conversation. To get to that stage we aren't talking about a couple of extra glasses of wine. He would have had to have drunk a staggering amount of alcohol, enough as Sgt Barber said to have killed most people. He would have to stay in custody until he was sober enough to charge and as I took him to his cell he asked.

"You aren't going to put me in the same cell as the wife are you?"

"Er.....no, I don't think that would be a good idea do you".

"Thank God for that, thank you".

PC Mick Murphy had been on Green Relief for a few months now and he had a particularly dry sense of humour which, coupled to the South African twang from his accent seemed to make him particularly amusing. He was also very astute and the only constable I knew who read The Times every day. He rarely raised his voice preferring to baffle others with a dry one liner that would cripple most of us. He lived almost opposite the nick in Hereford Road, a narrow side street that had a number of rather nice detached Victorian houses in what was now a conservation area. For some months he had wanted to build a garage and driveway at the side of his house because on-street parking was becoming very difficult and more often than not he couldn't park outside his own house. He obviously went to the time, trouble and considerable expense in having the plans drawn up and submitted to the planning department at Portsmouth City Council. Part of their brief was to consult a number of Mick's neighbours, whom Mick had already spoken to personally and they had given him their assurances that they had no objections. However when those same neighbours were approached by the planners they all changed their minds and objected to the garage and Mick's application was subsequently denied. But he didn't shout about it, in fact he just shrugged his shoulders and said he was considering his options.

A couple of weeks later he sold his car and bought a smaller one, in fact you couldn't get much smaller. He bought a red Fiat 850, one of those little rear engined things, often referred to as a hair dryer. But he still needed to park it somewhere. So he purchased a large but very tatty looking Transit Luton van, which was taxed, insured and MOT'd and parked it right outside his house. He then hand painted the words 'Garage' in huge white letters along both sides of the van and by using a set of steel ramps would drive the Fiat into the van each night. That's class.

The early hours of a quiet night shift can be awful. No matter how hard you try it can be difficult to keep your eyes open at times. We would therefore park up in a place where there was a decent amount of passing traffic so that we could at least keep ourselves occupied with the occasional stop check. It was 4 o'clock in the morning and Geoff and I parked up close to Velder Avenue roundabout.

Charlie-One to Victor Sierra 51

Victor Sierra 51 go ahead

Make the QEQM students residence please, two males seen trying the ground floor windows. Informant is the caretaker.

Victor Sierra 51, Roger

The Queen Elizabeth, Queen Mary halls of residence consisted of a couple of high rise blocks that housed university students. It quite often had break ins and thefts of and from the students cars. As we arrived I dropped Geoff off by the gate so that he could walk around the back whilst I drove in through the front. I'd done a quick lap of the car park which was clear and was heading back towards the gate where I knew the caretakers lodge was. I then saw a male come from a hedge on my nearside and walk across the front of the patrol car and walk away. I stopped the car and jumped out asking him to stop.

"Its OK mate I'm a copper" he said as he continued to walk away. I called him back and then another male popped out of the same hedge. They were both in their very early 20s.

"What are you doing here then?" I asked.

"What the fucks it got to do with you" came the reply, which wasn't the sort of reaction I expected from a colleague.

I explained about the call we had received and he just laughed. I asked to see his warrant card just to confirm his story. He was PC Simon Sard from Havant nick. I asked him again what he was doing here at four in the morning. He reluctantly told me that they were looking for a couple of girls. Geoff arrived and I asked him to stay with the pair whilst I went and spoke to the caretaker. He was very matter of fact that he had seen these two trying all the ground floor windows on the main block before he challenged them. Sard then flashed his warrant card at the man and said he was drugs squad and working under cover.

"Of course I didn't believe he was a copper which is why I called you lot" he continued.

Oh just great, how very embarrassing. How am I going to explain to him that actually this guy really is a Police officer?

I went back to the car and ascertained that Sard had just over two years service. I told him what the caretaker had said and he just laughed. He had been drinking but I wouldn't say he was drunk, just belligerent. In the end I told him and his mate, who was a student teacher and hadn't said a word, to just disappear and that I would smooth things over with the caretaker.

"No I'm not going anywhere" came the reply.

"What? What do you mean you aren't going anywhere, just get out of here will you, you've caused us enough embarrassment as it is". I said incredulously.

"Fuck off I ain't going anywhere" he said in a much more aggressive manner.

I pointed out that he'd actually committed enough offences to warrant being arrested and that he was being totally out of order. Geoff intervened and repeated much of what I'd already said but Sard just refused to leave.

"I tell you what Mr Sard perhaps you would care to explain yourself to my sergeant and he can decide what to do with you" I said, hoping he might just take the threat of a senior officer attending into doing the decent thing and buggering off.

"Do what you fucking like you wanker" he replied, folding his arms in a defiant and defensive manner.

I called Sgt Moorse to attend and he stated that he was less than two minutes away in the van. He arrived a short time later and I spoke to him through the driver's window. Mick told me to give him one more chance to leave or nick him. I was aware whilst talking to him that Geoff was continuing in his efforts to get him to leave. I went back to Sard and gave him his options, to leave or get arrested. His mate was pleading with him to leave. Sard turned to face me and I knew the look. He was going to hit me. His eyes bulged slightly and I saw his fist clench and with that he took a wild swing at my face, before losing his balance and falling to the ground. Geoff and I grabbed him, cuffed him and threw him in the back of the van. I couldn't believe it. I was incensed and all of us were in a state of shock that one of our own could behave in such a manner. Mick suggested we take him back to Southsea rather than Central custody whilst he contacted the night duty Inspector.

"Who is it?" I asked.

"Bob Allen" came the reply. I smiled to myself.

Sard was still gobbing off at Geoff and I as we arrived at Southsea and shoved him into the detained persons room. Mick Moorse had called for Bob Allen to attend from Central and upon his arrival we explained the circumstances to him. He sat on the edge of the table in the front office mulling things over for a minute, then stood up and said.

"Fuck it, charge the little twat".

Geoff and I then set about writing lengthy statements and concluded them with the line that this was, without doubt, the most embarrassing moment of our careers. An hour or so later and Bob Allen entered the room to say he had just been into the cell for a chat with Sard who was now crying like a baby and wanted to apologise to us. I looked at Geoff and he screwed his nose up and I'm glad because that's exactly how I felt about it. We declined the offer which Bob Allen fully understood. He then went on to ask us if we would be happy not to charge Sard but to have him taken up to HQ for 0900 that morning (which was less than three hours away by now) to explain himself to the Deputy Chief Constable John Hoddinott. Mr Allen went on to explain that getting a bollocking from the DCC was ten times worse than appearing in court and that even he wouldn't fancy facing the wrath of Mr Hoddinott, so it must be one hell of an experience! We agreed and handed over our statements so that the DCC could read them first.

Sard was in fact in the second year of his probation and I understand that the DCC extended it by another six months, placed him on weekly reports, fined him the maximum two weeks pay and apparently stood directly in front of him whilst bellowing in his face for a full 20 minutes.

Three months later we learned that a local beat bobby had received complaints about two cars parked outside a house at Eastney. Neither of them were taxed, MOT'd or insured and the officer was given mouthfuls of abuse by the owner when challenged about them. The owner was Simon Sard and within 24 hours he had been sacked.

It had been a particularly busy Friday night and we didn't get back to the nick for our grub until after 3.30 am. I parked the Volvo on the pad outside and we went in for our meal. An hour or so later we came out of the station and just stared in disbelief at the area car. Somebody had sprayed 6.57 in red aerosol paint right across the bonnet. I was furious and took it as a personal insult. Thankfully it was a workshop spare car and not our own one. Geoff and I stopped everything that moved for the rest of the night, looking for any signs of red paint or aerosol cans but didn't find anything. Cheeky bastards!

Is nothing sacred? The 6.57 Crew leave their mark on the area car.

Football violence was still rife and if anything it was getting worse. When Pompey played Birmingham City in April the full scale of the 6.57 Crews organisational ability came to the fore for the first time. Around mid day on the Saturday I was single crewed on early turn and wasn't even doing a football duty.

Charlie-One to any available city units to attend the town railway station to meet a train containing a few noisy Birmingham supporters.

Victor Sierra 51 attending

About six of us met the train a few minutes later and were horrified to find that around 300 Birmingham supporters got off. They were nearly all black and completely ignored the Police instructions they were given. Our plan was to box them up and escort them straight to the ground but in total silence they moved as one from the station and walked directly across the road to the Guildhall Square. We knew something was going to happen, you could sense it. They entered the Guildhall Square and stopped at the steps, where they all sat down in a tight group, as if on the terraces. Then they started a zulu warrior type chant that quite literally made the hair on the back of my neck stand on end. It started slowly and quietly with no apparent orchestration. I have to confess that it was superbly done and the six of us stood in a neat semi circle in front of them for several minutes. The chanting grew to a crescendo and then as one, they all stood up and with their right arms pointed across the Guildhall Square and shouted Z-U-L-U. I turned around and saw some 200 or so Portsmouth youths spread out in a long line across the square by Guildhall Walk. I mouthed quietly to myself 'Oh-my-God' and immediately felt akin to General Custer! A huge roar went up from across the square and both groups then ran at full pace towards each other. A massive fight followed with serious injuries being inflicted on both sides. We were powerless to prevent the vast majority from doing their worst and only a handful of arrests were made. After half an hour or so they all split up and ran off in different directions and there was sporadic fighting in various streets right up to kick off at three. Inevitably questions were asked in the days that followed. How did the Birmingham supporters know where to go? Who gathered that many Portsmouth youths together in one place at a certain time? Who gave them the instructions to line up across the square?

There's no such thing as a good chase was one of the things my instructor kept telling me on my standard car course. The possibility of something going wrong is extremely high and every pursuit is a danger to me, my crew mate, the target vehicle and most important of all, the public. Rod and I were on nights and had just finished dealing with a minor RTA on the Eastern Road. It was just coming up to midnight.

Charlie-One to Victor Sierra 51

Victor Sierra 51 go ahead

Are you still on the Eastern Road?

Answer yes

Traffic are pursuing a stolen motorcycle at Copnor and its currently heading east along Tangiers Road towards your location. Can you assist them please?

Victor Sierra 51, Roger

We just made it in time and as I turned left into Tangiers Road so the Honda CB 750 arrived at the junction at great speed. I could see the blue lights from the Traffic car about 500 yards away so it was some considerable distance behind. The bike turned left and headed north up the Eastern Road with us directly behind it. It accelerated away flat out but it was a bit of a rat bike and wasn't as fast as it should have been. I was quite close behind it at 80 mph when there was a loud bang from the bike and suddenly our windscreen went completely black. I instinctively hit the wipers which was the worst thing I could have done because the screen was now covered in engine oil from the bike. The wipers merely smudged the oil into an opaque shield that reduced my visibility to almost zero. Thankfully the wiper blade on the driver's side had a slight defect and it failed to wipe a one inch wide arc that wasn't covered in oil and was just wide enough to see through. The loss of oil had an adverse affect on the performance of the bike which now sounded terrible and couldn't exceed 60 mph. The Traffic BMW overtook us and took up position as the lead car. In hind sight I should have stood down from here but I didn't and I latched on to the rear of the BMW. The bike went up onto Portsdown Hill where it turned west for several miles before descending into Portchester where the rider lost control and fell off. He put up one hell of a fight in being detained and was eventually placed in the rear of a dog van, complete with Police dog and he still wanted to fight!

The following month and we took delivery of a brand new Volvo 240 Police Special with twin blue lights and a smart looking Police/Stop box on the boot. It was always nice to drive brand new cars but this one just felt so good and it drove beautifully. We were on early turn and were asked to keep a look out for a matt black, large capacity motorcycle that had failed to stop a couple of days before for the late turn area car crew. Geoff and I were doing some much needed paperwork but by 8 o'clock I was starving hungry and in need of some breakfast. I hadn't brought anything in with me and decided I would nip home and grab a bite to eat. So I left Geoff at the nick and headed towards the Copnor area where I lived.

As I negotiated the mini roundabout at Velder Avenue and headed north towards the Eastern Road I saw a black Suzuki GT750 approach the roundabout from Milton Road. As I gave it a good look the rider stared back towards me and I just knew this was the bike that my colleagues had been looking for. I did a very quick U turn and headed back to the roundabout and as I did so, I saw the Suzuki accelerate across the roundabout with its front wheel high in the air. It was two-up and without doubt this was the bike.

It was the middle of the morning rush hour and the traffic was very heavy. Milton Road is two lanes in both direction and the bike accelerated hard right down the middle. By now I had the blue lights and two-tones on and was quickly joined by Romeo Foxtrot 51, which was Fratton's area car, driven by PC Rick Bennett. The bike turned right into Priory Crescent and as it took the long left hand bend that circumnavigates Milton Park it was all over the place and wobbled badly from side to side. At the crossroads with Goldsmith Avenue there were cars everywhere and the Suzuki slowed to about 30 mph but just went straight across the crossroads without stopping. After a hundred yards or so it turned right into a side road and then travelled through a whole series of narrow residential streets at 50 mph or more before emerging into Devonshire Avenue. Although still a residential road it is much wider and dissects a number of other residential streets. The Suzuki accelerated flat out with smoke pouring from its two-stroke engine and screaming in protest through its three exhaust pipes. Up ahead I knew that half the road was closed due to road works which had temporary traffic lights in operation. As the bike approached I could see that the lights were on red and that there were several vehicles waiting in the queue. At over 60 mph the Suzuki travelled down the outside of the queue, went straight through the red light and forced an oncoming vehicle to brake hard and swerve out of the way in an effort to avoid a head on collision. After exiting the roadworks the bike hit 80 mph and continued along Devonshire Avenue overtaking several vehicles as it did so. As we approached the major crossroads with Eastney Road the traffic lights were on red with several vehicles waiting at the junction. Again the bike travelled down the outside of the queue of traffic, went straight through the red lights and turned left onto Eastney Road which was jam packed full of traffic. Somehow the Suzuki carved a path through the traffic, weaving in and out narrowly missing several cars that had to swerve out of its way. As it approached the Y junction with Goldsmith Avenue it had hit 60 mph again and the traffic lights were on red with two lanes of traffic waiting at them. It braked hard and swerved left and rode up onto the pavement alongside the White House pub and into Goldsmith Avenue. There was no way we could follow obviously and so we were forced to travel the wrong side of the 'Keep Left' bollards and then turn left into Goldsmith Avenue.

The bike hit 80 mph along Goldsmith Avenue and shortly after passing Priory Crescent the back wheel locked solid with smoke pouring from underneath it and it turned sharp right into Frogmore Road and towards Fratton Park. At the end of the road it turned right into Carisbrooke Road where it hit 60 mph again before turning left and straight out into Priory Crescent forcing a Vauxhall Cavalier to brake so hard it spun 90 degrees sideways. The driver looked terrified. Within a hundred yards was the major T junction with Milton Road and there was traffic everywhere. The Suzuki travelled the wrong side of the 'Keep Left' bollards and turned left onto Milton Road forcing a double decker bus coming from the right to stand on its nose. The bike weaved its way back through the traffic north along Milton Road hitting 60 mph. It braked briefly as it approached the Velder Avenue roundabout and then went straight over the roundabout and accelerated away again reaching 70 mph.

Up ahead I could see that the pelican crossing lights outside St. Mary's Hospital were on red and there was a queue of traffic both sides. The Suzuki flew down the outside of the queue and as it did so I saw three nurses crossing from left to right. I screamed out loud as the bike just went straight through them, knocking one of them to the ground as the other two leapt backwards and out of its way.

"You absolute bastard" I shouted out.

There was no way this one was going to get away, not now. As the bike negotiated St. Mary's roundabout I saw the pillion passenger thumping the riders back and shouting at him. The bike exited the roundabout and continued northwards up Milton Road reaching 70 mph. As it approached Copnor Bridge I saw the passenger shouting at the rider again and making gestures with his hands. Copnor Bridge is basically a double bend on a bridge and as the Suzuki took the first left hander it did it way too fast and went right over to the wrong side of the road almost hitting the kerb with the foot pegs scraping the road surface sending up a shower of sparks. After the right hander the bike had slowed to 50 mph and the road ahead looked quite clear. Rick and I had already talked about boxing the bike in and this was our first opportunity. The other Volvo overtook me and the bike and pulled up beside it forcing it towards the kerb. Our speeds reduced to less than 15 mph but I could see the passenger talking to the rider and then the passenger started to climb off the bike. I knew that if the bike was solo we wouldn't have a cat-in-hells chance of staying with it, we could barely keep up with it as it was. Then the rider hit the brakes so hard that the bike stopped almost instantly. The front of my car hit the rear of the bike and both of them were thrown upwards and off the machine as it toppled over. I jumped out of the car and grabbed the rider before he even hit the ground. He struggled violently as I threw him against the Co-op Dairy wall. He growled out loud as we continued to fight and I wrestled him back across the pavement and over the bonnet of the area car, shouting at him that he was under arrest. He let out an almighty scream as I thrust his arms behind his back and cuffed him. The two-tones were still sounding on both area cars and as I looked up I saw about a dozen people standing at the bus stop on the other side of the road who had witnessed this entire final episode! They looked quite shocked.

Then I looked at the front of the brand new Volvo and saw that the rear light cluster from the bike had gone straight through the front nearside headlight and damaged some of the surrounding trim. It's never good to be the first to bend the new area car! We later traced the three nurses who were thankfully not injured but that was more by luck than judgement. Craig was the early turn Sgt from Fratton and he arrived to deal with the Police Vehicle Incident (PVI) and jokingly said that this sort of thing would never have happened if he'd still been crewed up with me! Piss taking git.

It transpired that the bike had been stolen several months before and was a ringer on false plates; in fact the rider was responsible for the thefts of several high powered and valuable bikes. He was also disqualified and uninsured plus the bike was in a terrible state and was being ridden on slick tyres with no rear brakes. Worst of all was that seat wasn't even fixed to the bike in any way so it's a miracle they managed to stay on it given the way it was being ridden! At Portsmouth Crown Court a few months later Ronald Amess was jailed for 12 months for what Judge David Smith QC said was the worst case of reckless driving he had ever dealt with.

In July the whole force had to attend a three day course at the old Cadet Training School at Bishops Waltham to introduce us to a major new piece of legislation; the Police and Criminal Evidence Act or PACE as it quickly became known, which was to replace Judges Rules. This single item of law was about to change the manner in which the Police not only investigated crime but in the way it managed prisoner's welfare. It was a huge change that took some real getting used to.

There had been a change of Chief Inspector at Southsea and we had inherited Malcolm Bully from Central. To say he was a bit of a character would be a massive understatement. I first met him a few months before when he was in charge at Central and I had to nip upstairs to his office from the custody centre to obtain his permission to charge a driver with reckless driving, which was a requirement at this time. His office was at the front of the station and over looked the big roundabout immediately outside. His door was ajar and I was just about to knock when I caught sight of him holding his arms out as if he was holding a rifle and he was shooting at passing cars! At the very least I thought he would stop through sheer embarrassment when I did knock but to my utter surprise he didn't. In fact he told me to come in and continued shooting at the public for another minute or so before turning towards me and saying.

"Yes son, how can I help you?"

He had spent several years in the Rhodesian Police and loved reminiscing about it, in fact once he started talking about that or any other subject close to his heart you were trapped for at least the next two hours! And I'm not exaggerating either.

Apart from shooting members of the public Mr Bully also indulged in running little campaigns for his troops to partake in, but they were always at the lower end of the scale. He would regularly tell us all that he got more letters from the public about cars parked on double yellow lines or people riding bikes on the pavement than he ever did about burglars, muggers and rapists. If he started a two week campaign on anything he absolutely insisted we take part and get results, it wasn't an option. His current campaign was pedal cycles; riding on the pavement, riding without lights or riding two-up, it didn't matter what they were doing but he expected us to go out and deal with it and not ignore them.

It was mid-way through the campaign and we were on parade at the start of a week of nights when the parade room door flew open and in walked Malcolm Bully. This must be serious, you never see a Chief Inspector when it's dark! He started ranting that Green Relief thus far had submitted the least number of check forms for his cycle campaign and that it had to change or else. He then turned to Geoff and me and pointed at us.

"As for you two wankers, you're the area car crew and so far you haven't submitted a fucking thing. You should be setting an example to the others and not just swanning about in your flashy new Volvo, good God my old aunty could do better than you two. Sort it out or you'll both be wearing a big hat and pounding Albert Road for the next six months. Understood?"

"Understood sir" we both replied and with that he left.

Like all good coppers we moaned and bitched about it but we knew he was serious when it came to wearing a big hat and neither of us fancied that and so out we went on a bike hunting expedition.

Half an hour later we were driving down Festing Grove towards Festing Road when across the end of the junction went a pedal cyclist being towed by a moped. Oh pennies from heaven. The cyclist saw us straight away and started singing "Nee, naa, nee, naa, nee, naa" so campaign or not he was going to get stopped. As a bonus the cyclist had no lights on either. As we pulled out behind them so the cyclist let go of his mates arm and peeled off right into Craneswater Park. He was peddling furiously as we pulled along side him and I wound down the window and requested him to stop.

He told me to "Fuck off".

This happened three times before I opened the passenger door and Geoff hit the brakes forcing our man to collide with the inside of the door and fall off. As he leapt to his feet he picked up the bike and threw it at me. I fended it off and it fell to the ground. With that he just went completely berserk, attacking the pair us, punching us in the face and body, kicking, scratching and resisting arrest. We eventually managed to throw him over the boot of the area car, breaking one of the radio aerials off in the process. Geoff's jacket got ripped as we both called for assistance and the van. We had just about got him subdued and handcuffed when the van arrived. We put him in the back and within seconds he had managed to pull his hands from behind him, under his feet and out the front, which I'd never seen done before. He was now like a caged animal and started punching at the wooden slatted seats with both his fists and his feet. We could hear the seats break and splinter and one by one he destroyed all three of them. Then he started kicking at the back doors and seconds later both the rear windows popped out of their seals onto the road. Thankfully the mesh grilles inside were strong enough to resist his madness and despite him bending them back and forth they managed to stay intact. We followed the van to

Central and were dreading the doors being opened the other end. We had a reception committee waiting for him but by then I think he had exhausted himself and agreed to come out quietly.

He was charged with two counts of assault Police, resisting arrest, affray, four counts of criminal damage totalling several hundred pounds and riding a pedal cycle without lights. Despite the custody sergeants protestations Geoff and I absolutely insisted on that one. We photo copied the charge sheet with all the offences on it, together with copies of our statements and with childish grins we left it on Malcolm Bully's desk for the morning with an additional note saying 'Sir, do you want us to do any more?'

We got the note back the following evening and in big red letters he had scrawled across it 'Don't you fucking dare'. He could be somewhat pedantic at times but he was also a man's man with a great sense of humour and we certainly respected him because of it.

Roger and I were quite excited at the prospect of three days on the Isle of Wight policing the national scooter rally. There had been some serious disorder the previous year when the stage was set on fire and thousands of Mods went on the rampage. There had been a huge resurgence in the Mod culture over the last couple of years and now scooters, the clothing and the music, thanks to groups like The Jam, The Specials and Madness were back in fashion. It was a big Police operation that would oversee more than 10,000 Mods descend on the island over the August bank holiday weekend. It was the Traffic Departments job to escort the scooters from the Fishbourne ferry to the camp site at Forest Road near Newport and then it was the responsibility of the RSG to ensure that the festival passed off peacefully.

It rained all day Thursday and by the time Roger and I assembled with the rest of our crew on Friday morning it was still raining heavily, although the forecast had predicted a dry weekend. Roger had brought our tennis ball just in case we got bored. We arrived at the ferry terminal in Portsmouth at lunchtime and it was packed with hundreds of scooters desperate to get on the car ferry. We had set up a weapons amnesty bin at the ferry port and it already contained a couple of dozen decent sized knives and a meat cleaver. It was pissing down with rain and the Mods were all soaked.

After arriving at Fishbourne we drove in convoy to Forest Road and entered the field that was the entrance to the rally site. There were in fact four fields. The lower field housed the organisers, together with the Police and Ambulance service and we had a decent sized marquee and a control van for the weekend. The next two fields up were to be the camping sites and the fourth field adjacent to the third housed the stage, the bars and the catering outlets. Our field was at the bottom of the slope and there was a single track road that linked all four fields. It was still pouring with rain and the entrance to the site was already a foot deep in mud as the organisers laid out large amounts of straw to soak it up with. Thankfully we had been pre-warned to bring wellies with us and I'm mighty glad we did. I looked on as a queue of scooters half a mile long waited patiently to enter the site. There were Lambrettas, Vespas and Piaggios as far as the eye could see all brilliantly decorated with dozens of mirrors, whip aerials and furry tails. Some had been stripped to the bare bones and were aptly called 'Skellies' whilst others had huge extended front forks that made the machine look incredibly unstable. Some of these scooters must have cost thousands and you couldn't help but admire their owner's dedication. Almost without exception the riders and their passengers wore green Parker coats with fur lined hoods and jeans, which given the weather conditions were just about the worst possible items of clothing you could possibly wear. Anybody who has owned a Parker, as I did at school in the early 1970s, will tell you that once it gets wet, it stays wet and very smelly, for days! And we all know what happens when jeans get soaked.

Roger and I teamed up to patrol the site and familiarise ourselves with the weekends surroundings. As we entered the top field I looked around at the Mods who were still arriving in their hundreds. Most of them were just kids, no more than 17 or 18 years old and loads of them just stood there, shivering with cold and wet just staring at the tents they had brought with them, not having a clue how to put them up. Most of the lads had girlfriends with them, many of whom didn't look a day over 15 and were now wondering why the hell they had agreed to travel down from Birmingham or Cardiff on the back of a 20 year old Lambretta whilst wearing nothing but jeans and a cardigan as it pee'd down with rain all day. It was a pathetic sight that was repeated everywhere we looked. And so we spent the next five or six hours erecting tents and giving out sound advice about how to look after yourself in such awful conditions. Those we helped were truly grateful if not a little bemused that the Old Bill could be so friendly and helpful. Still it pissed down with rain. All the fields were now covered in mud and the access road was nothing more than a river with scooters abandoned here, there and everywhere. After putting up something like a hundred tents between us Roger and I were hungry and needed to dry out a bit ourselves. We trudged back down to the marquee where several of our colleagues took the piss out of us because we were absolutely covered in mud and soaking wet. We had a couple of hours off and rekindled the art of hand tennis using a couple of trestle tables.

By now it was dark and the evening's entertainment on stage was kicking off. There were still new arrivals queuing to get in which probably meant there was more tent erecting to be done. Roger and I waded through the mud to the first camp site and were busy sorting out a young couple's tent when we were approached by a 15 year old girl who said her friend wasn't feeling very well and had fallen asleep in their tent and now she couldn't wake her up. Their tent was in the top field somewhere and despite our hurried efforts we couldn't find it. She was pretty clueless and unable to give us any landmarks to go by. After half an hour of searching we eventually found it. The girl was fully clothed inside a sodden sleeping back and her face was laying in an inch of water inside the tent. She was unconscious, blue and ice cold to the touch. We could barely feel her pulse. Roger and I dragged her out of the tent, picked her up inside the sleeping bag and we ran with her down through the field to the mud track where we must have fallen over a dozen times or more. We ran down through the next field shouting and screaming at hundreds of youngsters to get out of our way whilst using the girl's feet as a battering ram. We went straight to the stand-by ambulance where the ambulance crew stripped her off and wrapped her in one of those silver space blankets. Within a minute they were sliding their way out of the field on their way to St. Mary's Hospital. She was suffering from severe hypothermia and would almost certainly have died had her friend not found us. Roger and I were caked in mud and soaked to the skin. We were absolutely exhausted and stood there bent forward with our hands on our knees, huffing and puffing like a couple of old gits.

After a cup of Maxpax hot chocolate we set off up the hill again to resume our welfare mission and to check up on those who we thought might have been in a similar situation to the young girl. We found plenty of candidates who were just sat there in sodden clothing not really knowing what to do. Some of them hadn't even brought a change of clothes or if they had it was just as wet as the stuff they were wearing. The bands were playing in the field next door but a lot of them just weren't interested any more.

About midnight we were patrolling the edge of the top field when we saw a body under a hedge. It was rolled up inside a length of clear polythene sheeting and the face was pressed up so hard against the plastic that it had disfigured his features just as if he was wearing a stocking mask before robbing a bank. We shone our torches all over it but got no reaction and we were convinced we had our first dead body. Roger gave it a gentle kick.

"What, what do you want?" shouted the body as we leapt backwards in surprise.

"Just checking your alive mate" said Roger.

"Of course I'm alive, I was just having a kip till you disturbed me you twats".

"Night, night then" we said chuckling.

Things had settled down a bit and so we trudged back down to the marquee which was full of waifs and strays, all feeling very sorry for themselves. Some had lost tents en route to the island, others had been completely washed out or their friends had buggered off home already and left them behind. It was still raining heavily and we now had a sizeable stream running right through the centre of the marquee. There was a young lad laying on his side across a couple of chairs fast asleep. He was curled up in a ball with his arms folded over his chest, a position he had occupied in an effort to get warm. He suddenly rolled over and fell off the chairs and straight into the stream. Everybody laughed at the poor sod as he scrambled back to his feet and then sat back on the chairs looking really sorry for himself.

At 2 am we set off for our accommodation in an old school at Bembridge where we did our best to dry our own kit out. I might as well just throw my trousers away I thought, I'll never get them clean again.

By 1600 the next afternoon we were on our way back to the site and it was still raining although not quite as heavily as yesterday. What is it about August bank holidays that brings on such crap weather? The site was almost deserted and we wondered if most of them had abandoned ship and returned home but we learned that most of them had gone into Newport and Cowes to buy dry clothes or use the local launderettes. The fields still looked like a scene from Vietnam with laying water everywhere and the access road was virtually impassable.

Tonight would see the top acts appearing on stage and it was expected to be packed out. By dusk the place was heaving again and our patrols concentrated on the main field. Roger and I were becoming increasingly uncomfortable because of a combination of the crowds, the alcohol consumption and the fact that it was pitch black, you could hardly see a thing. The only lighting came from the stage area and that was a hundred yards away. We got called back to the marquee and from now on we were only to go in if called in by the organisers and then it would be en mass. By 2300 it was starting to descend into chaos, there were fights everywhere and then it happened, some idiot threw an axe at the group that was performing on the stage. It struck the drummer in the head, thankfully blunt end first, but it still caused him serious injury. We escorted the ambulance crew in and out and then left them to it. The atmosphere was extremely hostile and the irony of the whole situation wasn't lost on Roger and I. Only 24 hours previously we had been rescuing many of these youths and helping them get sorted and now they were threatening to kill us. Monday lunchtime couldn't come quick enough for us frankly, we were city boys after all and wading through muddy fields wearing wellies just wasn't our style.

I'm sure some criminals think that coppers either don't talk to each other or that we are just plain thick. Plenty of them are quite convinced that if they commit a crime in a town other than their own then the Police in that town will keep it all to themselves.

Charlie-One to all Kilo units, your attention is drawn to a light green VW Golf responsible for a shop lifting in Chichester, possibly heading west towards the Portsmouth area.

I had a sneaking suspicion about this one and was heading down Goldsmith Avenue towards the Locksway Road area because somebody I knew well had recently obtained a light green Golf. Within seconds I saw it heading in the opposite direction, two up and clearly not too pleased at seeing me. I stopped it a short while later.

"Afternoon George, been shopping have we?"

"Don't know what you mean Mr Woodward" replied George Scaberras.

On searching the car I found various solid brass ornaments which spookily enough were exactly what had been stolen from the store in Sussex. George and his mate Richard Saxton were arrested and all the property recovered. George was quite amenable towards me when we were talking on a one to one basis; we could even have a bit of a laugh. He showed a fair amount of respect and made full and frank confessions and generally always cooperated with me. Unless his family were anywhere near that is. Then he was a complete shit. He would attack me verbally at every opportunity and if he was with any of his younger brothers then it was even worse. Their mother merely encouraged her boys to attack the Police at every opportunity and would defend their criminal activity on every occasion. She would make official complaints every time one of them was arrested or phone to complain of Police harassment if they got stop checked for something. They rapidly became one of those families from hell and their respectable neighbours soon got fed up with their anti social behaviour in the small cul-de-sac where they lived.

During the day time a lot of the Eastney boys and others from various parts of the city would congregate at the fountain in Commercial Road precinct. There could be anything up to 50 of them there at any one time being a pain in the backside to every decent human being that merely wanted to go to the bank or to shop in peace. But to me they were far more than that; they were a direct threat to me and my family when I was off duty. Up until this moment in time if you met or passed a local villain in the street and you made eye contact you might actually greet each other in a sort of a begrudging manner, a nod here, a brief smile there, nothing more, each of us knowing that business was business and that was that. But this lot couldn't do that. They couldn't leave it and it was getting worse, so much so that I would avoid the fountain area completely, taking big detours to avoid any sort of confrontation.

Tricia and I were sitting in the Wimpy Bar in Commercial Road one lunchtime with our baby daughter in her buggy. We were sat by a window when I spotted George and Dolly Scaberras walking by. Unfortunately they spotted me to and stood right in front of the window making obscene gestures and shouting out.

"Woodward you cunt" and other such remarks.

There were hundreds of shoppers walking by and the Wimpy Bar was packed, all of them now looking in our direction. I was furious and started to get up to go and confront them. Tricia grabbed my hand and pulled me back down not wanting me to get involved.

But I was involved. They had over stepped the line. They stood right up close to the window mocking me further. I couldn't stand it any longer and got up and moved towards the door. Before I'd even got there the pair of them ran like frightened rabbits. Typical.

On September 12th I watched the news as Birmingham erupted into racial violence with full scale rioting.

"Shall I go and pack your bag then?" said Tricia.

She was getting used to seeing me disappear for days on end and it did seem that at the slightest sign of tension anywhere in the country we would be off to help sort it out. Within 24 hours we were at Southampton airport boarding another plane to head north to Birmingham. Hampshire Police took 100 officers to England's second city and our carriers were waiting for us on the tarmac upon our arrival. We were split into two groups of six units and we got our own local outriders for the entire weekend. They were riding Norton Interpol 2's with the rotary engine which coughed and farted every time they shut the throttle. I was driving the last of the six carriers which meant we needed to drive faster than everybody else but at least I'd got one of the new 3.0 litre V6s with power steering which was a real bonus compared to the older carriers. Our Sgt was our own Mick Moorse and our entire crew was made of Pompey officers which guaranteed we were going to have a great weekend. We went everywhere on blues and twos and the motorcyclists ensured that we didn't stop for anything, not red lights, not roundabouts, nothing. It was great.

We drove straight to our accommodation which was quite a distance away and was West Mercia Police's training school. Wow, what a place. Huge swimming pool, full gymnasium, five a side football pitches, snooker tables, a decent bar and a country pub about 200 yards outside the gates. But it was the food that took us by surprise. We would be doing the night shift for the whole weekend and so when we got up and needed breakfast all we had to do was come to the dining room and the canteen ladies there would cook us whatever we desired. Really? What, no sausage, egg, bacon and beans together with a take it or leave it attitude? Certainly not we were told. They were right, you could ask for almost anything and they'd cook it. And at 4 o'clock every day they served up afternoon tea with freshly baked cakes, scones and jam. There were transfer requests flying in all over the place!

But it wasn't really a holiday because there was the serious business of rioting and looting to contend with. We had numerous briefings and warnings about what to expect. It certainly sounded hairy and the West Midlands Police were superb in the way they had organised things at such short notice. The two Portsmouth vans got the night club area around the Bullring to look after. It was a bit like policing Southsea seafront only ten times bigger!

As we got into our carriers so Mick Moorse piped up.

"Hope you've checked the tyres?" he laughed.

Am I never going to be able to live that one down I thought. We set off towards Birmingham city centre with our two escort bikes screaming passed us and farting loudly as they throttled off to stop the traffic at the next junction. As we raced down a dual carriageway towards the city centre I suddenly swerved hard left and into lane one.

"What's up?" shouted Mick.

I merely pointed at the six JCBs lined up on the central reservation.

"Bastard"

"Touché"

We took up our positions in and around the Bullring Centre and to all intents and purposes it was just another ordinary Friday night in another city centre really. There was no tension here and the locals seemed pleased to see us even if they were somewhat bemused that we had flown up from the south coast.

My crew were out on foot patrol and I'd been left in the carrier on my own when two young Asian lads approached the driver's door.

"Have you lot come up here to beat the crap out of the niggers?" enquired one of them in a very broad Brummie accent. I was somewhat taken aback by the question.

"Erm......well, we've certainly come up to help sort out the problems you've got up here, yes" I replied somewhat nervously, not wishing to inflame the racial tension any further.

"Good" said the other one "Those fuckers need teaching a lesson, smashing up our city, who the fuck do they think they are" and with that they walked off.

I sat there for ages thinking about what they had said. On the one hand I was sitting opposite a couple of night clubs that seemed to be filled with predominantly white people who didn't seem to be too bothered about the rioting and then I get asked a question like that from a couple of Asian lads and meanwhile less than a couple of miles away in another section of the city there were black youths wrecking the place.

By midnight we were all back in the van and had been joined by a local officer who asked if we wanted a guided tour of the area. It seemed like a great idea and he took us to various sites, ending up in the red light district. It was based on what looked like a nice housing area with big houses around a sort of village green. There were girls in pairs on every street corner, dozens of them. There were red light bulbs in the hallways and porches of several of the houses, with some girls openly flaunting their wares at the window. Portsmouth doesn't have a red light district as such, which is surprising given that it is a Naval town, you'd think we would. I'm not saying we haven't got prostitutes, of course we have, but we haven't got anything like this. It was quite an eye opener. Our guide told me to pull over and stop on the corner where there were two ladies of the night standing having a fag. One of them was a white girl, in her late 20s I think, although it was difficult to tell exactly because it was clear she'd had a rough life. She had unkempt blonde hair and had several sores on her face. The other girl was black and must have weighed over 15 stone. She was a big unit. She was wearing a white tee shirt and had absolutely enormous tits, they were huge and she was bra-less. Our guide obviously knew both girls and they knew him by name. They chatted for a couple of minutes and he told them we had come up from Portsmouth to see the sights. He then turned to the black girl and offered her five quid if she'd lift her tee shirt for his guests. Her smile disappeared in an instant when one of the wags at the back of the carrier shouted out.

"And I'll give you a tenner if you keep it on love".

With that we drove off.

A convoy of Hampshire Police Transit carriers heads towards Birmingham city centre.

We stopped off at Park Lane nick, a huge place that looked like it must have been at least a hundred years old. We were taken down to a large hall in the basement where we got some tea and coffee. We had been there about half an hour when we were joined by about 50 officers from Sussex who had only just arrived in Birmingham having left Lewis at 4 o'clock that afternoon and driven up in a convoy of Landrovers at 40 mph. They were knackered and somewhat pissed off when they found out we'd flown up again!

The following night we were back at the Bullring watching the revellers enjoy themselves but we could hear on the radio that things were going badly wrong in the Lozells Road area of Handsworth again. This is what we came for. We were champing at the bit for a piece of the action and we kept volunteering our services, as did every other unit that was there but it kept being declined. It was really frustrating just sitting there. Eventually in the early hours we were called in straight to Handsworth. To our grave disappointment the rioting had long since been quelled and we were just needed to relieve those who had been involved and to patrol the streets to ensure there was no re-occurrence. It was now 4 am and we were posted in pairs every 50 feet or so along a two mile stretch of road. It seemed that every shop had been looted and smashed. There were several burnt out cars still smouldering, filling the still morning air with that acrid burnt rubber smell and the road was littered with bricks and rubble. It was a pretty run down area by the looks of things even before the rioting but now it looked like a scene from Beirut or Soweto. It was really quite depressing. We just stood in our pairs kicking our heels and whiling away the time and looking forward to tomorrow's breakfast.

Just as it was getting light so we could hear a strange noise coming from the far end of the road. Every single one of us looked to our right to see a V formation of a dozen Police motorcycles taking up the full width of the Lozells Road and moving at about 20 mph. The noise was the leading motorcyclist standing up on the foot pegs of his Norton playing the Post Horn Gallop on a full length horn! It was bloody superb and they got rapturous applause from us all.

Sunday night was incredibly quiet and by Monday morning the West Midlands Police stood us and the other foreign units down.

We drove to Birmingham airport and parked next to Concorde which alas, wasn't to be our plane home. Had it been, it would have crowned an already great weekend.

It wasn't quite perfect because I found out upon our return to Southsea that we were losing Mick Moorse as our Sgt. After less than 18 months he was transferring up to the control room having been told that it was unlikely he would ever be allowed back onto Traffic. He was philosophical about it all and as always left with a big smile on his face. Our new Sgt was to be Laurie Mullen, newly promoted having spent most of his career so far as a DC (Detective Constable).

Pompey were playing Tottenham in a Milk Cup game at Fratton Park. Everything was quiet leading up to the evening kick-off. I was sat in the area car on my own in Palmerston Road.

Charlie-One to Victor Sierra 51

Victor Sierra 51 go ahead

Make the Travellers Rest pub, Somers Road, large fight in progress

Victor Sierra 51, Roger

Charlie-One do I have any other units to back up 51 please?

Various others volunteered their services and headed towards as Charlie-One came back with updates that they were still receiving calls and it looked serious.

I was the first to arrive and it was carnage. Every window was smashed, there were tables and chairs outside on the street, the pool table was on its side in the doorway and there were pool balls strewn across the forecourt. There were several people with serious facial injuries, including one who had the thick end of a snooker cue sticking out the back of his skull. There was blood everywhere. As I and other officers tended the injured we came under fire from a barrage of stones and bottles being hurled by a mob of about 200 Spurs fans who had amassed in an adjacent side street. Football units arrived to clear them away and a handful of arrests were made. All the injured were from London. All the arrests were of Spurs supporters. It didn't make sense. Standing on the corner about 100 yards away I could see a couple of familiar faces. Paul Van Clerk and Froggy Ford seemed very interested in what was going on but didn't venture any closer. After leaving the pub I joined the football units in rounding up the Spurs fans to escort them to the ground. We cornered them outside the Bingo Hall at Bradford junction and they were hopping mad saying they had been set up by the Pompey boys and they were really pissed off about it. As we set about searching them we found a number of weapons dumped under parked cars and on a nearby window sill.

I later spoke to one of our football liaison officers Gary King and he was very interested in what I had to say on my observations. It transpired that a meeting had taken place in London the week before between the hierarchy of the 6.57 Crew and their opposite numbers at Tottenham. Over a friendly drink in a north London pub they drew up their battle plan. A group of Tottenham fans would be directed to the Travellers Rest pub where a group of Pompey fans would set about having a fight with them. Not those that were organising this you understand. No, no, it was rarely them that ever got involved; their job was to direct operations. However, such is the nature of the type of person we are dealing with here that it goes without saying that some double dealing went on as well, despite the apparent cordial relations amongst the upper element. On this particular evening the 6.57 Crew didn't just send a small group in to have a scrap. They sent a large group armed to the teeth with knives, cosh's and lumps of wood with nails protruding from them. In return the 200 or so Spurs fans that just happened to be in the right area at the right time must have been directed there by somebody?

Sometimes no matter how hard you try, you just can't help people. Some of them really don't want it and get quite agitated if you persist.

Charlie-One to Victor Sierra 51

Victor Sierra 51 go ahead

Somewhere in Palmerston Road precinct there is a tramp laying on a bench and passers by are rather worried about him because of the weather

Victor Sierra 51, Roger

It was just before midnight in early November and it was very cold. There was an early frost and tonight's temperatures were due to dip to -2 degrees. Geoff and I found our tramp laying out on a bench at the end of Palmerston Road. He was in his mid 60s I'd say but looked reasonably fit for his age. His swept back grey hair was somewhat unkempt as you'd expect and he wore an old tweed blazer, a cardigan and a pair of trousers that were appallingly short. He had a pair of shoes on but no socks. He wasn't one of our regular 'roadies' as we knew most of them quite well. He was well spoken and completely sober, but that's where the niceties ended. He wasn't at all pleased to see us even though we assured him that we weren't here to move him on. However we were very concerned about him because of the cold weather. He waved us away with his hand and said it wasn't really that cold and that we should come back in the winter when it gets really bad! We offered to take him up to the Mill House shelter which he flatly refused or to the Salvation Army hall in Albert Road and again he declined. He refused to tell us when he had last eaten or had a hot drink. He had no relatives or anybody that we could contact on his behalf. He certainly didn't fall into the category of mental health or vulnerable adult and therefore we couldn't force the issue. He was getting more and more angry with us and in the end told us not to concern ourselves with him, he was perfectly comfortable, now bugger off. We bid him good night and he lay back down again.

Two hours later and Geoff and I were sat on the seafront keeping watch on the out muster from the clubs when Laurie Mullen called up on the radio wishing to speak with us.

PS130 to Victor Sierra 51

Victor Sierra 51 go ahead

You know that tramp you checked in Palmerston Road earlier?

Answer yes

He's dead. Would you like to liaise with me back at the scene please?

At first we thought this was some kind of a wind up but it wasn't. He was laying exactly where we'd left him two hours previously. Sgt Mullen was obviously concerned about what we had or hadn't done to safe guard this man's well being and said that the Coroner would probably be even tougher on us. Geoff and I felt awful. We interrogated each other for the rest of the night about whether we could have done more or perhaps detained him to a place of safety but the more we questioned each other the less of an answer we seemed to have. We were put out of our misery a few days later when the post mortem report revealed that he had died from natural causes; a heart attack and not hypothermia. In truth it didn't make us feel any better about it.

CHAPTER 10

1986. You're grounded

I had a week's annual leave owing to me from last year together with several rest days that I had accumulated and took the best part of two weeks off at the start of the New Year. I was actually very tired, both physically and mentally. It had been a very busy few months at Southsea and I was up to my ears in work. My box was over flowing with more than 30 files on the go at once, I had done quite a lot of Acting Sgt duties too and at times I'd been the only area car driver on the Relief, so there really wasn't that much time for luxuries like paperwork.

I was sitting at home watching TV when the phone rang. It was Inspector Watson who asked where the file on Whitcher and Cairns was because it was in court tomorrow. I couldn't remember whether I'd submitted it or not so I volunteered to come in straight away and do it in my own time. I got to the nick about 7.30 and sure enough there it was sitting amongst all the other files. It took me about an hour to get it all sorted and once I'd got it signed up I gave it to one of the late shift to take it across to Central and drop it in the CPS box for tomorrows court. No sooner had I done that than I got called into Inspector Watson's office. He said he wouldn't tolerate files being late and that as far as he was concerned I had neglected my duty and he promptly reported me for just that. No amount of protesting from me about heavy work load, acting duties, only area car driver etc was going to wash with him and that the final decision on what my punishment might be would rest with the Superintendent. I didn't exactly enjoy the rest of my leave.

My first day back was on a special RSG operation but nobody knew what it was, other than it was only going to be a single night out and not a week away. After meeting at Fratton we travelled up to HQ at Winchester, where after yet another curry we were briefed about Operation Roger and the first escort of cruise missiles from RAF Greenham Common out onto Salisbury Plain. This was a top secret operation and from now on we weren't allowed to make any phone calls or talk to anybody not connected to this mission. Absolute secrecy was the key to this operation being a success. We then boarded our carriers and headed towards Newbury nick, where we had another briefing about the route and what the objective of the operation was. Just after midnight we entered the base via a rear gate and I caught my first sight of a cruise missile silo. Huge concrete and grass bunkers the size of two football pitches housed several enormous trucks that had about 50 wheels each. Each truck had a long tube like box on the back and inside each tube was a cruise missile. The night air was awash with exhaust smoke that seemed to hang in the stillness, punctuated only by another truck cutting a swathe through it. American accents barked their orders to one another as Hampshire Police's Traffic Department BMW 528's sat alongside a couple of USAF Police Chevrolet's. In all there were four missile trucks mixed in with several other army vehicles that were interspersed by RSG units from Hampshire, Wiltshire and Thames Valley Police. Traffic vehicles would lead and escort the whole lot and it wasn't to stop for anything until it reached its destination on Salisbury Plain. Shortly after midnight the convoy was ready to role and we headed out towards the main gate which had been secured by a hundred or more Thames Valley officers, desperately trying to keep the peace women at bay. They threw eggs and paint at the missile trucks as it headed out the gate and south onto the A34 towards Hampshire. As it headed down past a wooded area so more protesters leapt out from behind the trees and lay down in the road to stop it. As soon as the convoy stopped so the missile truck in front of us was invaded by dozens of protesters who clambered up the sides armed with hammers and an axe. Some daubed slogans in paint along the sides whilst others just hollered and whooped like Red Indians. We de-bussed and climbed up the sides of the truck and started throwing the protesters off, quite literally. It was really quite scary because it was at least 20 feet up and I certainly didn't fancy falling or being pushed off. As the convoy got moving again so we had to fend off the protesters and ended up running beside our truck for what seemed like miles and you know how much I hate cross country running! Having outrun the protesters we managed to jump back on board our carrier and headed down the A34 until we reached the major junction with the A303 at Bullington Cross which we had already been warned was likely to be the big flash point. At this stage the trucks would be at their slowest as they negotiated the tight bends that would take them up onto the A303. The intel was right, we got ambushed by about 300 protesters from all angles. They jumped onto the trucks, laid down in the road, threw paint and bricks and generally made life for the Police very, very difficult indeed. The convoy got stopped several times but slowly we managed to disperse them enough to get it moving again. The only other time we got ambushed after that was driving through some small village in rural Wiltshire somewhere but in comparison with the previous efforts it didn't take us long to clear them. After reaching Salisbury Plain we entered another army base with our load and as soon as the gates were slammed shut behind us we could all breath a sigh of relief. But what intrigued us most of all was that we had all be sworn to secrecy during our briefings and that nobody was to know any details in advance and yet the protesters knew exactly what was happening, what time it was leaving and even the route it was taking! I'm quite sure it wasn't supposed to be like that.

I'd been back at Southsea doing acting duties for two days when I got summoned upstairs to see Superintendent Bob Dawes. It was obviously about the paperwork issue. I sat in front of him and had to explain again why I hadn't submitted this file in good time and tried to convince him that we were short staffed and incredibly busy right now, that I was the only area car driver a lot of the time and was doing a lot more acting duties in recent months. Whilst I wasn't expecting too much in the way of sympathy I did at least expect him to acknowledge that we were very busy and somewhat down on staff numbers. It goes without saying that I was expecting a big bollocking but I was ready for that and would take it on the chin. I wasn't prepared for what came next though. He very calmly told me that my excuses were nothing more than that, just excuses and that he was tired of his officers constantly submitting files late and that it wasn't good enough. Therefore to teach me and everybody else here a lesson he was grounding me from driving for a month. He would have done less damage if he'd plunged a stake through my heart. I sat there completely speechless.

"That'll be all, you may go" he said wafting his arm in a get out of my office type gesture. I stood up still trying to come to terms with my punishment.

"I presume then sir that as I'm clearly not capable of supervising my own paperwork that you no longer require me to perform acting sergeant duties either?" I enquired; somewhat sarcastically it has to be said.

"No I still need you to do acting" he replied, not even bothering to lift his head and look at me. I thought about this for all of two seconds.

"I'm sorry sir but the answers no, if I'm not fit enough to drive then I'm not fit enough to supervise the Relief" I said somewhat belligerently.

"PC Woodward don't push your luck with me or I'll see to it that you never drive the area car again. I think you're right though in that you clearly aren't of the right calibre to perform acting duties so I'll find somebody else who is, now get out".

I stood outside his door fit to burst. I was absolutely furious. What an arrogant bastard I thought. If he spent a bit of time finding out what our problems are out on the street instead of spending his entire day flirting with every female that enters the building then he might have some idea what we are up against I fumed. Grounded from driving for a month, Jesus how am I going to cope with that? I went back downstairs and within an hour the whole Relief knew about it. Everyone's reactions were the same. Why? What's the point? How's that going to help the rest of us if we need the area car? If you'd been a beat bobby what would your punishment have been then, to take your bloody boot laces away? It was the lowest point of my career and I felt very hard done by.

The next day Laurie Mullen returned from leave and I had to explain what had occurred. He was brilliant and went straight upstairs to confront Bob Dawes who stood his ground and told Laurie that I could come and ask for my driving permit back in exactly one month. Laurie and I reached an agreement that I would spend the next week or so sorting out every single file in my box and would submit the whole lot in one go and dump it on Bob Dawes desk to give him some idea what we did on a daily basis. Geoff was due back from a course next week so at least we had an area car and Laurie was most insistent that I continue to crew it even if I couldn't drive it. For the sake of the Relief I reluctantly agreed but I was thoroughly pissed off about the whole thing.

Missing juveniles can often be a bit traumatic, especially for the parents obviously and no matter what resources we end up using it's rarely enough to satisfy an anxious mum and dad.

Charlie-One to Victor Sierra 51

Victor Sierra 51 go ahead

28 Delamere Road please, report of two very young mispers. They have been missing for over an hour already

Victor Sierra 51, Roger

Mum was absolutely frantic. Her seven year old daughter Katie and her ten year old friend Mandy had been playing 'shop' out in the front forecourt of their terraced house. They had been playing for a couple of hours and been in and out of the house borrowing tins of food to sell and using plastic coins and a cash register. But now they were gone and all the food and toys had been left in the forecourt. We searched the house, shed and garden first because kids have a habit of hiding from parents to scare them but there was no trace. We called in the rest of the Relief and did house to house and searched the neighbour's gardens but to no avail and of course we put out the girls descriptions to every unit in the city and beyond. The girl's details were immediately posted onto the PNC as missing. The other girl's parents arrived and there were lots of tears as Katie's mum continually apologised to Mandy's parents for not ensuring their daughters complete safety. The parents were openly talking of them being abducted although we did our best to reassure them that probably hadn't happened, although we had no evidence to back that up with, we were just hoping that wasn't the case. We'd been at the house for almost two hours now.

Charlie-One to Victor Sierra 51

Victor Sierra 51 go ahead

Are you free to speak?

This was always control room code to ensure that there were no prying ears because the follow-up transmission was going to be sensitive. I went outside into the street and listened intently to the message from Charlie-One before going back indoors to speak to the parents. The girls had been found.

"Oh my God, where?" both mums shrieked in unison.

"London" I replied with my eyebrows raised so high they almost shot off my forehead.

"London?" both women shrieked.

They were now safely in the hands of the Metropolitan Police at Kennington Police Station and they should get themselves up there as soon as possible to collect them. I didn't really have any further details but it was likely that we would have to return tomorrow to talk to them and the girls together to ascertain what happened. We all breathed huge sighs of relief as the parents quickly gathered their belongings and headed straight for London.

The next afternoon Geoff and I went to meet young Katie and her mum at Delaware Road. We all sat there open mouthed as she told us her story. She couldn't remember why they had decided to go to London or whose idea it was but they both thought it was a great idea. They walked the mile and a half from home to Portsmouth and Southsea railway station where they waited until they saw a couple together that could pass for the parents of two young girls. As the couple went through the turn stile so they tagged on right behind them, making it look like they were all together. They boarded the train and got off at Waterloo where they wondered around for a while. They then left the station and walked out into the big wide world that is London. After about half an hour they were approached by a lady who offered to cook them beans on toast and as they were very hungry by now they said yes and so the lady took them back to her house. There she cooked them beans on toast and then said they needed a bath because they looked a bit grubby. So she plonked them in the bath and whilst they were in there she phoned the Police who came and collected them. Geoff and I sat there in silence. Then Katie's mum told her to tell us about the alarm clock. Young Katie then told us that they had packed some spare clothes into a small pink ruck sack together with an alarm clock so that when they stayed the night in a hotel they could set the clock very early so they could get up and leave without paying! We both looked at the mother who shrugged her shoulders and held up her hands in an incredulous manner. Young Katie looked so sweet and innocent sat in the chair that surely this must have all been Mandy's idea because she was ten and Katie was only seven. But apparently not, it was all Katie's idea.

We then drove to Powerscourt Road to talk to Mandy and her parents and Mandy confirmed everything that Katie had said and all of us were just so relieved at the way things had panned out. It could so easily have become a tragedy, the sort of thing that hits the national headlines. We got back into the car and Geoff said.

"Kids eh, who'd have em?"

A month had passed and it was time for me to go upstairs and request my driving permit be returned. I nervously entered Bob Dawes office and felt like Oliver holding out the bowl and saying "Please sir, can I have some more?"

He didn't even lift his head as he quietly said.

"No, come back and see me next month".

"I'm sorry sir I don't quite understand, I thought you said this was for a month" I pleaded.

"What I actually said PC Woodward was that you could come and *ask* for it in a month, at no time did I say you were guaranteed it back in a month" he said chewing on the arm of his specs.

"So come back and see me next month and maybe we'll have another chat about it. Shut the door on your way out".

I stood at the top of the stairs again just boiling with rage. My fists were clenched and I was shaking all over. You spiteful bastard. What a sneaky, underhand and childish way to behave. I trudged downstairs and sat in the Sgts office close to tears. Laurie was speechless and said many of the things I'd already said to myself. I couldn't stand being in that station a moment longer, so I grabbed my big hat and went for a very long walk.

Southampton were playing Brighton in a cup game. This wouldn't normally affect us but the yobs got to find out that a lot of the Southampton fans who lived on the Isle of Wight were travelling to the ferry by train and that it would be passing through Fratton station at 1830 and they intended to do some damage to them as it stopped. About 30 of the Eastney mob were gathered on the approach road to the station as several units arrived to usher them away. We knew all of them, although some better than others. One youth in particular seemed very agitated by all this and although I had seen him on a number of occasions with the others I'd not actually dealt with him personally. He was 19 years old with a skin head hair cut and big jug ears. He had a foul mouth on him and was for all the world an out and out yob. Despite moving him away several times he kept coming back and eventually I arrested him for conduct likely to cause a breach of the peace. He went berserk and it took several of us to restrain him and throw him in a van. His name was Michael Nayler.

A week later I had to go to his house in Esslemont Road to serve some amended charges on him and he was extremely abusive the minute I walked through the door. He called me all the names under the sun and threatened to "get me" the next time he saw me out of uniform. Police officers are quite used to hearing such threats and take most of them with a very large pinch of salt but there was something slightly unhinged about Nayler and the manner in which he said it.

My second month in the wilderness had come to an end but I was extremely reluctant to go cap in hand back to Bob Dawes only to have him shove it in my face once again. I'd already spoken to Malcolm Bully who said that if the decision had been his he would have ripped my head off, made me walk Albert Road for a couple of days, asked me if I'd learned my lesson and then told me to bloody well get on with it "cos you're a damned good copper and I wish I had more like you". He went on to state that he would have a word with Mr Dawes on my behalf.

I told Laurie Mullen of my concerns and he agreed that I probably shouldn't be placed in that humiliating position again. He therefore went upstairs and returned a few minutes later with my driving permit. I've never been so glad to see a three inch square piece of laminated card in my life! I never understood quite why Bob Dawes treated me the way he did but what I do know is that what little respect I had for him the first time around completely evaporated second time around and that true leaders of men like Malcolm Bully earn the respect of their subordinates by being conciliatory and compassionate and never resort to bullying in order to enforce their rank.

Large scale public disorder was still a big problem all over the city at weekends with groups of youths starting fights in pubs and clubs or out on the streets somewhere. It was actually quite tiresome seeing the same old faces committing the same type of offences and then just getting their wrists slapped at court, only to be released straight back out onto the streets to wreak further havoc on the local populous.

It was interesting to watch court officials squirm as they themselves became the victims of the intimidation tactics used by these youths when in court. For them it was a good day out. It held no fear for them whatsoever and the whole process of British justice was treated with utter contempt. Each defendant would stand in the dock smirking and sniggering back towards a large group of his mates sat in the public gallery. These youths would constantly interrupt proceedings by coughing loudly, laughing or by making stupid noises, but the favourite game was to constantly get up and leave, usually two or three at a time. Then after a couple of minutes they would re-enter as a couple more got up to leave, thereby ensuring a constant stream of irritating back ground noise. It was particularly galling as a Police officer to have to sit there and watch this happen, powerless to intervene unless instructed to do so by the Bench, which they rarely did. Most of the Magistrates and the Clerk of the Court seemed to be somewhat overwhelmed by the behaviour they were experiencing but it rarely, if ever, seemed to enter their heads that this is exactly the sort of thing that the residents of Portsmouth were having to put up with day in and day out, although in truth it was always a lot worse than this. They probably had no idea that they were actually becoming victims of this mob rule themselves and inwardly felt rather threatened by their behaviour. What they should have done was only allow a maximum of two or maybe none at all to sit in the public gallery and then handed down some proper deterrent sentences to exercise some kind of control over them rather than it being the other way around.

The Palmerston Road and Osborne Road area could be a flash point of trouble as the pubs kicked out and hoards of people made their way to the night clubs. There was an assistance shout from a Central PC outside the Some Place Else Club in Palmerston Road and as we arrived I could see that the group involved was a mixture of the usual 6.57 Crew and many of the hangers-on. A couple of them had been arrested and then the others set upon the officers already there. We pushed and shoved the others away and one by one they filtered back towards the scene. I'd already spoken to Michael Nayler and his mate Michael Navrot. They'd had quite a lot to drink and Nayler in particular was his usual unpleasant self. It was almost as though he was begging us to arrest him; it gave him a bit of kudos in front of his mates I suppose. He kept on coming back and eventually I had no choice but to nick him. Straight away he started to fight and we ended up on the ground, rolling around on the pavement whilst Navrot and a few of the others screamed further encouragement towards him. Nayler was handcuffed and as I held him against the van he spat at me and shouted out.

"You're a fuckin dinlo Woodward, I'll have you next time I see you out on the street, do you hear me, you're a fuckin dinlo" he screamed.

Navrot and several others got arrested too but I was somewhat uneasy that Nayler now appeared to be deliberately targeting me during these confrontations. He wouldn't do it towards other officers, it didn't appear to be a general anti Police attitude he had, although he clearly was, but it was always me he fronted up to.

Criminal activity can sometimes be bad for your health. It's an occupational hazard that occasionally you might get hurt.

Charlie-One to Victor Sierra 51

Victor Sierra 51 go ahead

Make 17 Devonshire Avenue please, not quite sure what's going on but ambulance are attending a man with a severely cut leg.

Victor Sierra 51, Roger

It was only half ten in the morning so this was a slightly unusual call to receive. I was single crewed and as I pulled up outside the address I saw a young man sat on the garden path with one of his shoes off. There was blood everywhere. He was quite up front about the manner in which he had injured himself and confessed that he was burgling the house and in broad daylight he kicked the front door in. As he did so his foot went through the glass and as his foot was withdrawn so it scraped on a piece of glass that sliced the back of his heel open. The adrenaline was pumping and he hadn't noticed. He was busy ransacking the place and had gathered the stereo and the speakers together at the bottom of the stairs when he saw the blood coming from his right leg. Then of course he felt the pain and sat down to have a look. It transpired that he had completely severed his Achilles tendon and his right foot was now dangling like a limp flag.

As he was sitting on the stairs so the rather startled owner returned home. Our burglar casually apologised for the mess and asked him to phone for an ambulance. I arrested him for burglary and after I cautioned him he rather comically replied.

"Well I'm not going to do a runner am I"

I escorted the ambulance up to the QA hospital and sat in the cubicle with him as a number of hospital staff came and went to examine him. Word quickly spread through A&E that there was a patient with a severed Achilles tendon and doctors and nurses from various departments arrived to take a look. It was unusual because this type of injury is normally internal of course and so Billy Burglar quickly became a bit of a celebrity and boy, did he milk it. Most of the staff felt sorry for him until I deliberately pointed out how he had sustained it.

Geoff and I were on nights and for once it was fairly quiet. The pubs had kicked out without too much fuss and those who were making their way to the clubs seemed to be behaving themselves. We were just cruising around chatting away when we stopped at the traffic lights at the junction of Albert Road and Waverley Road. We had been there for about 30 seconds when we both noticed a young man standing in the middle of Albert Road about 50 yards ahead of us. He was standing in a shadow so it was difficult to make out precisely what was going on but it looked like he was urinating in a big arc in the middle of the street, a bit like small boys do at school when they have peeing up the wall competitions! Go on, admit it, you did it too. There were several other people on the pavement looking at this chap and then we saw a woman run across the road towards him and as she got to him so she turned away with her hands over her face screaming. The lights went green and I drove towards him and to our horror he wasn't peeing, he was bleeding. He had severed the artery in his wrist and there was a huge arc of blood pumping from his arm. He just stood there in shock not really knowing what to do with himself as the blood rose above his head and shot about five or six feet across the road. I grabbed his arm and held it above his head and we quickly but quietly walked him across the road and sat him down on the step to a nearby shop. Geoff went and moved the car from the middle of the road, grabbed the first aid kit, a blanket and called for an ambulance, seemingly all at the same time. The wound on the man's arm was about six inches long and it was a wide open clean wound. I clasped both my hands around it and tried to clamp it shut by exerting as much pressure as I could on it. I needed him to keep calm to reduce his heart rate and slow the stem of blood. I don't think I've ever seen so much come out of a human being who was still standing upright before. Geoff found a decent sized bandage and we wrapped it around the wound but within seconds it was sodden. The only way was for me to keep my hands clamped over it. Whilst we sat and waited for the ambulance so he calmly told us that he and his girlfriend had been arguing and that he had got very angry and punched a shop window. It smashed and his wrist was sliced open in the process. He was starting to become faint and his blood loss was really starting to concern us. Although I had managed to stem the worst of it, there was still a fair amount seeping through. At last the ambulance arrived and they wrapped a huge pad and bandage around his arm and whisked him off to hospital. Both Geoff and I were covered in blood and my hands in particular were sticky with the stuff. It took an hour to clean ourselves up. We found out later that he had lost so much blood that he ended up staying in hospital for over two weeks before he was fit enough to leave and had we not done what we did he would almost certainly have bled to death.

It was a baking hot Sunday afternoon; a real scorcher and Southsea seafront was packed with tourists and day trippers. The beaches were full to over flowing and there wasn't a single parking space to be found anywhere. I was single crewed as Geoff had arrested a breathalyser from an earlier RTA and so I sat outside Nero's night club facing the pier. It really was boiling hot, so hot in fact that parts of the road surface were actually beginning to melt and were turning into a black slush.

I was busily writing up my pocket book when I looked up and saw a yellow Datsun travelling along St. Helens Parade towards me, undertaking a line of queuing traffic. It then failed to give way at the junction and turned right towards me, accelerated hard, overtook a car, then braked hard and pulled across in front of it and stopped almost immediately on the pelican crossing outside the pier, forcing the car it had just overtaken to brake and swerve. I immediately recognised the car as belonging to one of the 6.57 Crew and then my suspicions were confirmed when I saw that the driver was Andy Bradford, otherwise known as 'Meathead'. He was a vicious bastard whose first three convictions were for GBH on Police officers. And he'd had plenty more since then. I then saw four youths run down the steps from the pier and scuffle with each other as they fought to get into the Datsun. Bradford kept driving forward and then slamming the brakes on and was laughing as he did it. Just as the last youth jumped into the car so Bradford drove away from the kerb but with the rear passenger door wide open and right at that moment there was a Ford Escort passing the Datsun and the collision was inevitable. The damage to the Escort was extensive and the rear bumper was ripped clean off and bounced across the road and into the gutter. Both cars pulled straight into the side of the road and I knew there was going to be trouble. Bradford and the others leapt out of the car and started shouting at the young driver in the Escort, thumping on the roof and bonnet whilst Bradford screamed at him to get out of the car. I ran over to them and before I had even got there I saw that there was a crowd of over 100 people gathered on the promenade just above the scene looking on. Bradford saw me coming across the road and shouted out.

"I don't need you, fuck off".

I moved the others away from the Escort and got the terrified driver out of the car to ensure he was not injured in any way. I explained to both of them that I had witnessed the accident and that they needed to exchange details and then Bradford started to get really irate, accusing me of lying and trying to stitch him up. As we argued over whose fault it was I became aware that the group of four youths who had been with him in the car now numbered more than a dozen, all in swim shorts having come from the beach and within another couple of minutes there must have been 30 of them. Most of them were from the Eastney group of youths with a few other faces I recognised. Bradford saw this as his chance to get away and jumped back in his car and started it up. I leant in through the driver's window and removed the keys. He leapt out of the car ranting and raving, demanding I give back the keys. This was rapidly getting out of control and I was now completely surrounded by this baying mob that were now shouting and screaming in my face. I was going to need some urgent assistance. In a flash I felt hands all over my body as my radio was whipped from the holster on my belt and my truncheon and handcuffs were grabbed and removed. My hat was knocked off my head and I took a kick in the back of my leg. They all laughed out loud and I felt incredibly vulnerable. Then I heard them say things like.

"Go on Meathead, get him on the deck and we can finish him off"

"Woodwards gonna die"

"Come on, this is exactly what we've been waiting for"

I had to stand my ground and not lose face. Even though my heart was pounding like never before I fronted them up and jabbed my finger into their faces as I growled out loud.

"I know each and everyone of you by name, I know your dates of birth and I know where you all live, so if any of you lay a single finger on me then you will all get lifted over the next few days and I'll do my fucking damnedest to ensure you all go down for it. Now back off".

To my complete surprise they did but there was Bradford with his hand out stretched beckoning me with his fingers.

"Keys" he said.

I had no choice and I dropped them into his hand and he jumped back into his car with the others and they drove off. The others drifted off back onto the beach as I turned to the young lad with the Escort who was crying uncontrollably. I felt like joining him to be honest. Within a few minutes a lady came across from the promenade with my radio. She'd seen one of them dump it into a bin and I was very grateful to have it back. I found my hat in the gutter but my truncheon and cuffs were never seen again, no doubt they were kept as some kind of trophy.

We were back on nights and were particularly short staffed, so much so that I had to crew the area car on my own. Geoff was out in the van with Ray Hallett and Roger was single crewed in a panda. Everyone else was either on leave, on a course or off sick. I didn't feel too good myself and was obviously coming down with something. It was a very warm and humid night, one of those where everybody complains the next morning because they couldn't sleep type of nights. By meal break I was feeling really rough but because we were so short decided I couldn't really go off sick, it wouldn't be fair on the others. I went out in the car and drove down to a place called The Circle where I wound the seat back a little and closed my eyes, I felt terrible.

A few minutes later I became aware of a set of headlights shining right in through the front of the car. I opened my eyes and saw it was Geoff and Ray in the van and they were killing themselves laughing at me. I gave them the finger and just drove off. I was feeling particularly grumpy by now and just wanted to curl up and sleep. I drove down to the Shell garage on Goldsmith Avenue and parked around the side of the building. It wasn't open and it was nice and quiet here so I won't be disturbed. It was so warm that I kept the drivers window wound right down to let some air in as I reclined the seat right back until it was almost flat. I was just nodding off when I thought I had better remove the keys from the ignition just in case somebody leans in and takes them. I dropped them onto the passenger seat and within seconds I was out for the count.

Charlie-One to Victor Sierra 51

Oh I don't fucking believe this.

Victor Sierra 51, yes go ahead I said very wearily

Make Locksway Road area please further to follow

Victor Sierra 51, Roger

Cursing and swearing I wound the seat back up and then went to start the car. No keys. Where are the keys I said to myself, still slightly comatosed. I looked at the ignition, no they weren't there, I felt my pockets, no they weren't there either. Then I remembered I'd put them on the passenger seat but as I felt around for them in the dark I couldn't find them. I put the light on, still I couldn't find them.

Charlie-One to Victor Sierra 51

Victor Sierra 51 go ahead

What's your ETA for Locksway Road please?

Erm.........About two or three minutes

I got out of the car and felt my pockets again, nothing. I bent back into the car and fished around on the floor for them, nothing. Where the hell are they?

Charlie-One to Victor Sierra 51

Victor Sierra 51 go ahead

Have you lost anything at all?

You bastards! Yes I'd been well and truly had. Within seconds the van turned up on the forecourt and they threw the keys at me. I was still feeling rough and merely drove back to the nick in a big huff and then took the last hour or so off sick.

Within 48 hours I was back and laughed out loud as they described finding me virtually unconscious in the Volvo. They could see the keys on the seat and used a coat hangar that we usually opened locked cars with, unfurled it and then passed it in through the window, hooked the keys up with it and cried with laughter as the keys literally passed my nose and out of the car. Their favourite bit was watching me desperately searching for them whilst being called by the control room that were obviously in on the joke as well. Tossers!

Over the last couple of years the south of England had been plagued by something called the Peace Convoy, where New Age Travellers, or NATS would lead the hippy life style at various music festivals and gatherings during the year and then they'd all descend on Stonehenge for the summer solstice in June. The trouble was that over a period of time a lot of damage had been done to the ancient stones and its surrounding area and so English Heritage applied to the High Court for a banning order and a four mile exclusion zone and thus conflict was inevitable. In the summer of 1985 this had resulted in mass confrontation between the NATS and Police units from Wiltshire and Hampshire in what was later labelled the 'Battle of the Beanfield'. The Police had corralled the hippies into a field and after a lengthy stand-off the Police moved in to evict the travellers and move them on. It resulted in a violent clash where the hippies were driving their trucks and buses straight into Police carriers to maximise the damage and cause injury. This resulted in the Police having to do what they could to prevent it from carrying on and to restore some kind of order. In the mayhem that ensued the press were quick to show Police officers wielding truncheons and smashing the windows on a bus to get at the driver. What the media failed to show was that same bus had just deliberately T boned a Police carrier and it had to be stopped from causing further damage. But it was the only clip that was ever shown on TV and it was repeated over and over again.

In June this year there were obvious concerns about a repeat performance. The national media were very much against the whole hippy invasion and questioned the legality of the vehicles these anarchic people were living in and then driving on the roads. There were further concerns over the welfare of their off-spring together with the fact that many were claiming benefits when the rest of the country was of the opinion that they weren't entitled to. The over riding concern though was that the numbers appeared to have doubled since last year and they had set up camp at Stoney Cross in the New Forest and would move towards Stonehenge later in the week.

All RSG units were required for a special operation and we all met up at the Support Headquarters at Netley, near Southampton. We were joined by hundreds of other officers from within Hampshire, together with units from Surrey, Wiltshire, Thames Valley and the Met. The hangar at the newly opened public order training facility at Netley was full as the Chief Constable John Duke welcomed us to Operation Daybreak. The press were there to record everything and after further briefings we boarded our carriers and headed west towards the New Forest in the biggest Police convoy I had ever seen. There were more than 150 carriers and numerous support vehicles weaving their way along the A31 towards Stoney Cross. We entered the encampment at day break and written eviction orders were served on every occupant to quit the site immediately. It took several hours to organise things but every single one of the vehicles that could be driven was then escorted from the site to a special compound near Cadnam some ten miles away. Here, specialist officers from the Traffic Department examined each and every vehicle for its road worthiness together with the owner to ensure that he or she was also legal. Whilst they were doing that so DSS officials were brought in to establish whether each individual was entitled to claim, given their current status and child welfare officers from Social Services examined the conditions these children were expected to live in and to interrogate their educational needs. It was the single biggest Police operation ever mounted in Hampshire and was a huge success. The timing of the operation together with the combined services approach really took the NATS by surprise and there was very little trouble.

I was part of the reception committee at Cadnam and was kept busy all day with over 200 vehicles being brought to the site by Traffic units. Each owner had to be photographed with their vehicle and then documented, assigned a parking area and then told to wait for the arrival of an examining officer. This process took over a week during which time I got to have a good look at the state of these vehicles and the very solid reasons behind Hampshire's stance in removing them from our roads.

The vehicles used by the NAT's are impounded.

I jumped on board a single decker bus of 1970s vintage. A lot of the floor was missing and wooden boards had been laid loose over the hole. There was a wood burning stove half way along the bus and a hole had been cut out of the bus roof so that the chimney stack could go through it. The stove itself wasn't even secured to the floor. At the rear was a pile of half a dozen mattresses and loads of blankets that I wouldn't have allowed a dog to use. In the far right corner there was a metal bucket that was the toilet. It was full to over flowing with urine and faeces and the smell was gut wrenching and I had to leave. I found out later that this bus was home to six people including two very small kids. On a double decker bus we found that they weren't even using a stove but had an open fire placed on a metal grate upstairs! The whole area was blackened with soot and the remains of charcoaled wood were strewn everywhere. Discarded meat bones littered the floor together with dozens of tin cans, milk cartons and unwashed cutlery. It was pure filth. The Traffic Department were having great fun though and discovering hitherto unheard of offences under the Construction and Use Regulations. Every hour it seemed that one of them could be heard saying things like.

"Bloody hell, come and have a look at this, you'll never guess what I've found now".

Invariably we would have to satisfy our curiosity and wonder over to see if this one beat the last one we looked at and mostly it did. On a crappy old Bedford SB coach it was discovered that the fuel pump didn't work so the inventive driver removed the engine cover that was placed next to the drivers seat, that was prevalent on coaches of that age, to reveal the naked engine and in particular the fuel injectors. To keep the coach on the move they had used a large plastic water container, turned it upside down and used a plastic pipe connected to the filler cap and run it straight into the injectors. The bottom of the carrier was then cut off and fuel was poured directly into the container from another can whilst on the move!

A Morris Minor van was found not to have a floor at all and instead a large sheet of cardboard covered the area where metal should have been welded. The front seats were bolted to a couple of planks of wood that were then wedged into the inner sills. And an old BMC van that had a rear axle containing four wheels was found to only have two tyres fitted, with the inner wheels left to just spin in the air! Others had seriously defective brakes and steering, in one case no brakes at all with the driver relying solely on the hand brake to slow the vehicle down! Most had bald tyres and countless other defects.

Needless to say most of the vehicles weren't insured or MOT'd and all but a few were prohibited from being allowed back on the road and were destroyed. It was a highly successful operation all round.

People with mental health issues quite often end up being dealt with by the Police. Section 136 of the Mental Health Act allows a Police officer to remove a vulnerable person to a place of safety for their own protection and that place of safety is usually a hospital or the Police station. The station is always the last resort when all other avenues out on the street have been exhausted and once back at the station the search for somewhere else starts all over again, because your custody Sgt isn't going to be too pleased with you for bringing such a person into the station! Dealing with mental health issues isn't easy because quite simply Police officers receive no training on the subject whatsoever. And yet we are expected to know how to handle every type of illness and psychological problem known to man as if we had. But the really frustrating aspect in dealing with such people is that when the Police call upon the services of other professionals to assist them they quite often say there is little or nothing wrong with them and that they should be released. This even happens at hospitals where after depositing somebody who clearly has problems they are released back into the community a few hours later, only for the cycle of despair to start all over again. This very situation used to bring me into conflict with my own wife on occasions because she was a psychiatric nurse at St. James's Hospital which was based on Southsea's patch and we would have regular 'discussions' about such incidents.

Charlie-One to Victor Sierra 51

Victor Sierra 51 go ahead

Eastern Road please, Betty Fleming is playing with the traffic again

Victor Sierra 51, Roger

In truth there wasn't much traffic because it was three in the morning but Betty was one of our regulars. In fact she was so regular that we would sometimes get half a dozen calls a day about her antics. She lived in a ground floor council flat and would do all manner of strange things that resulted in the Police being called. Standing in the middle of the four lane Eastern Road in her night dress was one of them, standing out in the front garden just screaming would be another, dialling 999 more than 50 times a day was a favourite as was banging on all her neighbours doors in the early hours and then just standing there in silence when they opened it. Her doctor had her sectioned to St. James's several times but they released her because she wasn't deemed to be ill enough. Social Services tried to rehouse her but failed and they also tried to find her permanent residency at St. James's and met with the same result. And every time she went home so the Police got called back again. Her flat was a squalid affair and she clearly couldn't look after her self adequately and we all found it frustrating that the system clearly let her down. It took more than two years of constant distress for her, constant hassle for the Police and constant disturbance for her neighbours before finally a place could be found for her in a residential home down in Sussex.

The system also let down a lady called Josephine. I have no idea where we inherited her from but she just materialised one day when we were sent to a small restaurant in Albert Road where she had consumed a nice meal and didn't have the money to pay for it. Despite our best efforts we couldn't ascertain where she lived, whether or not she had any relatives, nothing in fact that might assist us in helping her. She just babbled complete nonsense. The restaurant manager was very good and agreed not to press the point just so long as we took her away. Over the next few weeks it seemed like every job we got deployed to there was Josephine looking back at us. They were silly things like a newsagent had become concerned at her standing in his shop reading all the magazines, even the men's ones, for more than two hours, or kicking over the dustbins in one street or opening all the milk bottles on peoples door steps or entering Tesco's, filling a basket and then not having the means to pay. We detained her several times and took her back to the station, handing her over to Social Services who basically said there was nothing they could do for her, so out she went again. A succession of doctors examined her and they all said much the same thing and so Josephine, a very friendly 50 something lady just slipped through the net because she simply didn't tick all the right boxes. It was both sad and very frustrating because even if she were to be charged with anything just what would a magistrate do? They would have her assessed by the very same people we had and the same conclusion would be reached so it would achieve absolutely nothing. The trouble was in releasing her the Police would get called back time and time again because the buck invariably stops with us.

Charlie-One to Victor Sierra 51

Victor Sierra 51 go ahead

Sorry about this but can you attend Craneswater Junior School please,

Jospehine is standing in the play ground upsetting the kids
Victor Sierra 51, Roger

She wasn't really upsetting them other than just standing there staring at everyone. I suspect most of the kids found it rather amusing as only kids can. Geoff and I took her by the arm and led her out of the school grounds to the patrol car. She was quite chatty today and I ended up asking her when was the last time she'd had a holiday. She couldn't remember. Geoff looked at me inquisitively. I put her in the back of the area car and I drove to The Hard where I purchased a one-way ferry ticket to the Isle of Wight. As the three of us stood at the window to the ticket office so the ticket master looked at me over his half-moon specs.

"You did say a one way ticket didn't you?" he asked.

"Yes please" I replied "For my friend here".

"Right..............OK then, that's £1.30 please and the next ferry is in five minutes" he said suspiciously.

We walked Josephine down the platform and I told her that the island was lovely at this time of year but that if she got herself into difficulty then she needed to get herself to Whitecroft Hospital, which is the islands equivalent to St. James's. She was very excited about going on holiday and I gave her the last tenner from my wallet to buy some dinner with. We guided her up the ramp and made sure she was safely on board. She stood and waved to us as if on a cruise liner as the ferry pulled away from its mooring and headed towards Ryde.

"I can't believe you've just done that" said Geoff through gritted teeth as we both waved back to her.

"Neither can I" I replied as we both turned to walk back along the platform.

We never saw her again and I can only hope that the authorities on the Isle of Wight treated her in the manner that she should have been afforded on the mainland.

Some mental health issues are a little more straight forward to deal with even if the process to sort things out on their behalf takes forever. I'd started to notice that Robert Wootton, one of our better known tramps had taken to sitting on a bench in Goldsmith Avenue close to the foot bridge that leads to Fratton railway station. It was quite a good place to beg for money and fags I suppose which is possibly why he chose it. The bench itself had been positioned in a sort of lay-by area set back slightly from the main pavement. I passed him everyday en route to and from work and after about two weeks realised that he had been there for a very long time. He had also stopped sitting on the bench and was now sat on the concrete and leant against the base of the bench. He seemed happy enough but then we started getting complaints coming in that he was swearing at passers by whilst others were concerned for his welfare. The Police attended a number of times but he was adamant that he was alright where he was. Unbeknown to us the Social Services had also visited him and had tried persuading him to get up and come to St. James's where they had sorted out a bed for him. He refused. However they had become so concerned about him that they used powers under the Mental Health Act to forcibly remove him to a place of safety and so we got called in to assist them.

Chris Robinson and I took the van to Goldsmith Avenue; there was no way he was getting in the back of my area car! We met a number of concerned social worker types and a GP and we all stood in a semi circle in front of Robert who was far from pleased at seeing any of us. Even standing ten feet away from him he absolutely wreaked of stale urine and excrement. He refused to get up. He was wearing two old fashioned army style great coats and two pairs of trousers held together with string. In the end we told him that if he refused to get up then we would have no choice but to lift him up. He just sat there muttering under his breath. Chris and I moved forward, took an arm each and tried lifting him but couldn't, not because he was fat or anything but because his coat was stuck to the concrete. Over the last couple of weeks he had wet himself and defecated into his clothes and they had in turn welded themselves to the ground. He was stuck fast and no amount of pulling him upwards was going to shift him. And the smell was unbearable. Undressing him in public was declared to be too undignified, as if sitting in two weeks worth of shit and piss wasn't! So I ran across the road to a wood yard and borrowed their metal shovel. I then pushed it under Roberts clothing several times and literally dug him out of the pavement. There was a ripping sound as the woollen coat fabric was torn away from the ground and Robert was lifted to his feet for the first time in weeks and gently moved to the van. Everyone was turning their head away to gulp a lung full of fresh air and holding it for as long as they could so as not to breathe the stench that was emulating from Robert. There were fleas everywhere, bloody hundreds of the things leaping off his coats as if they were abandoning a ship. He couldn't sit on the bench seats in the van because he wasn't strong enough to be able to hold himself upright and so we laid him down on the floor. Poor old Chris and a social worker got in with him as I wound down the front windows on the van to let some air in and then drove the one mile to St. James's on blues and twos with my head hanging out of the window. I have never smelt anything quite so stomach churning in all my life. After depositing Robert at the hospital we got out of there as quickly as possible, constantly scratching ourselves because we were convinced that the fleas had leapt onto us.

The van was abandoned outside the nick and was fumigated by a professional company before it could be used again whilst Chris and I dumped most of our uniform into sealed plastic bags and they were incinerated. We all wondered how it was that a human being could allow himself to fall into such a non-human state but also that he was actually one of the lucky ones that had been rescued, albeit like some badly treated dog, but at least he got some help.

About three months later I got sent to Solent Ward at St. James's on an enquiry and whilst there I was asked by the staff nurse if I recognised the man sat at the table who was currently being spoon fed by a nurse? I had to confess that I didn't but it was Robert. He was dressed in pyjamas and a dressing gown, had neatly cut hair and no beard and a full set of newly fitted dentures, hence the puréed food. It was an amazing transformation and one of the real success stories where the authorities got it right.

I was on early turn and it was just past three o'clock in the morning when the phone rang. When you have a two year old child asleep in the room next door the last thing you want is for them to be woken up in the early hours and so I grabbed the bed side phone as quickly as I could.

"Woodward you cunt, gonna get you, you fuckin dirty pigs head, we've got your phone number you fuckin pigs head. Your gonna die you cunt" said the voice on the other end of the phone.

I recognised it straight away as Michael Nayler and there was another voice laughing in the back ground. I was horrified and put the phone down almost straight away. It rang again a few minutes later and this time it was even worse.

"Gonna do you Woodward and your fuckin wife and baby and then we'll do your fuckin house, you pigs head, dirty fuckin pigs head, gonna kill ya Woodward, you dirty fuckin pigs head, nice shiny red Volvo you've got, gonna do that as well you dirty fuckin pigs shit".

I was absolutely incensed but thought the best way to deal with it was to just casually say.

"Goodnight Nayler" and put the phone down.

At least that way he knew that I knew it was him and that he might stop. It rang again ten minutes later and the vile bastard continued to call me all the names under the sun. Tricia was obviously very upset that our home had now been invaded by this creep and I pulled the plug on the phone.

Having had my sleep disturbed meant I wasn't in the best of moods at six the next morning as I recalled the story to Laurie Mullen and Danny Daniels. I was all for going straight around to Naylers house, kicking his front door down and nicking him. But, as was rightly pointed out to me I was actually the victim in this and that lawfully at least I wasn't the right person to deal with it, even if morally it might have been the right thing to do. I was particularly concerned for Tricia because she was now three months pregnant and didn't need the stress that this involved. My job and the youths I dealt with had already ensured that we hadn't been shopping in Commercial Road now for over a year because of the manner in which I got targeted when we were in the Wimpy Bar. Danny Daniels made a number of phone calls and permission was obtained to place a recording device on my home phone to record any further calls for evidence. The rules of engagement were that I had to answer the call and press the record button but not to say anything in return other than acknowledging the call. I really wasn't happy about this but if it meant securing the evidence against Nayler then so be it, I'll just have to bite my tongue. I got a visit later that afternoon from Pete Kearly at Technical Services who came to install this recording device. Pete had been my instructor at Bishops Waltham when I was a cadet and I knew him very well. He was a truly great bloke with a wicked sense of humour and he managed to put Tricia and I at our ease about the equipment that was installed.

At 0230 the phone rang. It was Nayler and Michael Navrot. The personal abuse and threats continued for fully five minutes before I decided that I had heard enough and put the phone down. Five minutes later it rang again and half an hour later it rang again and I sat there having to listen to yet more of Naylers uncontrolled glee at being able to shout and scream at me without the likelihood of me putting my hands around his throat. After the third call I pulled the plug again so we could get some sleep, although that didn't seem very likely.

The next day I brought the tape into work thinking this would be enough to go and kick his door in. But a conference had taken place between CID and the CPS and it was decided that in order to secure a conviction they would need a substantial amount of taped evidence and therefore my wife and I would have to endure sleepless nights for some considerable time yet. I really wasn't very happy about this and seriously considered taking the law into my own hands on this one. The idea of arming myself with a baseball bat and meting out some summary justice were thoughts that constantly entered my head.

So we went to bed each night dreading the phone ringing and waking us up. It didn't ring every night and it transpired that on the nights it didn't Nayler was locked up at Central having committed other offences so we did get some respite.

About three weeks had passed and I collected the post from the door mat one morning and opened a brown envelope that contained two photos. Both had been taken from inside a car outside my house and showed Tricia and I leaving the house with our two year old daughter in my arms to get into our car. On the back of one of the photos were the words *'Now we know where you live'*. A shudder went down my spine because I had managed to reassure my wife that even though they had our phone number there was no way they could find out where we lived. But clearly I was wrong. I felt incredibly threatened and vulnerable and my natural instincts were to protect my family. Part of that protection was not to tell her what I'd just discovered; in fact it was many years before I did tell her. I placed the photos and the envelope into a plastic bag and took them into work to be finger printed. I also strategically placed certain items around the house that I might be able to use as weapons should the need arise. I was very much on edge and found myself constantly looking out of the windows at night or pricking my ears up at the slightest sound outside.

The phone calls continued and during one of them Nayler boasted that he knew where we lived. Evidentially it was priceless but for me personally the prospect of having my day with a baseball bat was growing ever closer. The final straw came when I was on nights. Tricia took the call where Nayler and Navrot tormented her because they knew she was on her own as they had just seen me on the sea front. She was terrified and who could blame her. We'd put up with this now for almost six weeks and it was time for it to stop. The equipment was removed and our phone number was changed. In the meantime, as part of the investigation a number of officers in other parts of the city were played parts of the tapes to see if they could identify the persons responsible. Six out of the ten officers positively identified Nayler and Navrot. The file was handed to the CPS who decreed that there was insufficient evidence to charge either of them. I was sick to the core, in fact I've never been so angry in my life, its no wonder the CPS is oft referred to as the Criminal Protection Society. But there was no changing their minds, the argument being that every single officer who had identified them had had previous dealings with them and therefore it could be argued that they had some kind of vendetta against them! What utter rubbish. What kind of system allows scum bags like Nayler and Navrot to get away with such things? That base ball bat was looking even more tempting now.

It was early December and we were back on nights. It was one of those cold but clear weeks with a mild night time frost. The Christmas parties and works do's were in full swing but generally they were all good natured and didn't cause us too many issues, in fact it was quite quiet for once. I woke up on the Tuesday afternoon to news that a murder enquiry was under way after the body of a young woman had been discovered on waste land at Merry Row on Fratton's patch. She had apparently been raped and then beaten to death.

That evening before parade as we gathered in the canteen for our tea it was obviously the hot topic of conversation and it became even more so as we learned that two Police officers including one from Green Relief had been arrested on suspicion of murder and were currently in custody! PC 1133 Pete Forster was only just out of his probation and he was a lovely, somewhat naïve, big oaf of a bloke who was incredibly shy and insecure about himself. He was doing a two week stint on Oscar Mike, the street offences squad with another more experienced PC from Central.

Merry Row was an area of waste land, an old war time bomb site adjacent to Lake Road and there was a rough concrete road running through its 150 yard length that was used as a short cut from Buckland through to Holbrook Road. Fozzie and the other PC were in plain clothes in an unmarked van sitting on the edge of the waste land keeping obs on a group of nearby shops because of intelligence reports suggesting that they might be burgled over night. They finished work at 2am and Fozzie was asleep in the section house at Fareham nick when his door came crashing in and he was arrested and thrown into a cell downstairs! The other officer was arrested in front of his wife and kids before being locked up. Trying to obtain any further details though was impossible and besides which we were going to be tasked with doing a full road check on the roundabout junction close to the murder scene for the next few hours.

Linda Cook's murder had obviously generated a lot of local interest and the area was busy with local people when we arrived at 2230 that night to stop every car and pedestrian that travelled through the area in an effort to ascertain if they had seen anything suspicious the previous night. We had been there for about half an hour when Traffic turned up with a brand new patrol car that was on trial. It was a MK3 Ford Granada Concept Police car that sported a weird looking pod on the roof with a blue strobe light in each corner, fancy blue and yellow diagonal graphics and all of Fords latest RS sports accessories. It drew a crowd like moths around a light bulb and all of a sudden the interest switched from the murder of this poor girl to the Old Bills latest toy, which clearly wasn't right. The Inspector in charge of the road check had no choice.

"Thanks for popping down to assist lads, now piss off" was his farewell speech and off they went.

We spent the rest of the night until the early hours stopping everything that moved, all the time looking at the white tent that covered the spot where the body had been discovered. It was quite a sobering thought to think that another human being had met such a brutal end less than 24 hours previously in that exact place.

The next evening we were relieved to learn that both Fozzie and the other officer had been released because it had been established that they had gone off duty before the woman was murdered. Fozzie though had been put back into uniform and joined us upstairs. He was clearly still very shaken and upset by his ordeal and it had changed his entire perspective of the job. He asked to speak to me privately before we went on parade and as we went into a side room he asked for my advice. Whilst he had been incarcerated so someone from the investigation team had quite literally ransacked his room and he wanted to know what he could do about it. He said to fully understand I really needed to look at his room and so after parade I drove him across to Fareham nick and we went upstairs to the single men's accommodation wing. Fozzie was right, it was just as if he had been burgled. Every drawer was out and turned upside down on the floor, as were the contents of his wardrobe. Personal items were strewn all over the place and it was obvious that absolutely everything he possessed had been pored over. Fozzie welled up and asked me why they would do this? I really didn't have an answer for him but suggested that if he wanted to take it further then we needed to photograph it right now and submit it with a duty report. We got a polaroid camera from the cell block downstairs and took three photos of the mess. It really was quite a despicable thing to do to anybody, let alone an innocent colleague. Fozzie spent the rest of the night compiling his report and having submitted it he did feel a little better but I doubt he ever really got over his ordeal.

It was Boxing Day morning and we were on earlies. Steve Moore and I decided that breakfast at my place would be a very acceptable idea and so we popped home just after 8.30 to fill our faces. We'd only been there about ten minutes when Chris Robinson got sent to a silent alarm at the video rental shop on the corner of Francis Avenue and Jessie Road. Alarm calls at that time of day are invariably staff on premises or a fault in the system so we left him to it. Within seconds of him arriving he screamed that he had one running from the scene of a break-in and he was chasing him on foot. Steve and I jumped into the area car and headed towards him. We were there within three minutes and by now the chase had reached a house in Esslemont Road; Michael Naylers house. There was a fight going on at the door between Chris, Nayler and his mother and brother. We all piled into the hallway and then into the front room as the fighting continued. Naylers mother screamed in protest as his younger brother did little more than try and prevent Michael from being dragged away. In the chaos that followed Nayler managed to scramble to his feet and ran through the house and into the kitchen, closely followed by me, leaving the others to role around on the front room floor. I just saw Nayler leave via the back door and as I followed him I saw him trying to open the shed door, which was locked. He turned to face me and picked up a two foot long piece of wood.

"Come on then Woodward you cunt, you and me right now, right here" he snarled.

I looked around me and saw that we were in a typical Pompey mid terraced rear garden, in that the house to my right overshadowed the garden we were in and therefore nobody could see us. He came at me and swung the lump of wood. I grabbed him and we fell to the ground with him on his front. He was roaring like an animal and then for the first time in my life I completely lost it. With what is commonly described as red mist descending I found myself completely and utterly over whelmed with anger. All that shit my wife and I had put up with for weeks on end and all the abuse this toe-rag had subjected me to on plenty of occasions prior to that just bubbled to the surface. I grabbed those big jug ears and as he thrashed about trying to get me off his back so I just beat his face into the garden path. Robbo and Steve pulled me off him and as they rolled him over so I saw blood coming from his nose and from grazing on his chin and cheeks. He spat blood out on the floor and as they were cuffing him he looked at me and laughed.

"I knows where you fuckin live Woodward, I knows where you live you cunt. Had to change ya phone number though didn't ya, you fuckin wanker" he screamed as Robbo clamped his hand over Naylers mouth and they led him away.

I stood there shaking as the adrenalin continued to pump through my body. He was the lowest form of life I'd ever dealt with and I was particularly annoyed with myself for allowing him to reduce me to his level for just a few seconds. It wasn't a nice feeling.

CHAPTER 11

1987. Vote Docker

Events over the past year or so were starting to have an adverse affect on me personally. Much as I loved my job I now found myself withdrawing slightly from being right at the forefront of regular conflict with the likes of Nayler and the Scaberras family. Not that they worried me in any way but I had to put my young family first and there was no way I was going to let them destroy the most precious thing on earth to me. So I took a very slight step backwards and allowed other officers to get in their faces when necessary. I was still there doing my bit when required but encouraged one or two others to get more involved than they had been. Besides which I was now doing Acting Sgt duties almost daily and so it was only right that I take a more supervisory role.

Subconsciously I was also starting to become a lot more involved in dealing with road traffic matters. Not because they were easy pickings but because I have a genuine interest in anything that has wheels. I found dealing with complicated RTAs fascinating, especially if there was an element of dangerous driving involved and that people had sustained serious injury because of it, I felt it my duty to prove that these people were responsible and needed to pay. I was becoming increasingly concerned to at the number of youngsters riding mopeds, scooters and motorcycles in a truly awful condition and decided to target them, not to prosecute and persecute but to educate them. I was astonished at their total lack of mechanical knowledge and the fact that they were cheerfully putting their own lives at risk through sheer ignorance and stupidity. For example I stopped a lad on a Vespa scooter that had poor brakes, a bald rear tyre and no horn. As I pressed the horn button several times he said that actually he did have a horn and he would show me. He then removed the keys from the ignition, unlocked the hinged seat and in a tray beneath the seat was one of those chrome horns with a black rubber squeegee ball on the end. He squeezed it with a big smile on his face as it emitted its trumpet sound. I then asked him how long it would take him to do all of this whilst actually riding, as the little old lady stepped off the pavement in front of him? He stopped smiling. But that was the type of person who I decided really needed some practical help. So I would point out the offences and give them one week to get it fixed and return to see me at a set time and date and if I was satisfied that they had rectified the problem then they wouldn't be prosecuted. I got a 100% success rate and they were truly grateful for both the advice and the second chance. I also enjoyed the experience and it made a pleasant change from being spat at or sworn at. I felt it was time for me to make a decision about my future and after getting the backing from Laurie Mullen and Chief Inspector Bully I submitted my application for transfer onto the Traffic Department. I passed the Traffic selection board but knew I might have to wait over a year before I got moved.

I sat at the bottom of Velder Avenue facing north towards the Eastern Road having just finished dealing with a minor RTA behind me on the roundabout. I was busily writing the T1 accident card when I happened to look up and saw a Rover heading south towards me. The car was towing a small yacht on a trailer but the owner had forgotten to remove and store the 20 foot high mast which was now pulling down all the telephone cables across Velder Avenue! As it hit each cable so the wheels on the trailer left the ground by about a foot, before the cable snapped and it drove towards the next one. I jumped out the car to stop him and he was completely oblivious to the damage he had caused. In total he had destroyed more than a dozen lines! He wasn't very popular.

In March I got a new partner in PC 1711 Pete O'Brien as Geoff moved on and took up a post with the Cycle Squad tracking down stolen bikes. Pete was a very quiet man, small in stature but a very efficient and competent copper. We built up a good relationship and had quite a laugh along the way.

I also did something in March that was to impact upon mine and my family's life for several years to come, although I didn't know it right then. Whilst reading the Portsmouth News one evening I saw an article concerning a local Scout Group whose Bandmaster had deserted them a few years previously and they wanted to restart their marching band. As a youth in the early 1970s I was a member of the 1st Newport Scout Band on the Isle of Wight and we enjoyed a huge amount of success at band contests all over the UK, winning many of them along the way and scooping trophies everywhere we went. We even made an LP record and received the Freedom of the Borough of Newport, so I can legitimately march down Newport High Street with my bayonet affixed! I'm not qualified in any way shape or form to teach music and played drums when in the band but I thought I might pop along to help out with the percussion side of things. I was interviewed one evening and then taken to the hall to inspect the facilities and the instruments, which were a bit battered and covered in dust and cob webs. I was told that they had other people to interview but would I like to come back on Friday evening to meet the boys themselves? OK then.

At this point I need to emphasise just how brilliant a youth activity marching bands are. It teaches boys and girls, of all abilities music, marching, self discipline, pride, respect, develops a competitive nature and ambition, but above all keeps them away from the TV and the street corner. The more I thought about this the more I thought I'd like to give teaching drums a go, because it would be a good thing to give something back to the youth on my patch and if they only ever experienced a tenth of what I did as a teenager then they'd love it.

So, on the Friday evening I walked into the hall in Fawcett Road, Southsea and stood in the small kitchen whilst the Group Scout Leader, Mike Bourner, the chap who had interviewed me went through the start of their evenings formalities. He then reminded them about the article that had been in the paper a couple of weeks ago and asked if they were still keen to restart the band? They clearly were and Mike then said he had some good news for them and without further ado, he'd like to introduce them to their new Bandmaster, Mr Steve Woodward, as I was beckoned out from the kitchen into the middle of the hall.

"What? Bandmaster?" I whispered to him through gritted teeth.

Apparently I was the only applicant! Yes, but I only know drums and it's been 12 years since I hit one of those. In front of these 30 young lads, all with expectant faces, Mike assured me that he had every faith that I was the right person for the job. You mean the only mug that bothered to respond! When I got home and told Tricia she fell on the floor laughing. The more I thought about it the more terrifying the prospect became, because it meant that I was going to take a bunch of complete beginners and teach them how to play trumpets, drums and other instruments, how to march, undertake complex display routines, buy and maintain instruments and uniforms, arrange travel, raise funds, attend meetings and join band type organisations. And that was only the beginning.

A month later I also got a new addition to my own family when Tricia gave birth to our son Daniel. So now I was responsible for two little bundles of joy.

Pompey got promoted to the top tier of English football which meant that from August onwards we would be hosting the likes of Chelsea, Manchester United and Liverpool on a regular basis. It was a far cry from Carlisle United. But most of all the Pompey boys were looking forward to playing the scummers again. They could lose every game; it really wouldn't matter, just so long as they beat "that lot up the road".

For several weeks now we had started to notice a lot of additional graffiti daubed on walls, doors, road signs and all the other usual places with stuff like 'Vote Docker' or 'Docker Hughes 6.57' but what the hell did it mean? There was a general election planned for June 11th but surely it didn't have anything to do with that? But then it was announced in The Portsmouth News that one of the 6.57 Crew, Martyn 'Docker' Hughes was to stand as an independent candidate for the '6.57 Party' in the Portsmouth South constituency. They can't be serious surely? Who the hell's this bloke Docker Hughes anyway?

We've never heard of him, he's certainly not one of our regulars.

The paper printed a photo of him on the front page and he certainly wasn't anyone I recognised. But it was the 6.57 Party's manifesto that really grabbed the headlines because it was a bit strange to say the least and included the following;

All magistrates to have served time in prison.

Dockers to have their own community policing owing to the inadequacies of the central boot boys (a reference to Central Police Station!).

Portsmouth out of Hampshire.

Duty Free goods to be available on the Gosport ferry.

To abolish 'Off Course' betting tax.

Skates and sinbads out of Portsmouth.

No Robson or Waddle type hair styles and no moustaches.

To create a race track on Southsea Common, to keep Portsdown Park, to save The Tricorn and keep Wimpy Homes out of Portsea.

Help Loyalist prisoners in Northern Ireland and have an Apprentice Boys of Derry march in Portsmouth.

Most of the press attention seemed to be on the duty free goods on the Gosport ferry item, which obviously raised a smile and almost a nod of approval from most, but generally speaking it seemed that the fair people of Portsmouth were somewhat bemused by the whole idea that their football hooligan element were actually pressing ahead with promoting themselves as a political party. Although many of the items on their manifesto were clearly included to amuse there were a couple that caused some upset, in particular the reference to holding a march on behalf of the Apprentice Boys of Derry which I understand they eventually withdrew.

We were on nights and Pete and I were driving south along Fratton Road about one in the morning when we saw a figure on the offside pavement. He was in his mid 30s I'd say, wearing a black donkey jacket and a flat hat. He had a newspaper tucked under one arm and was carrying an old carrier bag in the other. He walked with a rather peculiar gait, he sought of bounced and was rather round shouldered. As we drove slowly by he sought of nodded at us and grinned. It looked like that bloke Docker Hughes. We had to go and have a chat with him so I did a U turn and we pulled up beside him. Pete wound the window down to speak to him.

"Excuse me mate but are you Docker Hughes?" he asked.

"Yeah" came the reply. He stood there looking at us with this sort of smirk on his face. To be honest he looked like he might have escaped from somewhere.

"Are you serious about this election then?" asked Pete.

"Yeah" said Docker..

"So whose idea was it to come up with the duty free's on the Gosport ferry then?" laughed Pete.

"Dunno really" he sighed.

"Have you got your election speech ready yet?" enquired Pete.

"Not really thought about it" came the reply. The more I looked at him the more I thought he looked like a cross between the cartoon character from the Mad comics and Yoda from Star Wars.

"Are you going to win then?" asked Pete.

He just laughed quietly and clearly felt a bit awkward talking to the Old Bill. It probably wouldn't do his politics much good to be seen talking to associates of the central boot boys.

"Well it's been interesting talking to you" said Pete politely "And good luck to you next week".

He just smirked at us again and continued on his way, bouncing down Fratton Road. We drove off not really knowing what to think. Yes we laughed a bit, he was certainly a character but not in the way we had expected. I'm not sure if he was taking the piss out of us or not, it was a bit difficult to tell.

Come June 11th and a large number of RSG officers were required to police the Guildhall area because of the 6.57 Party's possible disruption to proceedings. Quite simply they were not going to be allowed to disrupt the voting process in any way whatsoever. We had been briefed earlier that a fair number of Pompey's finest had already been arrested during the afternoon at one of their favourite watering holes, namely the Sir Robert Peel pub, which was nothing short of an insult to us as Police officers! They had been arrested for various public order offences, most of them alcohol related and were unlikely to see tonight's result. The Guildhall was the busiest I'd seen it since Maggie's historic 1979 win. The bar area was packed with a large number of the 6.57 Party and they played the same tactic they employed in court by constantly walking in and out of the main hall, shouting, laughing and generally being a pain in the arse. Several of them were warned concerning their behaviour and they just became more excitable as the evening wore on. Portsmouth South was one of the most marginal seats in the country and inevitably there was a recount which just delayed things still further and meant that several more pints could be downed at the bar before the result was announced.

By 2 am it looked like they were ready to announce the result. With that about 100 of the group stood at the back of the main hall as if on the terraces at Fratton Park and started singing Pompey songs and chanting for Docker. The noise was incredible; it was just like being at the Fratton End on a Saturday afternoon. I have to confess that I stood there smiling at them but shaking my head in disbelief all at the same time. Here was a group of lads, some of them still in their teens who had dared, yes dared, to take on the very establishment they so despised and had used the very process to take the piss out it, big time. The irony wasn't lost on me and I couldn't help but admire their bollocks for doing it. What made it even funnier was the look on the faces of those from within the establishment who had clearly never before witnessed such scenes or such fervent noise. And here were the Police, who had put up with this mob, these geezers for years, just watching, almost in admiration.

Eventually the noise died down enough to announce the results. But they had to wake Docker up first; he'd fallen asleep in a chair on the stage. He was that excited! The Tories just shaded it from the SDP by a mere 205 votes, so it was mighty close. But what of The Docker? What did he poll? An incredible 455 votes. There was a huge roar and cheer from his party faithful as they burst into song yet again, this time chanting out Dockers name as they all pointed to him up on the stage. He stood there looking somewhat embarrassed and when it came to making his speech he said that polling just 455 votes was pathetic. He clearly hadn't put the effort into his election speech as Pete had suggested. But actually 455 votes wasn't pathetic at all, in fact it was quite worrying that he had reached that figure and it was a lot higher than many had predicted.

Things calmed down a bit as the 6.57 Party made its way outside into the Guildhall Square. Docker joined them as they once again chanted his name. Then they decided to give him the bumps in celebration. A couple of dozen grabbed his arms and legs and hurled him to the ground before giving him 21 bumps. As they lifted him skyward you could almost see his arms come out of their sockets and as he came back down on each occasion so his 'party' put the boot in. It was sickening to watch. On the final lift so they threw him as high as they could and then just stood back as he plummeted onto the paving stones with a bone crunching thud. He was clearly winded but then got to his feet and just laughed. Incredible.

Later that month we were back on nights and Pete and I were in the area car sat on the seafront. It was a Friday night and it had that 'feeling' you just knew that something was brewing.

Charlie-One to Romeo Foxtrot 51

Romeo Foxtrot 51 go ahead

Make Gatsby's at North End please, large group outside trying to gate crash a private function

Romeo Foxtrot 51, Roger

Other Fratton units started to make towards the area as Pete and I watched the queues for our own clubs starting to grow. One by one we heard the Fratton units arrive.

10/10 Gatsby's, urgent assistance required

It's automatic and its instant. You don't get asked to go, you just do it. If officers shout 10/10 they mean it and its serious. I started the Volvo and we headed north straight up Fratton Road and into Kingston Road with everything going. As we approached North End junction it was mayhem, absolute chaos with the main ruck kicking off close to the door at Gatsby's. There must have been over 150 of them fighting with the Fratton units and it was all the usual faces from the 6.57 Crew. There were two bodies laying in the road with nasty looking head injuries and there were women screaming everywhere. A lot of the youths scattered as several police units arrived from different directions all at the same time. There were officers struggling to detain a number of men and we went straight to their assistance first. As we put several into a van so the main group had gathered again and they charged at the van. We fought them off and another couple got detained but we needed more vans and more officers. As the van with the prisoners in it was clearly the centre of attention so it was decided to get rid of it to Central. As soon as it had gone so we started to disperse this mob who were clearly in the mood to do a lot of damage. It was strange tonight because there seemed to be a lot of girlfriends with them, which was something we hadn't noticed before, they hadn't ever had girls with them and I think it made matters even worse for us, because as we nicked a male so his girlfriend would attack us and as soon as we laid hands on her so the other males got even more violent and aggressive. We pushed and shoved them north and south along London Road in an effort to split them up. Every now and then a scuffle would break out between one of the groups and a police officer which meant the rest of us fending off the others as they charged towards us making whooping noises like Red Indians. After half an hour we had only managed to push them 50 yards south to the mini roundabout at North End junction and I saw car drivers visibly shaken as their cars were surrounded and jumped on whilst others managed to reverse away from the area at great speed.

Something caught my eye. I looked to my right and saw Pete laying on his side in a recessed shop doorway. He was unconscious and as I put him into the recovery position I shouted for an ambulance and further units, this was now completely out of control. I could hear shop windows being smashed a short distance away to. I stood up and turned around. There was a group of the Eastney boys stood in a neat semi circle outside the shop doorway. I was completely trapped but I had to protect Pete from any further damage. Well if I'm going to die here then I'm going to take at least one of you with me, I thought. Standing in the middle of the group was Jason Hartgill.

He had both his hands raised and beckoned me towards him and shouted.

"Come on then cunt, you and me right now, lets see how fucking big and brave you are now" he screamed.

The others shouted various threats but such was the noise that I really couldn't hear what they said. I lowered my right hand and slipped my thumb into the leather strap of my truncheon. I folded the strap over my hand and then whipped it out in a well rehearsed and aggressive manner, holding it upright and ready to defend myself. It felt wrong. I looked at my hand and all I had was the strap. The bloody thing had chosen that very moment to break. My truncheon was still in its pocket. I looked at the strap and then looked at the yobs. They were looking at the strap to and there was a sort of pregnant pause. Everything seemed to have gone into slow motion. The silence was broken by a horrendous scream and I saw one of the group leave the ground with a German Shepherd attached to his arse. It was Ajax. Oh how I loved that dog and how he and Rowdy were enjoying their work. The group immediately turned their attentions towards them. As I bent back down to tend to Pete so I saw one of them kick Ajax in the head. He bit back and managed to keep the yobs shoe. Good boy. Pete had come to and was now sat up against the window looking very dazed, but at least he was alright. I told him an ambulance was en route and he told me to get back out there and help sort things out.

"Can I borrow your stick then?" I asked "Had a bit of a problem with mine".

Brick rubble was now being thrown at us from Stubbington Avenue. They'd discovered a builders skip full of the stuff and so we charged them and they scattered into various side streets. Rowdy had been joined by PC Dave Owen and his dog Ben and between them they helped clear the worst of the trouble makers away. Another van was arriving from the south and before it had even arrived so it got surrounded by over 30 youths who tried to overturn it. Chairs and tables from a nearby pub forecourt were then hurled towards it smashing one of the side windows as we charged at them. I saw the ambulance arrive and ran back to guide them to the shop doorway that Pete was still sitting in.

I then ran back and assisted my colleagues in getting rid of this group and eventually we dispersed the whole lot. Mind you it took us almost two hours. It was without doubt the worst street disorder outside of a football match I had ever witnessed. It was the closest Portsmouth has ever come to rioting, in the legal sense.

Pete was taken up to the QA and treated for concussion. He had no idea what hit him other than it came from behind him. Several other officers were treated for minor cuts and abrasions, which considering the ferocity of the violence we had faced was nothing short of a miracle. At 0500 that morning I was called across to Central to identify Jason Hartgill who had been arrested by another unit as he made his way home after he had been seen committing various offences at the fracas. Over the next few days so CID officers made several early morning arrests at individuals houses and in November a three day trial at Magistrates Court was arranged for the 17 offenders who had been charged with affray and violent disorder.

We had heard that they had employed the services of three barristers to defend them and so somebody somewhere took the decision to bring in a Stipendiary Magistrate from London to hear the cases. This was the first time any of us could recall a professional Magistrate being brought in, instead of relying on the local Lay Magistrates. The very first thing he did was clear the public gallery of the 6.57 Crew and threatened them with jail if they dared come back in. Well it was a promising start. There were only 16 defendants. Hartgill was missing. The Judge immediately issued a warrant and instructed me to go and arrest him and bring him before the court today. This was looking good. I went to Hartgill's flat and found him still in bed. He couldn't care less that he was under arrest for failing to appear and treated the whole thing as a joke. I thought I'd leave the surprise of who was running today's court for him to experience in full when we got there. He was locked up in a cell and I returned to the court to inform the Judge that he was incarcerated downstairs. He halted the trial and instructed the court gaoler to bring Hartgill up to face him. You could hear the jangling of keys and doors slamming shut in the hollowness of the cells down stairs, followed by the foot steps coming up from down below. Hartgill appeared in the dock and smiled and laughed at his mates, who seemed rather subdued for once and didn't return his arrogant greetings. The Judge asked for an explanation for his non appearance. Hartgill started to explain that he'd had a late night watching a film, when the Judge halted his obvious bullshit, told him to sit down and that he would deal with him later.

"And take that baseball cap off in my court" he bellowed out.

Hartgill was getting the idea now. So was everyone else. I obviously now had to step out of court as evidence was being given by others, but those who had already been in were rubbing their hands with glee because the Stipendiary Magistrate was nobody's fool and was making mince meat of the three barristers. An hour or so later I was called in. I gave my evidence-in-chief and then one of the defence barristers started to ask me questions about the incident outside the pub where the van had been attacked, which I hadn't mentioned in my evidence because it wasn't relevant to Hartgill. Before I had a chance to answer, the Judge shouted at the barrister that I hadn't given evidence about this so I obviously didn't witness it.

"So ask him a more relevant question" he insisted.

"I have no other questions for this officer" he rather sheepishly replied.

"Good, sit down then" he barked.

"Thank you officer, I have no questions for you either" he smiled and he instructed me to sit at the back of the court.

This three day trial was over by 3 o'clock the first afternoon and he found all 17 of them guilty. There was no piss taking now, they all stood there with their heads bowed. Hartgill was the first to be sentenced. He stood there, still quite nonchalant. The Judge was looking at the sheet of paper that contained his previous history. He looked at him over his glasses.

"I've got your previous convictions in front of me and for a young man of 21 your record is appalling and its all public disorder related. I see the magistrates in this city have seen fit to deal with you in a rather lenient manner by giving you probation, conditional discharges, bind overs and oh, the occasional fine. Well let me tell you young man that changes as of today, you will go to prison for six months. And for failing to appear before me this morning 30 days in custody to run consecutively".

"What?" shouted Hartgill "You're having a fucking laugh you wanker".

"Make that an extra three months" said the Judge "and I'm quite happy to double it again if you continue with your out burst. Gaoler take him down".

There was a collective but very quiet "yes" from all the police officers sat at the back of the court as we sat there not quite believing our ears. One by one he sent all of them to prison, ranging from three months to two years. In that one instant this one man had done what countless magistrates had failed to do for the last two or three years and that was imprison the yobs that were terrorising the people of Portsmouth on a weekly basis. It worked to, because it killed off the mass violence for a very long time and apart from the occasional football skirmishes we didn't experience anything quite like the Gatsby's incident ever again.

In the days that followed it was suggested that perhaps bringing a Stipe into Portsmouth might have been politically motivated. Maybe someone upon high, at the election night at the Guildhall maybe, had realised just how 'big' the 6.57 Crew were becoming and that they really needed taking down a peg or two. It was an interesting theory because no other football hooligan firm anywhere in the country had ever tried taking on the establishment in a political manner and although the 6.57 Party did it very much tongue in cheek it might still have been seen as a step too far by some.

You can't help it; sometimes you've just got to laugh. Unfortunate for the victim I know, but sometimes there just is no choice.

Charlie-One to Victor Sierra 51

Victor Sierra 51 go ahead

RTA Eastney Esplanade, one vehicle has gone over the promenade apparently

Victor Sierra 51, Roger

It was just before ten on a quiet Sunday morning as Pete and I made our way to the far end of Eastney Esplanade, the slightly deserted end of Southsea seafront, which wasn't an area known for its RTA's. The sight that greeted us was bizarre because all we could see was the tail end of a VW Golf sticking out of the roof from a beach hut! Only the rear off side wheel was on the promenade with the rest of the car at 45 degrees inside the hut. The L plate on the boot lid gave us a clue.

Father and daughter were still in the car and unable to get out. The car looked secure enough and so we opened the tailgate and both of them crawled out the back of the car and onto the prom. Neither of them was injured and the car looked relatively unscathed. Whilst we waited for the recovery truck so we ascertained what had happened. It transpired dad was giving daughter her first driving lesson in his own car. They had started at the western end of the seafront almost five miles away and driven the virtually straight course to Eastney. But then they had to do a U turn. Half way through the manoeuvre dad told her to slow down, so she took her foot off the gas and then put it onto what she thought was the brake. It wasn't of course and the harder she pushed the pedal the faster the car went and it shot across the promenade and sailed off the edge and in through the roof of the beach hut. She now stood there as red as a beetroot with her hands over her face and he just shook his head in disbelief whilst we mocked them both. They took it in good spirit and no doubt dined out on the story for years.

George and Dolly Scaberras were both wanted on fail to appear warrants and had been for several weeks. For once they had been keeping their heads down which meant that things were a little quieter. We came in on early turn and were handed good information that both of them were currently at the parent's house. So half the Relief descended on the house at half six in the morning armed with two warrants. After a brief struggle at the door we went in whilst a couple of the Relief waited out the back fully expecting at least one of them to jump out the back window. Mrs Scaberras was her usual charming self and made all sorts of threats and allegations, mixed in with huge denials that either of her sons was in the house. It wasn't the first time we had been to the address and so we knew the layout of the place quite well. I took the lounge, a rather spartan room with old and threadbare settees, a coffee table, TV and not much else. I lifted up the settees, nothing, looked behind the curtains and the telly, nothing, no bodies in here. I then turned towards the door and saw a dart board hanging on the wall. There was no wall paper on this section of wall but there were three photos pinned to it, just on the edges of the dart board. One photo had Dave Brown on it, one had Rod Briggs on it and the third had me on it. All three photos appeared to have been taken down towards the fun fair area and I did recall some kind of fracas there about a year or so before involving the usual crowd. Scribbled all over the walls were various expletives with arrows drawn towards each of us and I had the words *'metal metal'* arrowed at me. This was their pet name for me which I always thought was pretty silly and rather childish but they seemed to find it hilarious. They would shout it out to me in the street as if I might take offence, but come on please, after all the things I've been called over the years metal-metal comes bottom of the list surely? I ripped the photos off the wall and put them in my pocket. At the very least they couldn't take the piss out of us with them any more. We found George in bed but Dolly was no-where to be found.

It was late summer and half the American fleet was moored in Portsmouth harbour for the weekend. Thousands of American sailors and marines came ashore to sample our pubs and our women. Plenty of girls from London and elsewhere arrived on mass to help entertain the American boys and to ensure that order was kept our own RN Provost were bolstered by American Shore Patrols who were armed with long night sticks and they weren't afraid to use them either. To be fair the overwhelming majority of US service personnel are incredibly polite and well behaved. Their discipline code means they daren't put a foot wrong, especially in a foreign country or they get dealt with rather harshly.

The seafront was packed by 10 pm with several hundred Americans and by half ten the clubs were already full and the staff were turning people away. It would be even worse in an hour after the pubs have chucked out. I had PC 908 Nigel Linford with me. He was a young proby with just over a years experience behind him. We left the seafront having been called away to a domestic dispute and had just resumed from that when there was an urgent assistance call from the seafront. As we arrived we could see about 30 black males, obviously from the American fleet congregated outside the door to Joanna's. They looked pretty angry at not being able to get into the club and one of them had been detained, hence the assistance call. A van had been called for and so Nigel and I set about moving the rest of them away from the door and the immediate vicinity. We gently ushered them away and most of them were happy to cooperate, except one. He was really short, but he was as wide across the shoulder as he was in height. He had huge biceps, a shaven head and bulging eyes. He was in a foul mood because they had been refused entry to Jo's. Both me and his friends were trying to get him to move on but he kept shouting and swearing and jabbing an angry finger towards the door staff.

"Take your friends advice and get back to your ship" I advised him.

"Fuck you man" he replied with a very southern twang.

"If you stay around here you may get yourself arrested, now get a cab and get yourself back on board" I said.

"No fucking way man, I want those mother fuckers in there to pay" he shouted in a very American way.

His eyes bulged and I saw his fists and biceps clench up. He stared straight into my eyes. He's going hit me I thought. And with that I saw his arm draw back and I saw his fist coming straight towards my face. I ducked and dropped to my knees and as his arm went flying past me I turned to see his fist connect with Nigel's face. It was a sickening thud and lifted Nigel clean off the ground. He was unconscious before he landed. I instinctively grabbed the marine's arms and wrestled him to the ground. I recall thinking that this was sheer madness, this bloke is built like a brick shit house and quite possibly one of America's best killing machines and I'm now rolling around on the floor with him. He was going berserk lashing out with his fists and feet and as another officer arrived to assist me he grabbed his arm and bent it back against the elbow joint. I shouted at him to let go but he just growled at me. I tried releasing his grip but he was just too strong so I hit his knuckles with my stick. It had no affect and so I hit him twice more before he released him. By now I had been joined by the RN and US Shore Patrols who thankfully were just driving past. It still took half a dozen of them to restrain this hulk of a bloke and throw him into a van. He got two

US officers for company. I crawled on my hands and knees over to Nigel who was out cold laying on his back in a star shape. I rolled him onto his side and into the recovery position and waited for the ambulance. He started making murmuring noises so I called him a tosser for not ducking. I think he told me to piss off.

After packing Nigel off to the QA, I went over to Central to sort out my marine who was from the USS Mc.Cloy. His name was one I'm never likely to forget. It was John Jackson Johnson Junior the Third and the following morning he was told to plead guilty by his commanders and got sentenced to 30 days imprisonment at court. After serving his time here he was driven from prison to Greenham Common where he was put on a transport plane and flown straight back to the USA. There he faced a Court Marshall and was sentenced to another 12 months imprisonment in an American Army prison and after serving that sentence he was dishonourably discharged from the US Marine Corps. They don't muck about do they?

The night of Thursday 15th and 16th of October started like any other night shift really. The usual collection of calls concerning drunks, youths damaging cars, a disturbance outside Joanna's, a raging domestic in Somers Town. Nothing unusual, just run-of-the-mill incidents that kept the clock ticking throughout the night. Before I left home that evening I don't recall watching the news or the weather forecast and therefore cannot lay claim to having seen Michael Fish, the BBC's chief weather forecaster of the time ridicule the lady viewer who had phoned the BBC earlier, because she had heard that there was a hurricane on it's way from the south. Even if I had, I doubt very much that I would have taken much notice of it. As I left my house at Copnor everything appeared to be quite normal. I kissed Tricia goodbye and looked in on the two kids tucked up in bed. It was a typical autumnal night, fairly warm, but with a stiff breeze.

After parade Dave Brown and I crewed the area car and set about the aforementioned calls. As the evening wore on the wind became stronger and stronger. By about 2330 it was too strong and blustery to wear your hat after getting out of the car. I started to notice small items of street debris blowing around, the occasional dustbin could be seen laying on its side on the footpath and the roads were awash with leaves blown from nearby trees.

We drove along Elm Grove just before midnight and saw a couple of shop front awnings had been ripped to shreds and were flapping in the breeze like flags. Although the wind was now very strong, we barely passed comment about it. Then the radio gave us the first clue of what was about to hit.

Charlie-One to Victor Sierra 51

Victor Sierra 51 go ahead

Make the Garden House Rest Home on South Parade, apparently the front of the building has collapsed and there are two residents trapped inside. Hampshire ambulance is also attending

Victor Sierra 51, Roger

It was now just after midnight and at the time we received that call we were heading south in Palmerston Road. I turned left onto Clarence Parade and immediately became aware of the strengthening wind. It buffeted the big, heavy Volvo 240 patrol car and made it difficult to hang onto. As we approached the Garden House Rest Home, which was situated on the junction of South Parade and a small side road known as Kirkstall Road, I saw the spray from the sea coming ashore. South Parade was soaked in salt water and with it came the shingle from the beach. The stones though weren't being tossed up by the water, but were being blown off the beach by the wind and inland towards us. The patrol car was then hit by hundreds of pebbles, all along the offside. The noise was deafening.

I could see the ambulance parked facing us, in South Parade. As I stopped in front of it I noticed, to my amazement, that it was leaning over at an acute angle, with its near side wheels a good foot off the road! Luckily it was leaning against some scaffolding, erected on the building next door. I had enormous difficulty opening my door to get out of the car, but adrenaline was now taking over and I heaved it open. As it slammed shut I was hit by a huge gust of wind that quite literally blew me off my feet across the bonnet of the area car and pummelled me into the railings of the rest home. I got to my feet and looked at the rest home. Sure enough the ground floor concrete bay window was missing. Two teenage girls, the night shift care assistants at the home, stood at the top of the steps, frantic with worry as there were two elderly female residents in that room. The problem was that the internal door to the room faced south and because of the combination of the wind now coming in through the large hole at the front of the building and a pile of rubble that had built up around the door, it was impossible for them to gain access. With brute force and ignorance Dave and I managed to force open the door and in we all went. The two old ladies were still in bed, absolutely covered in glass and concrete rubble. One of the window frames was laying on top of one of the beds and the two of them had sustained cuts to their hands and faces. They were very confused and upset and were taken to the QA for treatment. As we assisted the ambulance crew with carrying the two patient chairs to the ambulance, which was now back on all four wheels, we had to bodily protect the two residents from the flying pebbles which were still coming from the beach like bullets from a machine gun. Both the ambulance men were wearing officially distributed hard hats, which I had long taken the mickey about at previous incidents. Now all of a sudden I wanted one! After contacting the home owner and Portsmouth City Councils Central Depot on the Eastern Road to come and affect some emergency repairs to the building, we returned to the patrol car.

I looked at the offside of the area car and found that it was peppered with tiny little dents and that there was a neat pile of stones at the base of the car. We needed a cup of tea and a fag, so it was back to the nick. During our rescue efforts at the rest home I was conscious of other units in the city attending other unusual calls, concerning collapsed walls and other storm related damage. It was beginning to dawn on us that this was going to be a busy night.

Back at Southsea we took the unusual step of recalling the two foot walkers we had out on patrol and insisted that they now double up in the panda cars because it was just too dangerous to be out on foot.

We stood in the front office drinking our tea and recounted our tales and it was now about 0130 hours and there was a huge bang outside the station. We all ran outside and looked north towards Victoria Road North and Elm Grove junction. There didn't appear to be anything amiss until someone noticed that a scaffold pole had been blown from scaffolding outside the Victory Restaurant in Albert Road and through the window of Allen Brothers Tyres on the corner of Victoria Grove. No sooner had we become aware of this latest incident than the shop quite literally exploded in front us. The scaffold pole had punctured the glass, the wind got inside the premises and because both the front and sides of the building were made entirely of glass, it just disintegrated under the pressure from the wind. We all dived to the ground as glass flew everywhere and various expletives were muttered as we lay there! After getting to our feet and brushing ourselves down we stared in utter amazement at a car, with no driver that was being blown by the wind out of Elm Grove across the junction to Outram Road where it mounted the pavement and very slowly bumped into the front of Threshers Wine Store. By now we realised that this storm was something rather different.

We were just about to go and do something about the car when there was a huge cracking sound, followed by another big bang, coming from the other side of the station in Victoria Road South. We ran around the side of the nick but could see nothing. Then we heard a woman screaming and looked across the road directly opposite the station. I looked up and saw an enormous hole in the roof of a large Victorian house on the corner of Hereford Road. The screaming was coming from the house. We ran across the road and into the front garden. We were being pelted with red clay roof tiles that were still falling from the roof as we desperately tried to gain access to the house by battering down the front door. I can't remember how we got in, but I do recall that as we entered the hallway to the house I was being choked by brick dust and being unable to use the lights as the electric had gone. I could still hear the sound of falling masonry and the screams of a woman in obvious trouble. We found the stairs and followed the pleas for help. As we opened a bedroom door and shone a torch into the room I saw the woman, clinging by her fingertips to a windowsill. Her husband was in a similar position at another window. They looked like a couple of cartoon characters being hung from those ancient wall rings! We shone the torch towards the floor. There wasn't one. It had gone. Above us was that huge hole and the night sky, with clouds racing passed at an unbelievable speed. The woman was in her late 50s and dressed in her nightie, her husband of a similar age and dressed in striped pyjamas.

How had they come to be in such a position? Like us, they had heard the bang of the scaffold pole going through the window across the street. This was the first they were aware of any storm outside and they both got out of bed to see what was going on. They were watching us, watching the car come out of Elm Grove, when the large brick chimney stack came down through the roof, onto their double bed, through the bedroom floor, down through the kitchen and into the basement. Everything in the bedroom had gone, all the furniture, the carpet, everything. We stood in the doorway and they clung to the windowsill on the other side of the room. How were we going to get them out? I cannot recall whose idea it was, or how we came to the decision we did, but we could see that just under the ladies feet there was a hole, where a floor joist had once been. A length of wood was found amongst the debris; probably one of the joists and this was slid across the void and pushed into the hole. The other end was placed on the floor of the doorway and we shouted to the woman to come over. Without hesitation and in bare foot, on a rough sawn piece of timber, she ran across the black hole, with just the aid of our torch light, to safety. Her husband struggled to reach the timber and had to grab it with his hands and then hang upside down and crawl, commando style. We shouted at him constantly not to give up. He made it and we hauled him up and into the arms of his now hysterical wife. The fire service arrived and the ladies only concern now was her budgie that was in its cage in the kitchen. We looked down into the hole that used to be her kitchen. No chance. I did hear later that by some miracle, the budgie did survive to tweet another day, although its cage had been vastly reduced in size! We then left the house and had to dodge more tiles still falling from the roof.

Charlie-One to Victor Sierra 51

Victor Sierra 51 go ahead

Make the maternity unit at St. Mary's hospital apparently the roof is coming off and they need help in evacuating the top two floors of the building

Victor Sierra 51, Roger

We headed north up Victoria Road North and right into Goldsmith Avenue where I came to an abrupt halt. Large wooden advertising hoardings had been blown into the road and as we attempted to clear them we were hit by flying debris. I was now very concerned for my own welfare, there was just so much debris that we were at real risk from serious injury or worse. Everything now seemed to be airborne. Fence panels, roof slates, conservatory roofs, dustbins, glass, stones, tree branches, road signs, in fact everywhere you looked, something was either damaged or in the process of being ripped from its mountings. After clearing the road, we continued along Goldsmith Avenue and turned left into Priory Crescent where I stopped again. A large tree had fallen from Milton Park and was now blocking the road. We informed Charlie-One. I reversed back into Goldsmith Avenue and headed east down to the White House pub, where I turned left into Milton Road and saw that another tree had fallen across the road, but there appeared to be a gap big enough to get through on the offside pavement. I was just about to move forward when Dave screamed out.

"Shit, look at that".

He pointed towards a large oak tree positioned on the edge of Milton Park. It was visibly shaking at its base. Then, like a Saturn 5 rocket, it took off, slowly being pulled from the ground taking the footpath and attached fencing with it. After it left the ground by a couple of feet it seemed to get tossed around like a matchstick before being flung into the park with an enormous crash.

"Sod this, I'm off".

I slammed the car into reverse and got as far away from the trees as possible. Our only safe route now was via Locksway Road, Euston Road and Velder Avenue. En route I heard the following radio transmission.

Charlie-One to Romeo Foxtrot station, can someone take the van out to an urgent job please?

Romeo Foxtrot station, we would, but it's laying on its side in the yard!

On arrival at St. Mary's we were greeted by one of the porters who stated that all was now well and that they had managed without us. It was now almost impossible to stand up on your own without having to take hold of something. You couldn't talk normally to someone, you had to really shout to make yourself heard because the wind was now just a constant roar, the noise it made was just incredible and the strangest thing of all was that it was actually quite warm, not the usual cold winter type of wind. But it was the overall sound of it, together with the noise of the debris that I remember most of all. We were about to leave when I was approached by a taxi driver, who explained to me that he had driven a doctor in a white coat all the way from Worthing to St. Mary's to perform some life saving operation. He went on to say that he didn't really believe the man's story and anyway, it was now over two hours since he dropped him off and the clock was still ticking and he hadn't returned. The porter overheard all this and then announced that they had been searching the hospital, prior to the maternity unit crisis, because of various reports of a bogus doctor doing his rounds in the hospital. We felt compelled to conduct a brief search in an effort to find him. I remember thinking "bloody marvellous, the whole world is falling down out there and here we are searching for a lunatic in a white coat".

Needless to say there was no trace and I broke the bad news to the taxi driver. I then really made his day by telling him that the roads back to Sussex were now completely impassable because of fallen trees and that he had no choice but to get his head down in his cab. He was not a happy man.

I then received a personal call on the radio from the station.

Apparently my house was falling down, my wife and kids had been evacuated across the road and could I attend? The patrol car seemed to fly up the Eastern Road towards my house. I quickly glanced at the damage; part of the main roof gone, the rear extension roof gone and about sixty feet of garden wall now laying on its side. Tricia and the kids were across the road at Doug and Dorothy Corney's house, an elderly couple whose son Roger was a Scenes of Crime officer at Cosham. The house was full of other evacuees and Dorothy was there with her big teapot and she loved it. It was just like the war, she kept saying and I suppose in many respects it was. Tricia eventually opted to take the kids back across the road and they all slept downstairs in the lounge, although I'm sure she didn't get much sleep. The house would have to wait.

Charlie-One to Victor Sierra 51

Victor Sierra 51 go ahead

Albert Road, Fawcett Road area please, report of four males in a red Ford Cortina who are smashing shop windows and looting the stores

Victor Sierra 51, Roger

We really didn't need this but I suppose you can always rely on the criminal element to rub salt into the wound. En route back down the Eastern Road we found a yacht parked on the grass verge. Funny place to leave it, I thought! Sure enough we found half a dozen shop premises with broken windows, but then it was difficult to decide whether they had been looted or was just subject to storm damage. The sound of shop alarms now filled the air and added to the overall noise factor.

Charlie-One to Victor Sierra 51

Victor Sierra 51 go ahead

Make Granada Road report of building collapse, believe persons trapped, fire service en route

Victor Sierra 51, Roger

On arrival a couple of minutes later we found dozens of people stood out in the street all looking up at the top of a large Victorian house that was used as bed-sits. The roof and gable end of the house had gone and had completely crushed a car parked at the side of the building. Everybody was accounted for except for the guy who lived in the top floor bed-sit. There was no reply from his door. Dave kicked the door and in we went fully expecting him to be out. We were greeted by one of the strangest things I've ever seen. All that was left of the room were four walls. The roof and ceiling had vanished; clouds could be seen rushing passed our heads again. Pictures on the walls swung violently from side to side, personal papers seemed to be swirling around us, as if caught up in mini tornadoes. There was rubble everywhere and the noise from the wind was truly frightening. And there in the corner of this tiny room was the bed. I could see a body in it and I feared the worst. I shone my torch at it and shook it by the shoulder and shouted something. To my astonishment he rolled over onto his back and screamed! I told him we were the Police and that it was time for him to leave. The poor man was totally confused. He just didn't understand what was going on. Most of his possessions had been sucked out of the room when the roof came off. His clothes had gone and he had nothing to put on his feet and he really could not get to grips with that noise, what the hell was it? We threw a blanket over him and bundled him down stairs to a waiting ambulance. If heavy sleeping ever becomes an Olympic sport then that young man would definitely win the gold medal for us!

It was now about 0500 hours and we spent the rest of our time removing debris from the roads. Large fence panels and wooden roofs were littered everywhere. People were up and about, there were lights on in houses that wouldn't normally be up at this hour and Charlie-One was still deploying units all over the city to various emergency calls. Getting to your destination proved tricky no matter where you went because of the number of fallen trees. We drove down to the sea front area. Most of the beach seemed to have landed on Southsea Esplanade and I lost count of the number of felled trees along Ladies Mile on Southsea Common and everywhere you looked there was devastation. The weirdest thing to comprehend was the indiscriminate damage that the wind appeared to have done. You could look at a group of five large trees and see that four of them were all right but that the one in the middle had been snapped in two, halfway up its huge trunk. The power involved in that kind of destruction is awesome. One of the saddest sights I saw was the enormous oak tree on the corner of Pier Road and Duisberg Way which was now laying on its side. Its huge root structure was now standing erect and was easily thirty feet across. That tree must have been at least a hundred years old and had probably witnessed all manner of historical occasions and would grace the landscape no more.

The wind still howled, but it had eased somewhat. The patrol car was still being hit by bits of debris that made Dave and I duck down behind the dashboard each time. We drove passed St. Vincent Road and saw a Volvo estate car that had been completely crushed by a fallen wall. We made our way slowly back to the station. As we stopped outside we saw Roger looking down at the rear of his Ford Escort panda car. The rear bumper and valance area had been folded underneath the car and appeared to have been crushed. Roger then related the story that he had been sent to another building collapse in Burgoyne Road and had parked the car facing south towards the sea front. After dealing with the incident he went to get back into the car but the wind was so strong he just couldn't open the driver's door. He then managed to open the rear tailgate of the vehicle and clambered inside. Just as he started the engine the car was hit by a huge gust of wind that lifted the front of the car clean off the ground. Roger reckoned the car was quite literally standing upright on its rear bumper and looking at the damage to it I fully believed him. The car was held in that position for just a couple of seconds, although I'm sure it felt longer than that to Roger, before the wind dropped and the car crashed back down to the ground. He was visibly shaken and felt lucky to be alive.

Green Relief came back one by one and we sat on the floor in the front office recalling the night's events. It had gone 0600 and none of the early turn had come in. It then dawned on us that perhaps they couldn't get in because of the huge number of blocked roads. A quick look at the duty sheet revealed that most of the early turn

Relief lived out of town, so it was likely that they were all having difficulty getting in. More important than that though was how were we going to get home? No one could phone us because all the phone lines were down and it really did look like we would all have to stay on duty. We were all totally exhausted and I personally didn't want to do any more, I'd had enough. Just before 7 am one of the early turn made it in. He had come from Hayling Island on his motorcycle and said he knew it was rough when he was overtaken on Langstone Bridge by a catamaran! Slowly but surely they all drifted in and after briefing them on the nights events and what they could expect to have to put up with for the rest of the day we all left to pick our own way home.

I drove home very slowly, dodging all the bits of wood and tree branches that were still rolling around in the carriageway. People were standing on street corners talking to each other, many of them armed with shovels and brooms. Others just stared in disbelief at a shattered tree or telegraph pole. I have to admit to feeling very numb and on hindsight was clearly in a state of shock. Dorothy was right. It was just like the war, it certainly looked like it and people's reactions to it all were probably very similar.

As I drove home I reflected on the horrendous things I have faced as a Police officer, many of them life threatening or dangerous, but I have nearly always felt in control of those situations until tonight. I can honestly say that I have never been so frightened in my life, because I was powerless to stop it. If the 'great storm' as it was later dubbed had struck during daylight hours, then I shudder to think of the consequences, hundreds would have died, instead of the unfortunate dozens who did during that night. I hope I never live to see another one.

The following month we lost our beloved Volvo 240 because it was up on mileage. Every now and then you get a car you just love and this was one of them, every one of us that drove it had affection for it. It was quick, reliable, comfortable and just brilliant to drive and B211 WPX was going to be a very hard act to follow. Its replacement was some idiot's idea of a new style 'city area car' a Volvo 360 GLEi.

What a heap of crap. It only had a 2.0 litre engine instead of the previous 2.3 litre power unit, no power steering, atrocious handling, a poor turning circle and pathetic performance. It was an old man's car, the sort of thing you tow a small caravan with. About the only thing that was missing from it were a couple of tartan rugs! We moaned and dripped about it everyday and after one memorable shout in it I actually kicked it hard up the backside, I was so frustrated with it. Whenever it went in for a service or repair and we got a workshop spare 240 in its place it would be at least a week or more before we took it back. I think our record was 10 days!

In mid December I escaped from Southsea to do a two week Traffic Aid at Havant. If this was the direction I wanted to go then the next couple of weeks would give me a better idea of whether we were suited to one another or not. I felt like the new boy at school again as I found the Traffic office, which was a tiny little place not much bigger than a broom cupboard at the furthest end of the ground floor corridor. I knocked and went in and met Sgt Phil Horne who greeted me with.

"Are you the chap from Southsea doing a Traffic Aid?"

After confirming that yes I was he said they were a bit short this afternoon which is why there was no-one for me to crew up with.

"So help yourself to a car, the kettles over there, I'm off home, good night".

With that he left. Oh, OK then, not quite what I was expecting so I'll just make the most of it I suppose. I made myself a coffee and then looked at the key board. Hmmn, Jaguar XJ6 or BMW 528i? Decisions, decisions. I'll take the Beemer, always fancied driving one of those I thought. With that I went out into the yard and found the car parked right in the middle of it. Havant nick is basically four buildings arranged around a central yard with a single entrance and exit point. I jumped into the BMW and started to familiarise myself with all the kit inside. I could work out most of it except for a bright orange pull-out type knob. So I pulled it and immediately activated the tri-sound siren. I pushed it straight back in to turn it off but it kept going, it just wouldn't stop! Oh crap. I kept on pulling it out, pushing it in but nothing happened. Faces started to appear at the upstairs windows. Then a couple of heads opened the windows and shouted at me to turn the bloody thing off. I would if I could. This is so embarrassing, what a great start. The passenger door on the car opened and a hand came in, pushed the knob in and twisted it to the right and the noise stopped. It was George Wenman, a long since retired Traffic man who was now confined to a desk job in the Process Unit. He just looked at me and walked off. At least I know how it works now then!

I went out on patrol, not really knowing where I was going but thought I'd cruise up and down some of the motorway network first of all. The hardest part was listening to two different radio systems at the same time. I had Charlie-One on local of course but now also had 'Mike' control, which was the motorway network on the VHF channel operated from HQ at Winchester. I was dreading getting a motorway call to be honest because I'd not been trained to do any motorway work and I knew it was an entirely different type of policing. But it wasn't the motorway that got me in a flap.

Charlie-One to Juliet Mike 04

Juliet Mike 04 go ahead

RTA Linkenholt Road, Leigh Park, car versus child pedestrian

Juliet Mike 04, Roger

Leigh Park? Oh no, its reputation as the worst area in Hampshire preceded it and besides which it was a rabbit warren if you didn't know where you were going and I didn't. It was the largest housing estate in Europe and had an awful reputation. I asked Charlie-One for directions but it still took me about 20 minutes to find it. Thankfully the area car was already in attendance and the young lad's injuries were very minor which let me off the hook somewhat. Learning a new area was always going to be a challenge but learning several new areas seemed impossible. The Traffic Department covered so many different sub-divisions that you needed to have a good working knowledge of all of them to enable you to get from one place to the next relatively quickly. It was a bit different to Southsea's two square miles!

A few days later and I was on late turn with a legend of the Traffic Department,   PC 2262 George Scammell. George was a Pompey boy through and through, Paulsgrove born and bred to be precise. He was a gruff character with a fuse shorter than John McEnroe, which quite often got him into a lot of trouble with the public and his colleagues. He had a tendency to open his mouth before engaging his brain and shouted a lot. But you couldn't fault his eagerness to do the job, he was as keen as mustard.

It had been a fairly quiet evening and we were just starting to think about heading back to the office about eleven o'clock.

Charlie-One to Juliet Mike 04

Juliet Mike 04 go ahead

Haslemere Road, Southsea serious RTA, van overturned

Juliet Mike 04, Roger

How ironic that the first really serious RTA I get sent to is actually back on my own patch! We arrived before the ambulance and found a white Transit van had overturned after colliding with several parked cars in the residential street. I could see a few residents gathered at the front of the van and so ran to their location. I was horrified to see the driver laying on his back underneath the front of the van, with his legs poking out from under the bonnet. People were just staring at him in silence. I crawled into the upturned cab and from inside I could see that his head was underneath the roof of the van with the top of the windscreen frame pressing down on his throat. Because the actual windscreen had popped out it gave me access to his body and I grabbed his arm and felt a slight pulse. He was alive. I screamed at the others to lift up the front of the van and became incredibly frustrated that they couldn't because it was wedged sideways between two parked vehicles with the rear of the van resting on the roof of a parked Talbot. They couldn't turn it because it would undoubtedly cause further injury to the driver. I felt his pulse stop. I punched his chest because it was the only part of his body that I could access and his pulse started up again. This was desperate and I was frantic that we were going to lose him. His pulse stopped again. George and the locals were all trying their best to move the van but it just wouldn't budge. I punched his chest several times and then kept massaging his heart area as his pulse restarted again. Then it stopped. The ambulance crew arrived and took over from me but within a few minutes they had declared that he was dead. I sat on the edge of the pavement staring at the body. I was really quite upset and felt I'd failed.

However in the days that followed we learned that he had been out celebrating his birthday at a nearby pub and despite the best efforts of the landlord he refused a taxi, ran out the pub and jumped into his van. He'd only driven 200 yards when he hit the parked cars and the crash was heard from inside the pub. The subsequent post mortem found that he had died from a broken neck and was three times over the drink drive limit. What a waste.

For the remainder of my attachment I crewed up with several experienced Traffic officers, including Howard Marrs who had transferred onto Traffic about 18 months previously and they all helped me with a few basics. It was a steep learning curve but a thoroughly enjoyable one. Dealing with motorway incidents, serious RTAs and defective vehicles and drivers was exactly what I was hoping it would be like. This was definitely the path for me to take.

CHAPTER 12

1988. Black Rat beckons

Much of the talk over the Christmas and New Year period had been about Pompey's forthcoming visit to Southampton on January 2nd. Here was the opportunity for the 6.57 Crew and the rest of Pompey's fans to do their worst at The Dell. I wondered if us old K Division officers might also be welcomed with a warmer smile this time as I felt sure they were not looking forward to having the Portsmouth fans in town and might just need our assistance. To be fair most of that underlying tension seemed to have past over since some of the older city officers had retired. And not before time either. This was the first competitive meeting between the two clubs in Southampton for many years and we wondered just how much damage and mayhem the Portsmouth mob might do. At the very least we expected them to systematically destroy The Dell and go on the rampage through Commercial Road. I did hear that there were a few Pompey boys who point blank refused to go because they couldn't stomach the thought of actually setting foot inside Southampton. They were so anti, so diametrically opposed, that the very thought of being in Scumhampton, even to wreck the place, would mean that they would somehow become tainted. Most of the estimated 3000 fans were travelling the 15 miles by train and we met them at the station and herded them into the box to escort them up Hill Lane before turning right into Archers Road and past the big pub that was always occupied by the Southampton youths. This was going to be the first flash point but a wall of Police officers outside the pub ensured that the two groups merely threw abuse at each other rather than anything else. It has to be said that Southampton didn't have a hooligan problem like Pompey and never have had. Yes they had a few trouble makers but nothing on the organised scale of the 6.57 Crew. I don't think they could ever mass up a recognised mob of 300 to 500 virtually every weekend to go and wreak havoc somewhere and leave the place in no doubt as to who had just been in town.

We corralled the Pompey fans into the cage at the Archers Road end of The Dell, often referred to as a flea pit. It was a hideous little football ground that was incredibly difficult to police and the cage was an extremely claustrophobic and oppressive place to incarcerate an already angry and potentially violent group. Today the football did the policing for us because Pompey won 2-0 and their fans were ecstatic. It meant that in their first season in Division 1 they hadn't lost to the scummers, having previously drawn the home match two-all. The bragging rights went to Portsmouth and that was crucial to most of them.

After the match we let the whole lot out at once, boxed them up and walked them back down Hill Lane towards the train station. There were a few minor skirmishes en route but nothing major. As we arrived at the station so a few Southampton youths made towards the Pompey fans but were chased away by Police dogs and nothing happened. The Dell remained intact and not a single window got broken in Commercial Road or anywhere else. I have to confess I was somewhat surprised by this because they would happily run riot through Fratton Road or any number of residential streets in their own city and smash everything they could but didn't do the same or worse in the city they professed to hate to the core. It didn't make sense to me.

I think it's probably a very British thing that we tend to have a fondness for the lovable rogue type, the cheeky chappy that can charm the pants from a rhinoceros. Deep down we'd all like to have the bottle to do a naughty deed and hopefully get away with it but because we are basically too honest we don't indulge but for some reason we find that we cannot help but admire those that do. However, they have to be funny or cute or possess a cheeky smile or some other endearing feature that warms us towards them. If they are nasty, tasteless or aggressive that leaning never works. I have to confess I had only ever come across one such character and I'd known him for several years now, in fact almost as long as I'd been in the job. His name was Charlie Fry and even his name conjures up an image in most peoples minds, even if they've never met him, he just sounds cheeky.

I first came across him when he would ride crappy old mopeds without L plates on. Unfortunately for him he was one of those people who I came across at the time JB was giving me a hard time and insisted I return each day with five names in my book. I think Charlie was in there most weeks. To his credit he never swore at me, never got aggressive, always took it on the chin and even laughed about it. But he never learned from it. Instead of going and buying some L plates, doing the chin strap up on his helmet, fixing the horn on his bike or replacing the headlight bulb he'd just leave it and hoped he wouldn't ever get stopped again. But of course he did. We struck up quite a rapport and he was amazed when I no longer needed to ask him his date of birth or his full address because I knew it off by heart! It got to the stage where I would openly take the piss out of him and he'd laugh and throw a few lines back at me. It wasn't long before he got disqualified and guess what? He really didn't think we'd notice him riding the same bike and so inevitably he'd end up getting arrested and so it went on and on. He progressed onto other things, a bit of shop lifting and a couple of drunk and disorderly's but nothing too bad. Then one night whilst I was off duty I received a call from the nick because Charlie had been arrested for criminal damage to a caravan window and the only officer he would talk to was me. Somewhat reluctantly I drove into work and Charlie confessed his sins to me and got charged. Whilst there I had to ask him why he would only speak to me and none of my colleagues and he said I had always treated him right and that he "didn't want no hassle from the other coppers, you knows wot I mean mush" he said with a wry smile. Actually I didn't.

Then one morning I came out from the station in the area car and headed along Albert Road. I was single crewed and had just gone past the Kings Theatre when I saw a bright yellow JCB coming towards me. I did a double take on the driver because it was Charlie Fry. He waved at me and smiled. But he's disqualified. You cheeky sod. I immediately called the station on my radio and requested somebody come out straight away because this JCB would be outside the nick within the next few seconds. In the meantime I was desperately trying to turn the Volvo around but was thwarted by the traffic. Then PC Dave Murray piped up.

1855 to Victor Sierra 51

Victor Sierra 51 go ahead

I'm standing outside the nick, no JCB as yet, are you sure it was heading this way?

Victor Sierra 51, answer yes

Within seconds I had stopped outside the station and spoke to Dave. He hadn't seen it at all. Charlie must have turned left into Exmouth Road then, that's the only side road between here and where I saw it. I doubled back and searched everywhere for a bright yellow JCB. Nothing. In the end I gave up. By the time I returned to the station an hour or so later the story had been embellished to such a degree that apparently, even as an established area car driver, shortly to go onto Traffic, I couldn't keep up with Charlie Fry in a JCB and that he out drove me and I lost the pursuit! The story took on such epic proportions, fuelled still further by Dave Murray's glee that at last he'd got one over on me, that it was in danger of eclipsing the bald tyres on the area car saga. I never saw Charlie Fry again and never got to find out where he went on that day.

I was in my usual early turn daze, feeling somewhat numb because getting up at 0515 hours still didn't agree with me. I was hungry to and although it wasn't even half eight yet I decided to head into the nick for breakfast. I was single crewed because Pete was doing some paperwork and as I sauntered slowly up from the seafront and along Waverley Road so I suddenly saw an elderly man step off the pavement in front of me frantically waving his arms.

"Can you help me officer, my sister's gone and done something really stupid" he pleaded.

As I got out of the car he quickly explained that she was in her 80s and suffered from depression and had slashed her wrists. I called for an ambulance before I even went into the house and as I entered he stopped and said he couldn't go upstairs because he couldn't stand the sight of blood and that what she had done he found very upsetting. I ran upstairs and opened the bedroom door. The sight that greeted me was truly pitiful. This elderly lady was dressed in her nightie and sat on the edge of her bed. She was painfully thin and very pale. She had cut both her wrists lengthways, about three inches each and had made several attempts at cutting her own throat and the kitchen knife was still embedded in the side of her neck! Her heart rate was so low and her pulse so weak that the blood flow from her wrists wasn't quite what you might expect. Yes it spurted out but it was only every 20 seconds or so and was a fairly modest amount. The wounds from her throat were superficial in comparison but there was plenty of blood coming from where the knife was and it was running down her front. She looked like something from a horror movie. I tried talking to her but she didn't acknowledge me at all, she just stared blankly at the floor. I needed to stem the flow of blood but I only had two hands and despite me shouting for the brother to come and help me he failed to materialise. I clamped my hands over both her wrists but that seemed to make the blood flow quicker from her neck and throat. I asked Charlie-One to chase up the ambulance. I needed to stop her bleeding, but how? There were no towels handy and anyway I daren't let go of her wrists. She still wouldn't respond to me. I had no choice in the end but to gently lay her back down on the bed and placed her arms down by her sides with her wrists turned upwards. I then straddled her and put my knees over the cuts in her wrists and then placed both my hands around her throat! It seemed to work and I just knelt there for another five minutes before I heard the ambulance arriving outside. I heard them coming up the stairs and as they entered the bedroom so they just stood there, mouths wide open. I must have made an interesting sight!

"Not a word, do you hear me, not a bloody word" I called out.

"I'm just going to go and get my camera" said one of them as if making for the door.

It was late February and Pete and I were on nights. It had been uncannily quiet but then the first couple of months after Christmas usually are. Everybody's broke, the weathers crap and it seems like months before we can look forward to blue skies and some sunshine. Consequently there are fewer people out and about, especially in the early hours and occasionally you can go the whole night without receiving a single call. It didn't happen very often and we moaned about it when it did. It was just gone 4 am and this was our first call of the night.

Charlie-One to Victor Sierra 51

Victor Sierra 51 go ahead

Make Ferry Road please, RTA, car overturned

Victor Sierra 51, Roger

How on earth do you roll a car in Ferry Road we asked ourselves, its barely the width of one car. Ferry Road was little more than a loosely tarmacked track that led to the Glory Hole and the Hayling Island ferry and we were approaching it from the Eastney end of the seafront. We turned right into the unlit road and almost instantly found the scene. A Renault Fuego was laying on its side with the roof area wrapped around an eight foot high steel gate post at the entrance to an old car park that overlooked the beach. The car was virtually U shaped and we doubted if anyone had survived. We shone torches through the windscreen and thought there might be somebody inside but it was very difficult to tell because of the level of damage and the car did seem to be filled with a lot of junk. We called out but got no reply. Armed with my torch I climbed up onto the side of the car because I could see that the passenger window was smashed. I shone my torch inside and sure enough there was somebody in there and they were moving slightly and moaning. I called out again and a male voice came back with.

"Get me out, get me out". I recognised the voice and then I saw the ears.

"Is that you Michael?" I asked.

"Is that Woodward, ah fuckin hell no, well you can fuck off, I don't need you, you fuckin dinny twat" he shouted back.

"Well I think right now Mr Nayler you need me a lot more than I need you. Are you trapped by your legs?" I enquired.

"I ain't telling you fuck all, now piss off, go on, I don't need you here you fuckin mong" he continued.

"Despite our differences Mr Nayler I'm here to help you whether you like it or not, now can you move at all?" I asked.

"I'm telling you I don't want your help now fuck off" he screamed.

I clambered down from the side of the car and winked at Pete.

"OK Michael if you insist we'll clear off then. Goodnight" and with that we walked back towards the area car, which was just out of sight from the overturned Renault. We opened the patrol car doors and then just shut them again as we stood by the car.

"Please don't go Mr Woodward, you know I don't mean it, please don't leave me here, Mr Woodward please" came the whimper from inside the Renault.

We called the Fire and Ambulance services to the scene and as we waited discovered that the Renault was stolen, which we weren't entirely surprised about. The Fire service arrived and set about cutting him out of the car. Despite the fact that these guys had been dragged from their beds in the early hours to come and rescue him, Nayler gave them nothing but verbal abuse. He continually swore at them, calling them every name imaginable. I had no choice but to intervene several times and warn him about his behaviour, which generally made him even worse. Thankfully it only took them about 20 minutes to cut away the front of the car and untangle his feet and legs from the steering column and to our utter amazement he escaped from the wreckage virtually unscathed, bar a few minor cuts and bruises. It's always the same; they seemingly always get away with it. If that had been an innocent member of the public they'd be dead or at the very least maimed for life. But not the car thief, or the drink driver or the hardened criminal, they somehow survive with barely a scratch. It's just so bloody unfair. I let Pete have the pleasure of nicking him; I couldn't bare the thought of dealing with him. He laughed out loud and then shouted at me.

"Thought it was your lucky night didn't you Woodward, thought I was fuckin dead, well you was wrong, I'm still ere and you don't fuckin like it do ya. Changed ya phone number lately" and he burst out laughing.

"Friend of yours is he?" asked one of the firemen.

"Definitely not" I replied. Maybe I should have left him to rot in the wreckage.

Deep down though I knew that fairly soon I would no longer be working at Southsea, because once my transfer onto Traffic came through I'd be gone and I wouldn't have to put up with the likes of Nayler and one or two others ever again. I took another very large step towards achieving that in May when I attended my four week Advanced Driving Course at Maidstone in Kent. Due to financial cuts Hampshire had closed its driving school a couple of years ago and we now had to attend the Maidstone unit. After pulling your driving standard to pieces they set about rebuilding us, bit by bit, little by little as we drove various cars like the MK2 Ford Granada 2.8i, the Ford Sierra XR4x4, Rover 827i and the BMW 528i. They had a very special dark green MK2 Granada 2.8i that had all sorts of trick bits on it and which they called the Green Goddess. It was a fantastic car to drive and really boosted your confidence and we all wanted it for our final drive but sadly it was broken during our final week, so we had to make do with the standard 2.8i. We would travel all over the country at some incredible speeds. From Maidstone we would drive to Ipswich for lunch and then via Hertfordshire and Surrey return to Maidstone in time for dinner without touching a motorway once as virtually all the driving was done on A and B roads. On another occasion we drove to Cardiff for lunch! Inevitably there was lots of theory work to be done to and I would spend hours and hours learning definitions and passages from the bible, otherwise known as Road Craft, the Police drivers hand book. I really wanted my Class 1 Advanced certificate. It had been my ambition since the day I joined and I wouldn't be satisfied until I'd got it. Getting a Class 2 wasn't an option. I would see that as failure, not quite good enough, second best, must try harder. There was a fun element to it as well though because Maidstone had its very own skid pan and apart from the official training we did on there we were sometimes allowed to use it in the evenings to practice further. I took every advantage I could to do just that, sometimes I would be the only person on it and would spend two hours there some nights. It was exhausting especially after the intense driving you would be expected to do during the day but it was definitely worth it.

Come the day of the final drive we drew lots to see which order we would drive in. I drew the short straw and got the last drive of the day. Bollocks, I really didn't want that, a middle order drive would have been better. One by one our course went out and completed their drive, which on average took about 50 minutes to an hour. The last but one officer went out which meant it was me next. I smoked about half a dozen fags as I paced up and down. After an hour and a half they hadn't returned which only made my stress levels worse. They eventually came back, having been caught up in the tailback from a crash on the M20. Now it was my turn and we headed out of Maidstone and into the countryside. It was going fairly well I thought until I was instructed to do the next section under commentary. This was never my favourite aspect and sometimes I made a bit of a hash of it and today wasn't much better. As I flew down the outside lane of a dual carriageway I was so busy concentrating on my driving and the commentary I missed the examiner telling me to take the first exit at the next roundabout. I heard him speak but didn't register what he said. He clearly realised what had happened as I hadn't changed course and repeated the instruction as we headed towards the roundabout. I somehow managed to squeeze in between two cars and then saw my gap on the roundabout and took the first exit. I thought I'd blown it right there and then, but gave myself a good slap and pressed on. As we shot down past the Meridian TV studios I went for an overtake on two cars but as I was half way passed the first one I saw a warning sign for a right turn ahead junction. So I moved straight back in, made sure the examiner knew why I'd done it and then seamlessly moved straight back out for the second overtake as we passed the junction to our right. I knew then I'd passed the course. But was it good enough to get the coveted Class 1 and become what is known in the trade as a 'graded grain'? After that overtake everything just clicked into place and I thoroughly enjoyed the drive, it was one of those that just felt right.

We gathered in the class room back at the driving school, the nine of us probably more nervous than we had ever been in our careers thus far. Sgt Dick Shepherd who was the Chief Examiner at Maidstone stood at the front and in the order that each pupil had taken the test, read out his result and whether he would receive a Class 1 or Class 2 certificate. To obtain a one, you had to score 88 or above. The maximum was 94, but few if any ever achieved that. Yet again I was last to hear the news.

"PC Woodward, 92, Class 1, top of the course, congratulations" he smiled.

Top of the course. Me? I've never come top in anything. But to come top on the advanced course just made me feel very good about myself. I couldn't have wished for better. The sheer kudos of becoming a Class 1 Advanced Police driver was an amazing feeling but better than that was having the ability to drive in a manner that many people can only dream of. The Police 'system' of car control is so much more than being able to drive fast, it is driving in art form, aiming to make every drive better, smoother, quicker and in a manner that is totally in control no matter what. I was on cloud nine.

The following month I got a phone call from headquarters, there was a vacancy coming up at Andover Traffic, did I want it? Andover? You must be joking, that's about as far away from Portsmouth as you can possibly get without crossing the border into Wiltshire. I turned it down but got warned that I would go to the bottom of the waiting list and might have to wait some considerable time before getting something closer to home. I'll have to wait then.

Two weeks later I received a form AD2 informing me that I was being posted to Cosham Traffic Department as from 4th July. It was the perfect move for me as Cosham is based just on the outskirts of Portsmouth and polices the largest area of motorway in the county. Becoming a Traffic Officer, to don the white hat and become a 'black rat' had been my dream for years. I couldn't wait to get started.

I'd been at Kilo Sierra now for ten years and in that time I think I'd grown from being a completely wet behind the ears no hoper into something resembling a half decent street policeman. I arrived in a city that I had listed bottom of the areas I wanted to work at and in the end fell in love with the place and many of its people. It was my honour and my privilege to have served the decent citizens of Portsmouth, for there are many of them and to help protect them from some of the criminal element that all too often blighted their lives and neighbourhoods. It was also my distinct pleasure to have worked with some of the most professional people on the planet, who put their lives on the line, without hesitation, every single day. The city of the star and crescent is a unique place; there really is nowhere else quite like it. There is an immense pride amongst its people, they are fiercely loyal towards one another and towards the city itself. Some of it stems from its football club but much of it I think comes from the fact that it is an island, with a definite boundary, a border and therein lays its firm identity and its inner strength. Other cities may be bigger, richer, more contemporary or cosmopolitan, but none of them can compete with Portsmouth's pride and the more you try to put it down the harder Pompey people fight back. That's just the way they are.

Before I left Southsea for pastures new, albeit only five miles away, I had a lot of goodbyes to make. On my last day I didn't drive the area car, I didn't want to. Instead I put on my tunic and a big hat and went out on foot patrol, something I hadn't done for a very long time. I patrolled Albert Road, the seafront, Palmerston Road, Elm Grove and many areas in between saying 'good morning' to the people and waving to shop keepers and many others. It was thoroughly enjoyable and made me realise just how important that day to day contact with the public really is. As much as having Police officers in cars attending emergency calls is vital in order to serve the public in an instant when they need it the most, the fact is that the Bobby-on-the-Beat type officer, that Dixon of Dock Green presence is as essential today as its always been. A succession of politicians and senior Police officers have got it horribly wrong over the years by tinkering with the service in a manner that achieves little or nothing at street level. Beat officers like Mick Smith who everybody on his beat knew by name are the key to good policing, combined with a good working knowledge of the area. As JB constantly rammed down my throat "there ain't no substitute for experience in this job young Stephen, now go out and find some".

Green Relief reunion in 2007
L to R from the back
Steve Woodward, Steve Moore, Dave Martin, Chris Robinson, Geoff Tarvin,
Ray Hallett and Dave Randell
L to R at the front
Steve Brockbank, Craig McIntosh, Mick 'yob' Smith, Mick Keating

If you enjoyed this book then keep a look out for Steve Woodwards second volume that charts his next 10 years in 'the job'. If you thought this book was traumatic just wait until you read **'Charlie Mike Zero Seven'**.

ABOUT THE AUTHOR

STEVE WOODWARD served in the Hampshire Constabulary from 1975 to 2008. He was one of the stars of the BBC TV series 'Traffic Cops' and made other appearances in 'Real Rescues' and 'Southern Crime Stoppers' together with a drama documentary on 'The Great Storm'. He is an accomplished author and organiser of a large number of charitable events and emergency service shows. He decided to write this book because he says, the Police service, as an organization, fails to tell the public about the fantastic work its frontline officers do on a daily basis.